Celebrate Liberty!
Famous Patriotic Speeches & Sermons

compiled with historical annotations by
David Barton

WallBuilder
PRESS

Aledo, Texas

Celebrate Liberty: Famous Patriotic Speeches & Sermons
Copyright 2003, David Barton
Third Printing, April 2010

Additional materials available from:
WallBuilders, Inc., Post Office Box 397, Aledo, Texas 76008-0397, (817) 441-6044, www.wallbuilders.com

Cover painting:
"Evacuation Day" by E. P. and L. Restein
Courtesy Library of Congress

Cover design:
Jeremiah Pent
Lincoln-Jackson
383 Walden Dr.
Franklin, TN 37064

Library of Congress Cataloging-in-Publication Data

323.4
Barton, David
Celebrate Liberty! Aledo, TX:
WallBuilder Press 2003
52 p; 21 cm.
ISBN 10: 1-932225-09-9
ISBN 13: 978-1-932225-09-9
Endnotes and price list included.
PN6122
1. American Speeches   2. Patriotism   3. Freedom of Speech
4. Democracy
I. Title

Printed in the United States of America

Table of Contents

Introduction & Acknowledgments

These orations are timeless – they reflect principles that inspire mankind both in patriotism and in love for liberty. However, the language in which these principles are expressed has changed dramatically over the past two centuries, resulting in a need to annotate this work. Additionally, a few simplifications have been made to the format of the orations so that modern readers can fully appreciate both the rhetoric and insight of previous generations.

Simplifications

Since the content of these historic orations is more important than their style, we have taken minor editorial liberties in three areas.

1. Spelling

All spellings have been modernized (i.e., "draft" instead of "draught"; "Savior" for "Saviour"; "burden" for "burthened"; etc.).

2. Punctuation & Capitalization

In earlier generations, commas and other punctuation marks were used very profusely, and virtually every noun was capitalized. In this work, modern rules of capitalization and punctuation have been applied to the original text.

3. Grammatical Structure

The language syntax and sentence formation used in early orations is much more complex then that of today. Consequently, a single sentence then might run for 10-12 lines and a single paragraph may run for several pages. For this work, those overly long sentences have been broken into multiple sentences, and lengthy paragraphs have been divided into shorter paragraphs according to modern rules.

Additionally, some parts of the oration in which the orator greatly expounds on a single point have been shortened. In such cases, ellipses (. . .) are always inserted to indicate to the reader that some content from the original text has been omitted; however, care has been taken in such instances to ensure that the meaning of the original remains unchanged. (The reader may resort to the original version – available in many libraries – to view the oration in its entirety.)

While these superficial changes will improve readability, they will not affect the content of the message; the original meaning is intact and reflects the genius of the orator.

Annotations

1. Word Definitions

Many words used in earlier generations by all ages and educational levels are today primarily found only in graduate level programs. Therefore, some words in the original will be followed by its definition appearing in brackets. For example, "panegyric" is followed by [public praise]; "toscin" [alarm bell]; "acedama" [burial ground]; "relumed" [rekindled]; etc. (In order to preserve the original meaning of these words as used in the context of the orations, they have been defined using Webster's 1828 Dictionary rather than contemporary dictionaries.)

2. Time-Dated Jargon

Many phrases used in early America are unknown today (e.g., "fly up and kick the beam" or "yield the palm"). Annotations are inserted at the bottom of pages to explain such idioms.

3. Classical and Political Literacy

In past generations, the average citizen's knowledge of classical literature, world history, and American political intrigues was both broad and deep. For example, citizens knew why Americans revered the names of Camden and Chatham; they could list the "Gallic heroes" that fell in defense of America; they understood how the "Gordian knot" of Greek mythology applied to the American Revolution and why the "lyre of Orpheus" (also from Greek mythology) was pertinent to the symbols on the American flag; and the common man could recite by memory lengthy quotes from English poets such as Pope, Dryden, or Milton.

In contrast, contemporary studies reveal that only six percent of Americans today can name the freedoms secured through our First Amendment; graduating seniors can identify an average of only seven States on a blank map of the United States; and not one of the top fifty-five elite colleges and universities in America required a single course in American history for graduation! For this reason, historical annotations have been inserted at the bottom of pages to explain names, events, or issues largely unknown to Americans today.

$$- \, - \, - \, \bullet \bullet \, - \, - \, -$$

Researching the hundreds of tidbits of historical knowledge that appear in these annotations was both an extensive and intense task. While only my name appears on the cover as the historical editor and annotator, it would be erroneous to conclude that this work was solely my product. The arduous task of modernizing some of the most profound of early American orations on liberty has been the work of an excellent team of invaluable researchers and editors – individuals such as Nathan Lehman, Becca Douglas, Joni Gingles, Damaris Barton, Steele Brand, Tom Smiley, Grady Barton, Callie Fowler, Zac Kester, Whitney Fowler, Katie Schonhoff, Barbara Smiley, Rose Barton, and others. I would be foolish to take credit for what this work represents: the contributions of numerous workers – both seen and Unseen – without whose assistance this book would not exist either with its current content or format. To all of those who helped, in both the human and Divine realms, I offer a sincere and heartfelt, "Thank you!"

David Barton
July 2003

✴✴✴✴✴✴✴

An Oration by

David Ramsay

1794

AN

O R A T I O N,

DELIVERED IN

St. MICHAEL's CHURCH,

BEFORE THE INHABITANTS OF

CHARLESTON, SOUTH-CAROLINA,

ON THE FOURTH OF JULY, 1794,

IN COMMEMORATION OF

American Independence,

By the Appointment of the

AMERICAN REVOLUTION SOCIETY,

AND PUBLISHED AT THE REQUEST OF THAT SOCIETY,

AND ALSO OF THE

SOUTH-CAROLINA STATE SOCIETY

OF

C I N C I N N A T I.

By DAVID RAMSAY, M. D.
Prefident of the Senate of South-Carolina.

CHARLESTON—PRINTED BY W. P. YOUNG,
NO. 43, BROAD-STREET.

Dr. David Ramsay

David Ramsay

(1749-1815)

David Ramsay was directly involved in achieving American independence and establishing America's government. Not only was he a national political leader but he was also a noted historian, being an eyewitness to many of its momentous events and a fellow-laborer for liberty with its most important leaders.

Ramsay graduated in 1765 from the college which became known as Princeton. He pursued the study of medicine under the great Princeton alumnus Dr. Benjamin Rush, later a signer of the Declaration of Independence and a surgeon-general of the Continental Army. Dr. Rush declared that Ramsay was "far superior to any person" graduated from Princeton.

Ramsay moved to South Carolina to practice medicine, and in 1776 was elected as a patriot leader to the State legislature. (He also served as a field surgeon during the Revolution.) South Carolina was a center of activity during the Revolution (the site of 137 battles), and when British General Henry Clinton captured the region in 1780, Ramsay was forced to flee. Two years later when American Generals Nathanael Greene and Francis Marion (the "Swamp Fox") recaptured the State, Ramsay returned. He was elected to the Continental Congress and was serving in that body when the final peace treaty with Great Britain was negotiated. He then returned home and was elected as the leader of the State Senate (the position he held at the time of this oration).

Notwithstanding his significant political and medical contributions, Ramsay is best known as an historian of the American Revolution. He penned the *History of the American Revolution* (1789), the *Life of George Washington* (1807), and the *History of the United States* (published in 1816, shortly after his death). His works of history are unique for several reasons: he used many original materials that he had personally collected during the Revolution; he had an excellent memory for details; he maintained an impartiality in the telling of events; and he wrote from personal experience about many of the principal actors in the important scenes of American independence.

Ramsay's life – renowned for its benevolence, piety, and patriotism – came to an untimely end when he was assassinated by an insane maniac. Shot at close range with a pistol, Ramsay lingered several painful days before his death. In addition to his own manner of dying, Ramsay had faced many other tragedies in his life, including the untimely death of his beloved wife. Despite these misfortunes, Ramsay always retained a cheerful optimism because of his Christian faith.

Ramsay delivered this oration in 1794 in Charleston – a booming coastal town by the standards of that day with a population of over 16,000. The city (one of America's earliest) was named "Charles Town" in honor of King Charles II who had granted the original charter for the Carolina Colony in 1663. Charles Town was the first settlement in the new colony and became its capital; and when Carolina was divided into two colonies in 1712, it remained the capital of South Carolina.

Charles Town was an uncommonly cosmopolitan city for its time: it was home to the first theater building in America (1736) and home of the nation's second oldest bank (1798). Charles Town also welcomed religious settlers from all faiths and denominations, housing one of

CHARLESTON DURING THE AMERICAN REVOLUTION

the largest Jewish communities (and the oldest Jewish synagogue) in America, not to mention an Anglican church founded in 1682 and an African-American church founded in 1791. (Charles Town's black population was almost twice as large as its white population.)

At the end of the American Revolution, although the city's name was changed from Charles Town to Charleston, it still remained the capital of the State. However, in 1788, when the State Convention to ratify the new US Constitution was meeting in the Capitol building, a fire broke out and destroyed the complex. The State capital was then moved permanently to the city of Columbia.

Ramsay delivered this oration in one of the most famous of all American churches: St. Michael's Episcopal Church (named for the Archangel Michael, the warrior angel considered the guardian of the heavenly heights). The church (still active today) is one of America's oldest church structures: its cornerstone was laid in 1752, the clock in the tower dates from 1764, and the church organ is from 1768. St. Michael's was also one of Charleston's most impressive structures and dominated the city skyline. The steeple of the church (an amazing 186 feet high with a weathervane 7 1/2 feet long) served for years as a lighthouse maintained by the government. The church was also a center of community life, and even President George Washington had stopped to worship there on a presidential tour through the South.

ST. MICHAEL'S EPISCOPAL CHURCH

At the time Ramsay delivered this oration, George Washington was in his second term as President and the nation was becoming convinced that it would survive under its new Constitution – despite the internal feud raging between Secretary of State Thomas Jefferson and Secretary of the Treasury Alexander Hamilton. At home, the State's Governor was William Moultrie – a revolutionary patriot who had been a Major General in the Continental Army under George Washington.

Also at the time of this oration, the eyes of the entire nation were focused on South Carolina. Citizen Edmond Charles Genet, a French envoy to America, had sought American intervention for France in the European war but President Washington refused and instead issued a proclamation of neutrality. An enraged Genet then went to South Carolina and began to issue French authorizations for American ships to attack and seize the ships of France's enemies (e.g., Great Britain, Prussia, Russia, etc.) as well as to attack Spanish forts in Florida and Mississippi, thus urging Americans to ignore President Washington. While Genet had intended this ploy to force America to help France, it almost caused America to go to war against her. Another momentous event of a much different import was also occurring at the same time: Eli Whitney had just developed the cotton gin at the home of South Carolina patriot, Major General Nathanael Greene, thereby revolutionizing agricultural productivity throughout the nation.

Ramsay's oration looked at how America had been blessed with a form of government superior to any other in the world. He examined the qualities that made America different from all other nations and showed how the spirit of liberty had survived the centuries, overcoming the most oppressive tyranny. He correctly identified the fruits of liberty in America and challenged future generations to cherish and preserve its unique principles and values.

Ramsay's oration on liberty is all the more impressive in that it heralds liberty as a gift of God – in a State that was pro-slavery and therefore had an insufficient view of liberty. Ramsay was anti-slavery and owned no slaves; and his boldness in speaking out against that evil subjected him to heavy personal pressure. Nevertheless, he delivers a view of liberty that is complete and mature, based on what God intended rather than what some men at that time permitted.

1776
+ 18
1794

®ration.

FRIENDS, COUNTRYMEN, AND FELLOW CITIZENS:

On this day eighteen years [ago], a nation was born at once – a new order of things arose and an illustrious era in the history of human affairs commenced. The ties which before had joined us to Great Britain were severed and we assumed a place among the powers of the earth. Having delivered the first oration that was spoken in the United States to celebrate this great event, [†] I feel myself doubly honored in being again called upon – after a lapse of sixteen years – to perform the same duty. . . .

I will not wound your ears on this festive day by a repetition of the many injuries received by this country from Great Britain which forced us to cut the Gordian knot which before had joined us together. [††] Suffice it to observe that for the twelve years preceding the fourth of

---

† David Ramsay delivered America's first-ever public Independence Day Oration on July 4th 1778 (David Ramsay, *An Oration on the Advantages of American Independence; Spoken before a Publick Assembly of the Inhabitants of Charlestown in South-Carolina, on the Second Anniversary of that Glorious Aera* (Charleston, S.C., 1778)). Some argue that the first oration was actually delivered by the Rev. William Gordon (1728-1807) in Boston on July 4th, 1777 (William Gordon, *The Separation of the Jewish Tribes, After the Death of Solomon, Accounted for, and Applied to the Present Day, in a Sermon Preached before the General Court, on Friday, July the 4th, 1777. Being the Anniversary of the Declaration of Independency. By William Gordon. Pastor of the Third Church in Roxbury* (Boston, 1777)), but there is a slight distinction in that the Rev. Gordon's sermon was delivered before the General Court of Massachusetts (i.e., State government officials) whereas Ramsay's was delivered as a public oration before the entire community. Regardless of whether Ramsay's oration was officially the first, or the second, or simply the first before a public gathering, Ramsay nevertheless holds a distinguished place in American history with this remarkable accomplishment.

†† According to Greek legend, a poor peasant named Gordius came to Phrygia in an ox cart. The people in that vicinity embraced an ancient prophecy that their future king would arrive riding a wagon, so believing Gordius to be its fulfillment, they made him king. Gordius was so grateful that he dedicated his ox cart to Zeus. He tied his ox cart with an intricate knot and, according to the legend, whoever untied that knot would rule all of Asia. No one was able to solve the puzzle and untie the knot, but in 333 BC, Alexander the Great simply took his sword and cut through the knot; he became the ruler of Asia. In a similar fashion, America had severed the elaborate connection that long fastened her to Great Britain and had thus "cut the Gordian knot."

July, 1776, claim rose on claim, injury followed injury, and oppression trod on the heels of oppression till we had no alternative left but that of abject slavery or complete independence. The spirit of freedom decided in favor of the latter. Heaven smiled on our exertions. After an eight years war in which our countrymen displayed the patience, the perseverance, and the magnanimity [bravery] of republicans struggling for every thing that is dear to freemen, their most sanguine [optimistic] wishes were realized. . . . Such a triumph of liberty could not fail of vibrating round the world. . . .

On this anniversary of independence, it cannot be improper to show that this has actually been done and that in consequence thereof we enjoy advantages, rights, and privileges superior to most if not to all of the human race. Bear with me, then, while I attempt to demonstrate this by a detail of particulars.

In entering on this subject, where shall I begin? Where shall I end? Proofs are unnecessary. I need only appeal to experience. I have a witness in the breast of everyone who hears me and who knows the condition of the common people in other countries. In the United States, the blessings of society are enjoyed with the least possible relinquishment of personal liberty. We have hit the happy medium between despotism and anarchy. Every citizen is perfectly free of the will of every other citizen while all are equally subject to the laws. Among us no one can exercise any authority by virtue of birth. All start equal in the race of life. No man is born a legislator. We are not bound by any laws but those to which we have consented. We are not called upon to pay our money to support the idleness and extravagance of court favorites. No burdens are imposed on us but such as the public good requires. No enormous salaries are received by the few at the expense of the many. No taxes are levied but such as are laid equally on the legislator and private citizen. No man can be deprived of his life, liberty, or property but by operation of laws freely, fairly, and by common consent previously enacted.

The liberty of the press is enjoyed in these States in a manner that is unknown in other countries. Each citizen thinks what he pleases and speaks and writes what he thinks. Pardon me, illustrious Washington, that I have inwardly rejoiced on seeing thy much respected name abused in our newspapers. Slander against thy adamantine character [character as pure and impenetrable as a polished diamond] are as harmless as pointless arrows shot from broken bows – but they prove that our printing presses are free. The doors of our legislative assemblies are open and the conduct of our State officers may be safely questioned before the bar of the public by any private citizen.

So great is the responsibility of men in high stations among us that it is the fashion to rule well. We read of the rapacity [corruption], cruelty, and oppression of men in power but our rulers seem for the most part to be exempt from these vices. Such are the effects of governments formed on equal principles, that men in authority cannot easily forget that they are the servants of the community over which they preside. Our rulers, taken from the people (and at stated periods returning to them) have the strongest incitement to make the public will their guide and the public good their end.

Among the privileges enjoyed by the citizens of these States, we may reckon an exemption from ecclesiastical establishments.[†] These promote hypocrisy and uniformly have been engines of oppression. They have transmitted error from one generation to another and restrained that free spirit of inquiry which leads to improvement. In this country, no priest can decimate the fruits of our industry nor is any preference whatsoever given to one sect above another. Religious freedom – banished from almost every other corner of the globe – has fixed her standard among us and kindly invites the distressed from all quarters to repair [come] thither. In some places, fire and faggot [bundles of wood ready to burn – i.e., burning at the stake] await the man who presumes to exercise his reason in matters of faith. In others, a national creed is established and ex-

---

† "Ecclesiastical establishments" refers to those countries literally run by a specific church, without either freedom of religion or freedom of conscience – such as France or Spain with Catholic rulers, Great Britain with Anglican rulers, Geneva with Protestant rulers, etc. In America, no one religion or denomination possessed exclusive civil power or officially ran the government.

clusion from office is inflicted on all – however worthy – who dare
to dissent. In these happy States it is a fundamental constitutional
point "that no religious test shall ever be required as a qualification
to any office or public trust" [US CONSTITUTION, ARTICLE VI, CLAUSE 3].
The experience of eighteen years has proved that this universal
equality is the most effectual method of preserving peace among
contending sects. It has also demonstrated that the church and state
are distinct societies and can very well subsist without any alliance
or dependence on each other. While the government – without
partiality to any denomination – leaves all to stand on an equal
footing, none can prove successful but by the learning, virtue, and
piety of its professors.

Our political situation resulting from independence tends to exalt
and improve the minds of our citizens. Great occasions always produce great men. While we were subjects, the functions of government were performed for us but not by us. To administer the public
affairs of fifteen States † and of four millions of people, the military,
civil, and political talents of many will be necessary. Every office in
each of these multifarious [diverse] departments is open to every citizen who has the abilities requisite for the discharge of its duties. Such
prospects cannot fail of exciting a laudable ambition in our youth to
make themselves worthy of public confidence.

It is one of the peculiar privileges we enjoy in consequence of independence that no individual – no party interest – no foreign influence – can plunge us into war. Under our excellent Constitution,
that scourge of nations will be avoided unless unprovoked and unre-
dressed injuries rouse the body of the people. Had we not asserted
our rank among nations, we – as appendages to Great Britain – would
this day have been engaged in hostilities against France (though barely
struggling for the rights of man), and all this at the call of a foreign
master and without any voice or will of our own in the matter. Think
of the cruel war now carrying on by kings and nobles against the

---

† In addition to the original thirteen States, two more had been added by the time of this
oration: Vermont (1791) and Kentucky (1792).

equal rights of man – call to mind the slaughtered thousands whose blood is daily shedding on the plains of Europe [†] – and let your daily tribute of thanks ascend to the Common Parent of the Universe Who has established you in a separate government exempt from participating in these horrid scenes. . . .

If we are to judge of the excellence of a government from its fruits in the happiness of its subjects, we have abundant reason to be pleased with our own. Since the peace of 1783, our country has been in a state of progressive improvement. . . . Our exports and imports have overflowed all their ancient boundaries. A revenue sufficient to support national credit and to satisfy all other public exigencies [necessities] has been easily raised – and that without burdening the people. Upon an average, five of our citizens do not pay as much to the support of government as one European subject. The whole sum expended in administering the public affairs of the United States is not equal to the fourth part of what is annually spent in supporting one crowned head in Europe.

From the increase of our trade and population, new ports are daily opened and new towns and cities lift their heads in all directions. The wilderness on our western frontier is constantly lessening by the extension of new settlements. Many who now hear me have been witness to the legislature of a State comfortably accommodated in a place where seven years ago the trees of the forest had never experienced the ax of the husbandman. [††]

[†] Although the French Revolution then occurring had begun as a civil war between French citizens and their tyrannical king, a number of surrounding nations headed by monarchies had come to the aid of the French monarch in order to prevent any freedom movement from spreading beyond France into their own countries. Nations opposing France included Spain, Austria, Prussia, and even Naples and Sweden, thus causing Ramsay to note that it was a war carried on by "kings and nobles" (plural) "against the equal rights of man" in France. As a result, French revolutionaries were having to fight monarchies across Europe in battles from France to Italy.

[††] Although Vermont became a State in 1791, its capital city, Montpelier, had been founded in 1787 – only four years before its Statehood; hence, Ramsay's 1794 comment that the legislature of that State had been formed "in a place where seven years ago the trees of the forest had never experienced the ax of the husbandman."

It was hoped by our enemies – and feared by our friends – that the people of independent America would not readily coalesce under a government sufficiently energetic for the security of property and the preservation of internal peace, but they have both been disappointed. In these States there is a vigorous execution of the laws and an upright administration of justice. Property and personal rights are well secured. Criminals are easily brought to suffer the punishments due to their demerits, and no legal impediment exists in the way of creditors recovering the full amount of what is due to them. . . .

Time would fail to enumerate all the superior advantages our citizens enjoy under that free government to which independence gave birth. I may safely affirm in general, that as it proceeded from the people, it has been administered for their benefit. The public good has been the pole-star [guide] by which its operations have been directed.

That we may rightly prize our political condition, let us cast our eyes over the inhabitants of the Old World and contrast their situation with our own. A few among them are exalted to be more than men, but the great bulk of the people – bowed down under the galling yoke of oppression – are in a state of dependence which debases human nature. In the benighted [dark] regions of Asia and Africa, ignorance and despotism frown over the unhappy land. The lower classes are treated like beasts of burden and transferred without ceremony from one master to another. In some parts of Europe the condition of the peasantry is not quite so bad, but in what country are the rights and happiness of the common people so much respected as in these States? In this enumeration I purposely omit France. Her former government was one of the worst. We trust and hope that when peace is restored, her enlightened rulers will furnish a new and strong proof of the connection between liberty and happiness. †

Among the established governments of Europe, that of Great Britain deservedly stands high – what is faulty in that, we have avoided;

---

† At the time of this oration, the atrocities of the French Revolution were not yet public nor had the "Reign of Terror" begun. For this reason, Ramsay is the only orator in this collection to speak favorably of the French – a position he later changed when the extent of the French bloodbath became known.

what is excellent in it, we have transplanted into our own (with additions and improvements). Is trial by jury the pride of Britain? – it is in like manner the birthright of our citizens. † Do Englishmen boast of the privileges they enjoy by virtue of the act of Parliament commonly called the Habeas Corpus Act? †† – we enjoy the same, and with more facility [ease of use], for with us two magistrates (one of whom is of the quorum) are empowered to give all the relief to a confined citizen which is contemplated by that act. Do Englishmen glory in the revolution of 1688 and of the contemporary acts of Parliament which declared the rights and liberties of the subject? ††† – we have much more reason to be proud of our Constitution. Whoever examines these declaratory acts of the English Parliament will find that all the provisions in favor of liberty which they contain fly up and kick the beam when weighed against the following single sentence in our constitution: § "All power is originally vested in the people, and all free governments are founded on their authority, and instituted for their peace, safety and happiness." §§ . . .

---

† Trial by jury is guaranteed in the Bill of Rights – in the 7th Amendment to the Constitution.

†† Writs of Habeas Corpus are issued to keep a person from remaining in prison indefinitely. In many monarchies, an individual could be imprisoned for years and never come to trial or even be formally charged with a crime. A writ of habeas corpus is an order to bring a prisoner before a judge either to levy specific charges against him or release him.

††† The "Glorious Revolution" of 1688 forced a tyrannical James II from the throne when Prince William of Orange from Holland invaded the country with the support of many leading English political and military leaders. William became king (William III) and his wife Mary II became queen. They restored many civil and religious freedoms and enacted the first full British Bill of Rights protecting the rights of citizens, increasing the powers of Parliament, and reducing the power of the King.

§ This phrase ("fly up and kick the beam") was an old expression that meant something was of very little weight, comparatively speaking. It was derived from the use of balance pan scales: the beam was the cross member of the scales, and if there was a light pan on one side, then when weight was placed on the other pan, the less weighty pan would often "fly up and kick the beam." In this oration, Ramsay is saying that the provisions for liberty in the British Declaratory Acts – great as were those provisions – actually were lightweight when compared to just one sentence in the South Carolina State constitution.

§§ This quote is from the 1790 South Carolina Constitution (Article IX, Sec. 1) that Ramsay helped write.

Do Englishmen value themselves on what is called Magna Charta? †
In the preamble to this celebrated instrument, it is stated that "the
king, of his mere free will, gave and granted to all freemen of his realm,
the liberties" which are therein specified. What is thus said to be given
and granted by the free will of the sovereign [the King], we the people
of America hold in our own right. The sovereignty rests in ourselves;
and instead of receiving the privileges of free citizens as a boon [favor]
from the hands of our rulers, we defined their powers by a constitution
of our own framing which prescribed to them that thus far they might
go but no farther. All power not thus expressly delegated [to the gov-
ernment] is retained [by the people themselves]. . . .

With such a Constitution – and with such extensive territory as we
possess – to what height of national greatness may we not aspire?
Some of our large States have territory superior to the island of Great
Britain, and the whole together are little inferior to Europe itself. The
natural advantages of our country are many and great. We are not left
to depend on others for our support and strength. Our luxuriant soil
is capable of producing not only enough for the increasing multitude
that inhabits it but a surplusage for exportation sufficient to supply
the wants of hundreds of thousands in foreign countries. . . .

With pleasure I could dwell on the pleasing prospect of our rising
greatness, but I hasten to point out what is the line of conduct proper
to be pursued by those who are so highly favored. We ought, in the first
place, to be grateful to the all-wise Disposer of Events Who has given
us so great a portion of political happiness. To possess such a country
with the blessings of liberty and peace together with that security of
person and property which results from a well-ordered, efficient government is – or ought to be – [a] matter of constant thankfulness.

Industry, frugality, and temperance are virtues which we should
eminently cultivate. These are the only foundation on which a popular government can rest with safety. Republicans should be plain in

---

† The Magna Charta was enacted in 1215 AD by Englishmen demanding protection for
their persons and property against the arbitrary actions of King John. This document was
the first step in limiting governmental authority and securing rights to British citizens. The
Magna Charta was, in essence, the world's first Bill of Rights.

their apparel, their entertainments, their furniture, and their equipage [transportation]. Idleness, extravagance, and dissipation [immorality] of every kind should be banished from our borders. It is from the industrious alone that we can gather strength. The virtues now recommended are those which prepared infant Rome for all her greatness. It is only from the practice of them that we can expect to attain that rank among nations to which our growing numbers and extensive territory entitle us to aspire.

While we celebrate this day, we should call to recollection those who have nobly fallen in support of independence. Time would fail to do them justice individually. To mention the names of some seems a species of injury to others who are equally deserving of our praise. It is the business of the historian to recite their names and to tell their gallant deeds. Let us – while we recollect their virtues – be animated with the love of our country that like them, when called upon, we may die in its defense.

Many of those tried friends who bravely fought our battles or who wisely conducted our civil affairs through the late revolution have taken their leave of this earthly stage [†] and a new generation has nearly grown up in their places. On them it depends to finish what their fathers have begun.

Much is still wanting to perfect our internal police [lesser governments]. As our government rests on the broad base of the people, every exertion should be made to diffuse virtue and knowledge among them. The uninformed and misinformed are fit tools to subserve [carry out] the views of the turbulent and ambitious. Ignorance is the enemy of liberty – the nurse of despotism. . . .

Had I a voice that could be heard from New Hampshire to Georgia, it should be exerted in urging the necessity of disseminating

---

† By this point – barely a decade since the Revolution and only five years since the start of America's constitutional government – many great leaders had already died, including signers of the Declaration Benjamin Franklin, John Hancock, Roger Sherman, Francis Hopkinson (and others) as well as several signers of the Constitution and military generals. Nevertheless, many still remained alive, including George Washington, John Adams, Thomas Jefferson, and Charles Carroll.

virtue and knowledge among our citizens. On this subject, the policy of the eastern States is well worthy of imitation. The wise people of that extremity of the Union never form a new township without making arrangements that secure to its inhabitants the instruction of youth and the public preaching of the Gospel. Hence their children are early taught to know their rights and to respect themselves. They grow up good members of society and staunch defenders of their country's cause. No daring demagogue [†] – no crafty Cataline [††] – no ambitious Alexander [†††] can make any impression on the liberties of such an enlightened people. . . .

We should, above all things, study to promote the union and harmony of the different States. Perish the man who wishes to divide us into back country or low country, into a northern and southern, or into an eastern and western interest. Forming one empire we will be truly respectable; but divided into two or more, we must become the sport [mockery] of foreign nations and peace will be forever exiled from our borders. . . . We should consider the people of this country – from the Mississippi to the Atlantic, from New Hampshire to Georgia – as forming one whole, the interest of which should be preferred to that of every part. Even the prejudices, peculiarities, and local habits of the different States should be respected and tenderly dealt with.

The art of government has never yet been brought near to that degree of perfection of which it is capable. It is lamentably true that it seldom or never has been administered with an express view to its proper object: the happiness of the governed. We should be fired [motivated] with the generous ambition of teaching mankind by our example that the people are capable of governing themselves to better

---

† A demagogue is a leader who appeals not to sound principles but rather to the popular prejudices and passions of the people in order to gain a following and make himself their apparent indispensable leader. In short, a demagogue is a leader who inflames and incites rather than inspires.

†† Cataline (108-62 BC) led a revolution against the Roman Republic in 63 AD.

††† Alexander the Great (356-323 BC) was a conqueror who subdued nation after nation to build to himself a great empire.

purpose than it ever has been done by kings and privileged orders. Men of high rank in Europe have asserted that government formed at noon on the equal principles we have adopted, would terminate before the setting of the sun. This day begins the nineteenth year of ours and it [is] now stronger and more firmly established than it ever was. . . .

The eyes of the world are fixed on this country. . . . The abettors [helpers] of tyranny are anxiously looking for opportunities to discredit the new doctrines of the rights of man. They on every occasion represent them as leading to confusion and anarchy. Equality of rights and equality of property is – in their opinion – one and the same thing. Let the wisdom of our laws and the orderly conduct of our citizens disappoint their wishes and give the lie to their calumnies [disprove their false accusations]. Let us teach them by our example that genuine republicanism is friendly to order and a proper subordinating [self restraint] in society – that it is hostile to mobs and licentiousness of every kind but the firm supporter of constituted authorities – the guardian of property as well as of the rights of man. . . .

It remains for us to recommend free governments by the example of a peaceable, orderly, virtuous, and happy people. We should press forward in accomplishing everything that can add to the common stock of public good. While war with its horrid attendants is the pastime of kings, let it be the study of republicans to make unceasing advances in everything that can improve, refine, or embellish society. Animated with this noble ambition, the superior happiness of our country will amply repay us for the blood and treasure which independence has cost. May that ambition fire our breasts, and may that happiness increase and know no end, till time shall be no more. ■

✶ ✶ ✶ ✶ ✶ ✶ ✶

An Oration by

George Washington Adams

1824

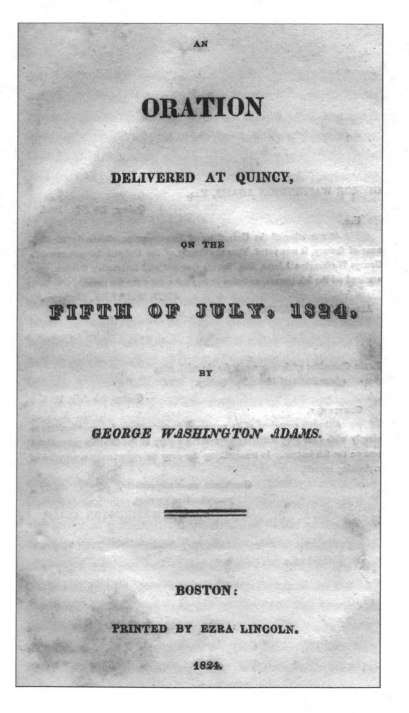

AN

ORATION

DELIVERED AT QUINCY,

ON THE

FIFTH OF JULY, 1824,

BY

GEORGE WASHINGTON ADAMS.

BOSTON:

PRINTED BY EZRA LINCOLN.

1824.

George Washington Adams

George Washington Adams
(1801-1829)

George Washington Adams (GWA) came from a long line of patriots and was part of a distinguished American family. His grandfather was John Adams (signer of the Declaration of Independence and 2nd President) and his father was John Quincy Adams (6th President). George was named by his parents, obviously, for George Washington, a close friend of the Adams family.

George's early biography cannot be separated from that of his famous father (John Quincy Adams). George was born in Berlin in 1801, the location of his father's diplomatic service at that time. His father had entered the foreign diplomatic corp under President Washington, and when John Adams became President, Washington urged Adams to retain JQA in the foreign service, declaring that he was "the most valuable public character we have abroad and . . . will prove himself to be the ablest of all our diplomatic corps." JQA therefore remained overseas as the minister to Prussia throughout the presidency of John Adams; and thus when George Washington Adams was born, it was in Berlin.

When Thomas Jefferson (considered by John Adams as his archnemesis) defeated Adams for the presidency, John Adams – as one of the his final acts before leaving office – recalled JQA (and therefore his family). The childhood years of GWA consequently were spent growing up in America.

When James Madison was elected President in 1809, he dispatched JQA as a diplomat to St. Petersburg, Russia. For this overseas assignment, JQA took part of his family with him but left GWA (along with GWA's younger brother, John) in Massachusetts, in the care of JQA's brother, Thomas Boyleston Adams.

JQA gave his brother, Thomas, explicit instructions about the training of the nine-year-old GWA, directing "sedentary learning" (the regular course of academic studies learned while sitting – e.g., math, grammar, etc.) as well as training in the "languages" (Greek, Latin, French), "classical studies," "drawing," "fencing," "fine arts," "the use and management of firearms," "horseback," "learn[ing] to [ice] skate," "speaking," "handwriting," "spelling," "letter writing," and "bodily fatigues" (exercise). JQA also warned his brother, "let him [George] be encouraged in nothing delicate or effeminate" and let there be "no cockering" (coddling or indulging). Today, this would be quite a rigorous plan of study for a nine-year-old, but it was not uncommon then.

Once JQA arrived in Russia, he began to correspond directly with George. Even though JQA fully trusted his brother Thomas to educate George, he nevertheless wanted to provide his own personal influence on his son. He therefore wrote him a number of letters instructing him on the study of the Bible. Interestingly, those letters were reprinted in 1848 as a book: *The Letters of John Quincy Adams to His Son on the Bible and its Teachings*. The preface of that book explained: "The following letters were written by Mr. Adams, while ambassador at St. Petersburg, to one of his sons [George] who was at school in Massachusetts. Their purpose is the inculcation of a love and reverence for the Holy Scriptures and a delight in their perusal and study."

LETTERS

OF

JOHN QUINCY ADAMS,

TO HIS SON,

ON

THE BIBLE AND ITS TEACHINGS.

Auburn, N. Y.:
DERBY, MILLER, & CO.

1848.

In 1814, three years after these letters were written (and while America was in the latter stages of the War of 1812), President Madison dispatched JQA to England to negotiate a final peace treaty to the war. On his arrival, JQA sent for George and John, who sailed to London to be with the rest of his family. In 1817 when James Monroe was elected President, Monroe appointed JQA as his Secretary of State, so the Adamses left England after a three year stay.

On his return to America, George was admitted to and graduated from Harvard, the *alma mater* of both his father and grandfather. He became an attorney (he studied under the tutelage of the great Daniel Webster) and was elected to the Massachusetts legislature.

George Washington Adams suffered a tragic and untimely end to his promising life. While on a steamer bound for New York, he went overboard in Long Island Sound and drowned. His body was found washed ashore weeks later.

George delivered this oration five years before his death, while only twenty-three years old. It was delivered in Quincy, an area where both his father and grandfather had been born. Quincy was at that time a small town whose commerce relied on agriculture, grist mills, and iron furnaces. Its population was less than 4,000, but it was on the verge of rapid growth with the forthcoming addition of two new industries: shipbuilding and granite quarrying.

On the national scene, James Monroe was President and the nation was experiencing what today's historians describe as the "Era of Good Feelings" – a period marked by a lack of partisan political feeling. Indiana, Illinois, and Maine had just been added as States; America had obtained the Florida territory; Stephen Austin was leading settlers into Texas; the Seminole War had just been ended by General Andrew Jackson; Philadelphia organized the first school for African-Americans; and Liberia had been founded so that free blacks in America who wished to do so might return to their homeland.

On the religious front, the territory of North Dakota had opened its first church, Connecticut had disestablished the Congregational Church, the American Tract Society was formed to distribute Gospel literature, and the American Sunday School Union had just been founded to organize Sunday Schools across the nation.

Internationally, many nations – inspired by the American example – were attempting to throw off monarchy, tyranny, and despotism; some were successful, some not.

In this oration, George acknowledged the Providence of God in the founding of America and the establishment of its liberties, be-

ginning with the discovery of the continent by Christopher Columbus and proceeding forward. Adams particularly noted God's hand
in the Reformation – how those teachings directly impacted the Pilgrims and the Puritans, and how their Christian faith affected the
growth of both representative government and quality education in
America. He then honored the heroes of the Revolution – especially
John Hancock and Samuel Adams – and concluded with a look at
how American liberty had affected the rest of the world. His oration
was an inspiring look at the causes of American liberty and its effects at home and abroad.

Oration.

The causes of great events, those events themselves, and their extensive consequences, are subjects worthy the attention of enlightened and intelligent minds. We have assembled, fellow citizens, to celebrate the anniversary of a day justly memorable in the records of our country's history – a day glorious to this nation as the festival of its nativity – glorious to humanity for the expression of principles proportionate to its exalted privileges. It is the intention of our celebration to signify our adherence to those sublime principles "which are not of an age but for all time," [†] and it is delightful to reflect upon the countless multitude of free Americans who with this purpose have watched this morning's dawn. . . .

Whence is this general joy? It arises from our independent freedom which has made known to us the value of our institutions planted by the energies and secured to us by the virtuous efforts of our ancestors. Let their energy be to us an example, and their efforts motives for unfailing gratitude to Him who prospered them.

The Declaration of Independence was an advance in the progress of mind – a point in human history to which the important occurrences of preceding ages led and from which consequences of high import have proceeded.

The Christian Revelation – that mild and beautiful religion which has taught man his duties and his hopes – is the true source of human happiness. With its establishment commenced the course of improvement which succeeding ages and wonderful events have carried onward to our own age and time. The contemplation of the steps by which it has advanced affords much matter of instructive thought and many reasons for just admiration. America has done and is do-

---

† This line is from a work by English poet and actor Ben Jonson (1572-1637), who – in honor of his friend and contemporary – wrote "Lines to the Memory of Shakespeare" that included:

> He was not of an age, but for all time!
> And all the Muses still were in their prime
> When, like Apollo, he came forth to warm
> Our ears, or like a Mercury to charm!

ing her share in the great work; and from the hour of the discovery up to the present moment has shown a proud example to the world.

Past history justifies the reflection that undertakings of magnitude are accomplished only through toil and suffering and perilous endurance. This vast continent, unknown for centuries, was discovered from the fortunate conjecture [foresight] of an enlightened mind; yet the history of its discoverer is a history of injuries – injuries during his life and neglect after his death.

Born in a republic, Christopher Columbus was brought up upon the bosom of the wave and fitted for the mighty object of his life. Having conceived that object, he imparted it first to the people of his native land. Censured by his own countrymen [the Portuguese] as a visionary projector, rejected by nation after nation to whom he had applied, Columbus persevered in his design with assiduity [diligence] and firmness truly admirable. † At length the Spanish sovereigns [King Ferdinand and Queen Isabella] risked the experiment, furnished the daring navigator with a miserable squadron, and assisted him with slight encouragement; ill-appointed and badly-manned, he sailed to find a world!

Tried by the dangers of the ocean, distrusted by his men, conflicting twice with mutiny and rage, the promise was wrung from him that in three days if land were not discovered he would return

---

† Columbus, in his own writings, speaks not only of the rejection and scorn he suffered from others but also of why he was willing to persevere in his goal:

> [O]ur Lord opened to my understanding (I could sense his hand upon me) so it became clear to me that it [the voyage] was feasible. . . . All those who heard about my enterprise rejected it with laughter, scoffing at me. . . . Who doubts that this illumination was from the Holy Spirit? I attest that He [the Spirit], with marvelous rays of light, consoled me through the holy and sacred Scriptures . . . they inflame me with a sense of great urgency. . . . No one should be afraid to take on any enterprise in the name of our Savior if it is right and if the purpose is purely for His holy service. . . . And I say that the sign which convinces me that our Lord is hastening the end of the world is the preaching of the Gospel recently in so many lands.

Given the motivation and assurance Columbus found in the Scriptures, he overcame the "censure of his own countrymen" and "persevered in his design."

to Spain. His life, his all was on the cast [gamble – that is, it all depended on the figurative throw or "cast" of the dice that he would discover land within three days]; but his own fortitude supported him. On the evening after he gave the promise, a distant light pierced the dark waste of waters; Columbus saw and marked the glimmering signal; it was a moment of intense interest; to his aspiring mind, another world was found! His triumph was complete; that little beam revived the fainting spirits of his crew and relumed [rekindled] the rays of hope. . . .

The discovery of America by Columbus in 1492 – succeeded by that of a shorter passage to the East Indies in 1497 by Vasco de Gama – exposed to European avarice [greed] the sources of unlooked-for wealth. From their full fountains, the Indies poured the precious metals into Europe like a flood. With them went luxury and its concomitant [accompanying] vices, but with them went also the means of knowledge. . . . [T]he Reformation followed, and this . . . event, rousing men's passions as its march went on, caused a continued emigration from the Old World to the New for other purposes than those of wealth and plunder till the poor Pilgrim crossed the deep waters to find a home where he might worship God as his own conscience taught and where he might be free from persecuting power.

The Reformation – emanating from Germany – passed into England, and owing to the fortunate conjuncture [circumstances] of the times was there established; but it was not in the intention of her "hard-ruled king" † to part with his supremacy and hence arose wide differences of opinion. Tyrant power wielded the sword and used it bloodily, designing not to silence but to extirpate [totally exterminate] religious opposition, and the sanguinary [bloodthirsty] measures thence adopted hardened the non-conformists [e.g., Pilgrims, Puritans, etc.] in their

---

† The phrase "hard-ruled king" was taken from William Shakespeare's (1564-1615) play, *Henry the VIII*, in which Henry was called "our hard ruled-king." Henry VIII came to the throne in 1509; Luther nailed his 95 Theses to the door in 1517, thus beginning the Protestant Reformation; and Henry VIII made himself the head of the Church of England (the Anglican Church) in 1534. This was a "hard-ruled" era in which religious non-conformists and reformers were declared heretics and often exiled or put to death.

faith. [†] Persecution was opposed by bigotry, suffering was paralleled by obstinacy, till the temper [attitude] of the age grew cruel, unrelenting, merciless; men's minds were soured and all parties assuming the rigorous rule of uniformity while they believed their own opinions right, held every departure from them heresy and sin.

In this state of things, our forefathers – tired of a fruitless struggle with the dominant power and harassed by domestic sorrows – sought an asylum here. Heaven seems to strengthen the human faculties proportionably to the obstacles to be encountered; obstacles multiplied before our fathers and were surmounted; Plymouth was settled and in the rock the tree of liberty was rooted. Bound by their religious covenant, the Pilgrims bound themselves by a political constitution. [††] By a charter to the Plymouth Council under a royal grant based on discovery and implied conquest, they came hither, but their

---

[†] The reaction to the Reformation by English leaders indeed was often bloody, reflecting their intent to eradicate religious opposition through the most oppressive measures. For example, Henry VIII (1491-1547) declared himself the head of the church in England and began eradicating those of differing beliefs. Dutch Anabaptists were burned at the stake; other religious leaders were charged with treason and executed; and Henry seized the property of churches not affiliated with the Church of England. Queen Mary continued the purge, executing John Rogers, who had assisted in the publication of Tyndale's English translations of the Scriptures. Subsequent kings, including King James, conducted similar purges, mutilating, hanging, or disemboweling religious non-conformists right up until (and after) the time that the non-conformist Pilgrims and Puritans left for America in search of religious freedom. These "bloodthirsty measures" simply "strengthened the non-conformists in their faith" and made the Pilgrims and Puritans even more committed to their own beliefs.

[††] That political constitution was the "Mayflower Compact" – the first government charter drafted solely in America. In November of 1620, the Pilgrims had arrived in America on the Mayflower, and before disembarking into a new area with no established civil government, in December 1620 they drafted and signed the Mayflower Compact, declaring: "Having undertaken for the glory of God and advancement of the Christian faith . . . [we] combine ourselves together into a civil body politic for . . . furtherance behind the ends aforesaid." William Bradford, one of their leaders, confirmed the religious purpose of their political constitution when he explained that the Pilgrims had come to the New World because "a great hope and inward zeal they had of laying some good foundation, or at least to make some way thereunto, for the propagating and advancing the Gospel of the kingdom of Christ in those remote parts of the world." Their desire resulted both in a new religious order with religious freedoms, and a new political order with new political freedoms. The Mayflower Compact was the first document of self-government in America in which the citizens replaced nobility and aristocracy with local government and community self-rule.

best title was afterwards acquired by purchase from the natives of the soil † and subsequent efficient labor on the land.

Hardly had they completed the outline of their town before the indiscretion of their countrymen surrounded them with dangers. . . . [Settlers] unlike their Plymouth neighbors [the Pilgrims], and unrestrained by conscientious virtue, gave themselves up to wild licentiousness. . . . [and] plunged deeper into reckless dissipation [pleasure seeking]; [they] gathered the flowers of spring to wreath their garlands, and – like the victims of the Roman altars – knew not the fate that was impending over them; strange! †† . . .

---

† An infrequently told story (and an often neglected aspect of the early settlements in America) is that religious leaders and colonists often *purchased* land from the Indians – at the price set by the Indians. Such, for example, was the case with the Pilgrims (Plymouth Plantation), Puritans (Massachusetts Bay Colony), New Haven Colony (later Connecticut), Pennsylvania, and others.

†† In 1625 in area near the Pilgrims, Captain Thomas Wollaston and 30 indentured servants arrived and founded a settlement named "Mt. Wollaston." When Wollaston later left the region, Thomas Morton – in search of treasures and easy riches – moved in and occupied the area, renaming it Merry Mount. He and his followers did indeed make "merry" on the "mount" and therefore were firmly opposed by the devout Pilgrims who held the charter to the area. As described by Pilgrim Governor William Bradford: "[Morton and his followers] set up a Maypole, drinking and dancing about it many days together, inviting the Indian women for their consorts, dancing and frisking together (like so many fairies, or furies rather) and worse practices. As if they had anew revived and celebrated the feasts of ye Roman goddess Flora, or ye beastly practices of ye mad Bacchanalians" [the Greek deities of wine and reveling].

Morton gave his weapons to the local Indians so that they could hunt food for him and his men while his group spent its time in party and drunkenness. The Indians came to despise their own weapons and to treasure the new ones supplied them by Morton. They also so imbibed Morton's self-gratifying lifestyle that they became willing to go to any lengths to obtain more of the weapons and goods like those lavished on them by Morton. The result was that – following years of good relations with the settlers – the Indians began to kill the colonists in order to obtain their weapons and goods. In the eyes of the civil leaders in the area, Morton had sowed the seeds of destruction of the colonists.

Because of the licentiousness and debauchery of Morton and his men, military leader Myles Standish had him seized (ironically, Morton's own men were too drunk to resist Standish or to defend Morton) and placed Morton on a deserted island until a passing English ship could pick him up and take him back to London.

In London, Morton used his pen to attack the Pilgrims and Puritans. In 1637, he published *New English Canaan* in which he described America's lavish bounty but maligned the Puritan settlers as repressive incompetent bunglers. He returned to the Massachusetts area several times and reveled in being a constant "thorn in the flesh" to local leaders.

The Pilgrims of Plymouth and the primitive settlers of New England came over to enjoy unmolested the exercise of a simple and unadulterated form of worship. To obtain this religious freedom, they left a land over which Nature had profusely scattered her most attractive graces – a land which has been beautifully called

"A precious stone set in the silver sea" [†]

where were the tombs of their fathers and the homes of their kindred – where their earliest affections had grown and their dearest recollections lingered; but it was no longer the home of liberty; Astraea [††] had deserted it and left green Albion [†††] a barren waste girt with a triple wall of regal tyranny. What was the beauty of the earth to them, deprived of liberty of conscience? For this they could forego this "pleasant land of their nativity" [RUTH 2:11] – for this they could restrain those feelings which might not be entirely destroyed, estrange [separate] themselves from home and friends and kindred to become acquainted with the rude savage of the wilderness. [§] They brought with them the rigid principles for which they had contended and the stern spirit which they had imbibed.

Religion was the platform of their political state and they respected its ordinances and its ministers. These exerted a favorable influence upon the public morals, watching them with scrutinizing jealousy; the people possessed an operative suffrage [right to vote] in their

---

† This line is taken from William Shakespeare's (1564-1615) play, *Richard II* (Act II, Scene 1).

†† Astraea was the Greek goddess of innocence, purity, and justice. In Greek mythology, she withdrew from earth because of the wickedness of man and became the constellation Virgo ("The Virgin") in the heavens. Interestingly, ancient Babylonian and Egyptian depictions of the constellation Virgo include this symbolic virgin holding an infant, Horus, whose name means "He Who Comes Forth," symbolizing the virgin birth of Christ. This affirms the truth of Psalm 19:1: "The heavens declare the glory of God; the skies proclaim the work of His hands."

††† Albion was the ancient and literary name of England. In fact, in 1579 San Francisco Bay was briefly named "New Albion" (New England) by English explorer Sir Francis Drake.

§ Adams is noting that after the departure of Astraea (justice) from Albion (England), the English became steadily more tyrannical in their government thus providing the Pilgrims with just cause to repair to the New World despite the hardships they would face.

church government and were familiar with polemic controversy [a rebuttal argument against a person's belief or opinion]: they sifted doctrines and decided for themselves contested points. . . .

Accustomed to judge for themselves in matters of theology, they began to feel it as their right to judge in those of government. Acknowledging themselves to be English subjects, they drew nice distinctions in defining that subjection in order that it might not prejudice [injure] their privileges. With no nobility to check the growth of equal systems – no hierarchy to hold out a lure to clerical ambition or to sustain royal pretensions to supremacy in religion – no courts supported by the forfeitures decreed by their own judges – they grew up in the enjoyment of republican rights. . . . Their immediate executive was elective and thus responsible to them; indeed, the wise and virtuous men who took the lead in their affairs encouraged the republican immunities of the people and supported the established charter rule of annual elections from their own conviction of its value, sensible

> That nobler is a limited command
> Given by the love of all your native land,
> Than a successive title, long and dark,
> Drawn from the moldy rolls of Noah's ark. †

To annual elections they soon added representation and improved on the practice of the Mother Country by equalizing the rule. This right of being represented was not granted by the first charters but it was adopted shortly after their arrival. . . . These rights were the elements of their high character, but there was another cause which added to their firmness and increased their privileges.

From the earliest settlement, they cultivated good learning and useful science. The controversies of theology could not be maintained without sufficient learning to oppose the arguments of learned orders of the [state-established] church laboring for its preservation. Controversy had been for years familiar as the daily food of life. The

---

† These four lines are from a 1681 work, *Absolom and Ahithophel* (Part I, line 299), by John Dryden (1631-1700) – named poet laureate of Great Britain (1668).

Reformation had – in the different sides which states and monarchs were compelled to take – opened the wide gates of speculative doubt and proved to mankind that they could think for themselves.

This point once gained, there was no limit to the interest which attended the investigation of religious questions; hence this interest extended throughout Europe and spread itself over the whole surface of society. The study of theology became the surest path to influence and honor, and learning was sought for as a weapon of controversy. Inexpressibly anxious about their eternal welfare, our fathers taught their children to "*search the scriptures*" [JOHN 5:39; ACTS 17:11], and thus laid the cornerstone of learning's proudest temple: a reading and reflecting community. They established schools and colleges for public education. While New England was a sterile wilderness, the halls of Harvard rose to educate a line of excellent men qualified to instruct their countrymen in wisdom, to seek her in her dearest treasuries [storehouses of abundance], to dispense to mankind the inestimable benefits of knowledge and virtue. †

> These are brighter, richer gems
> Than the stars of diadems.

The collective character of a people is composed of the same mixture of differing qualities which are discernible in individuals – it comprises the same liberality, generosity, honesty of intention, and the same stormy passions which, when roused, shake the whole happiness of private life. Our forefathers were a patient and persevering people; their devotion was simple but earnest; their theories were circumscribed [limited] but conscientious; their morality was rigorous but practical. They were from necessity frugal; from their position circumspect [cau-

---

† Not only did Harvard graduates in general have a distinct impact on the nation, but specifically Harvard graduates from Massachusetts were extremely influential. Massachusetts graduates included signers of the Declaration such as John Hancock and John Adams; signers of the Constitution such as Rufus King; Constitutional Convention delegates such as Caleb Strong and Elbridge Gerry; military officers such as Artemus Ward and Timothy Pickering; original US Supreme Court Justice William Cushing; and many others – and these were only the leaders in the civil arena. There were equally distinguished Harvard leaders in numerous other areas ranging from theology to education to business.

tious]; from their situation vigorous and hardy. Obliged alike to brave the savage and the European foe – acquainted equally with the implements of husbandry and with the weapons of war – they guarded the state till she had cleared the dangers of her infancy. Such was the early character of the people of New England. It shows a race of men fit to be free. History presents no parallel to such a people mid all her records of bloodstained laurels [trophies] and successful wrong – mid all her tales of daring enterprise and reckless valor, of learned lawgivers and grasping conquerors; she shows no other state originating in devotion and in liberty of thought – no other nation whose foundation was the pure worship of the living God.

In this character we may trace the progress of mind. Freedom opened the blossom of republican polity [elected representative government] which was in aftertimes to ripen into admirable fruit. The early systems of elections, of representation, and of property were improvements on the old modes – the former by limiting official power, increasing responsibility, and equalizing popular participation in government; the latter by securing to industry the profits it affords.

This character, which intercourse [discussion] and habit in the next generation had extended and confirmed, was not in good accordance with regal prerogative or parliamentary supremacy. It became necessary, therefore, that the Mother Country should counteract and check it by a plan of colonial policy. . . . [T]he people lost many of their most peculiar [cherished] privileges. The gloomy machinations of the last Stuarts extended to America and were mainly directed against the bold and independent spirit of New England. [†]

No longer empowered to elect their own executive, the colonists were holden at the mercy of the throne – a mercy burdened with

---

† The Stuarts were a line of the royal family of Great Britain that reigned from 1603-1713 – a line that included King James II, Queen Mary II, King William III, and Queen Anne. Throughout the Stuart reign, there was mismanagement of New England (such as when a despotic governor was appointed in Connecticut in 1665) thus causing much resistance to the crown from New England. As a result, the kings became even more hard-fisted in their efforts to subjugate the spirit of freedom and independence – the "bold and independent spirit" – that characterized New England.

such hard conditions as completely changed its office. Violent and arbitrary maxims of government (carried into execution by rulers strangers to the soil and its inhabitants) affecting the right of property, destroying the right of suffrage [voting], subverting [overthrowing] customs which had grown up with the people – were the "tender mercies" [c.f., PROVERBS 12:10] which the "nursing mother" administered to her distressed offspring. The same eclipse which had overshadowed the sun of British liberty portended [threatened] total darkness to the world, but under the merciful decree of Providence it passed away and left the orb [planet] more radiant than before. The British revolution saved mankind from projects deeply designed for their entire subjection † and forms another step in the advance of mind!

During the reigns of the last Charles and James, the value of the American plantations began to be appreciated. †† The Mother Country framed a system of colonial policy which depressed their energies and fettered their power. The Parliament – during the Commonwealth [under Cromwell] – had passed the act of navigation and subsequently added to it acts of trade by which the profits of the colonial

---

† Key to the British Revolution were the efforts of Oliver Cromwell (1599-1658), an opponent of the absolute power of the crown. A leading figure in the English Civil War (actually three distinct wars from 1638 to 1660, involving Scotland, Ireland, and Wales), Cromwell organized opposition military forces – including his famous "Ironside" regiment, a body of men that combined strong convictions with a religious enthusiasm in fighting. King Charles was eventually overthrown and executed.

Cromwell then attempted the establishment of a Puritan Commonwealth in place of the traditional monarchy, but his attempt eventually failed (after Cromwell's death, the government reverted back to a monarchy). Nevertheless, for a time Cromwell did remove hereditary monarchs from ruling over England and his efforts laid the foundations for the forthcoming Glorious Revolution (1688) that limited the power of kings, increased the powers of Parliament, and established a British Bill of Rights.

†† One indication of the help bestowed on "the American plantations" by Charles and James involved Pennsylvania. Both had been personal friends of Admiral Sir William Penn and promised the Admiral they would take care of his son, William. It was Charles that in 1681 granted Pennsylvania (named after William Penn's father) to the young William Penn, thus establishing one of the most important of the American colonies – a colony founded on complete religious liberty and on equitable relations with the Indians. (Charles had also granted the charter for Carolina in 1663.)

commerce were made returnable through the British market. † This commercial monopoly was vigorously enforced by one party [Great Britain] and artfully evaded by the other [America] till at length the power of the crown extorted a partial obedience. . . .

Was it to be imagined that a people such as we have shown – habitually jealous of their liberties – would tamely and quietly submit to such restrictions? Was it to be supposed that a hardy and enterprising race of men, skillful in calculation and shrewdly sensitive to honest profit, would willingly consent to let the price of their labor – the gains of their industry – slip from their hands? It would have been wholly foreign to the character of this people to have submitted without murmuring to this unfavorable scheme. They did not willingly submit; they lost the first charter for their opposition; †† they lost that right of choosing their own executive which had so long protected them in freedom. ††† . . .

---

† The Acts of Trade (and the Navigation Acts) – implemented under both the Tudor and Stuart line of British kings – eliminated free-market competition on many goods and created a British monopoly on trade. The alleged design of the Acts was the expansion of the British carrying trade against Dutch competition, but the result was the closing of markets and the raising of prices for Americans. The first Navigation Act was enacted in 1651 and forbade the importation of Asian and African commodities into America except on ships owned by the English. Also prohibited was the importation of European goods into England unless carried on British ships. In 1663, an act was passed requiring that *all* foreign goods destined for America – no matter their nation of origin – be shipped through British ports. With monopolies established and competition eliminated, the Americans suffered greatly. For example, the Molasses Act of 1733 forced Americans to buy the more expensive British West Indian sugar rather than the less expensive French West Indian sugar. The result was widespread smuggling by the Americans.

†† The charter for the colony was revoked in 1684 because the colonists persistently ignored royal orders. For example, despite orders to the contrary, they operated their own mint to coin money, refused to incorporate property prerequisites for voting, and did not give the English state-established Anglican church preferential treatment but rather discriminated against them in preference to the more numerous non-conformists and non-Anglican dissenters in the colony.

††† When the colony's charter was revoked in 1684, the people "lost that right of choosing their own executive." In 1691, the crown issued a new charter joining the Massachusetts Bay Colony, the Plymouth Plantation Colony, and the Maine Colony into the single Massachusetts Colony. The people were not allowed to choose a governor; instead, he was appointed by the crown. However, the people were still allowed (for the time-being, at least)

The revolution commenced with the resistance made to an order from the superior court of this province for writs of assistance to carry into execution the acts of trade. [†] These writs of assistance indicated the first speck in the horizon round which the clouds collected to burst in thunder over Britain and to purify the political atmosphere of the world. . . .

In this situation – when the British government had decided to exert the power of the empire and war hung lowering darkly over America – the Declaration of Independence was issued and received

---

to continue electing their legislature – a right they later lost.

In 1768, Samuel Adams – with the approval of the Massachusetts legislature – issued a paper attacking Parliament's practice of taxing the Colonies without allowing them representation; he called for a unified resistance of the Colonies to the Crown. In response, Massachusetts' crown-appointed Governor, Thomas Hutchinson, promptly dissolved the State legislature. When resistance continued on the part of the Colonists (culminating in the famous Boston Tea Party), Great Britain responded with the Massachusetts Government Act that removed _all_ elections from the people.

† Writs of Assistance (to enforce the Acts of Trade) was an outrageous British measure that was met with great opposition and resistance in America. The Writs of Assistance were vague warrants issued by British magistrates to allow British officials to search for smuggled goods within any home or premise. James Otis (the mentor of John Hancock and Samuel Adams) argued vigorously against these writs, showing that they were unconstitutional even under the then existing British laws. These writs did not enumerate specific items for which authorities would search but instead were often completely blank except for the signature of a magistrate at the bottom of the writ. The authorities then would break into homes and search for "contraband" under the authority of these vague warrants; if smuggled goods were found, the authorities would then fill in the blanks on the writ *after* the discovery; however, if nothing was found, they would keep the writ and carry it with them to their next point of search – a clear abuse of the writs, abridging the very protections for which the writ laws originally had been enacted. (As noted previously, the Acts of Trade helped enforce a British monopoly on trade, closing markets and raising prices for Americans, thus causing widespread "smuggling" (the purchasing of cheaper products by the Americans and resulting – according to the British – in the need for open-ended writs to search for illegal "contraband.") The abuse of liberties and rights under these writs was so great and so odious to Americans that when the Constitution was written, the Fourth Amendment specifically forbade such writs, declaring:

> The right of the people to be secure in their persons, houses, papers, and effects, against unreasonable searches and seizures shall not be violated, and no warrants shall issue but upon probable cause supported by oath or affirmation, and particularly describing the place to be searched and the persons or things to be seized. (AMENDMENT IV)

with acclamation throughout the Colonies. The arm of tyranny was palsied [paralyzed] by the blow – it cleft his lion helm [an armored helmet with a hinged visor] in twain and struck the feeble falchion [broad sword] from his hand. The Colonies had shaken off the chains by which they had been manacled and owned no longer an imperious [overbearing] master; they told the world that they were free; and in the reasons they assigned for this assertion of their freedom are to be found the soundest principles of public justice – the boldest theories of human rights.[†] These are the reasons why this sublime instrument marks an advancement of the human mind – these are the claims which have won for this day the annual tribute of a nation's joy – these are the sacred ties which hold together these increasing States [††] in the strict bonds of union and of harmony. . . .

The effects of this Declaration are now everywhere visible. Look through the country and behold our accumulated blessings: see nature robed in beauty, fertile in rich luxuriance; see health and plenty everywhere around you; see a dense and settled population stretch-

---

[†] The essence of these "boldest theories of human rights" and "soundest principles of public justice" are found in the first eighty-five words of the second paragraph of the Declaration of Independence:

> We hold these truths to be self-evident, that all men are created equal, that they are endowed by their Creator with certain unalienable rights, that among these are life, liberty and the pursuit of happiness. That to secure these rights, governments are instituted among men, deriving their just powers from the consent of the governed. That whenever any form of government becomes destructive of these ends, it is the right of the people to alter or to abolish it and to institute new government.

The "bold theories" here espoused include: God made all men equal; God bestowed equal rights on all men; God-given rights are unalienable; those unalienable rights include life, liberty, and the pursuit of happiness (among others); governments are created to protect God-given unalienable rights; legitimate governments operate only by the permission of the governed; and when governments become oppressive and cease to fulfill these God-ordained functions, the people have the right to create a new government. These were indeed "bold theories" regarding human rights in that day; they still remain revolutionary throughout most of the world today.

[††] At the time of this oration, the United States had increased from its thirteen original States to twenty-four, including the eleven new States of Alabama, Illinois, Indiana, Kentucky, Louisiana, Maine, Mississippi, Missouri, Ohio, Tennessee, and Vermont.

ing from the cold regions of the North to the exuberant [rich] valleys of the South, from the prolific intervals of the East to the flourishing prairies of the West; see your shores washed by two oceans and the soil your own. Are not these motives for rejoicing? The welcome of this day throughout the land gives our reply.

But beside the general national reasons for rejoicing in the benefits resulting from this proud day there are others, fellow citizens, which affect us peculiarly. We cannot forget that the great name which leads the illustrious catalogue upon that venerated instrument went forth from here [i.e., from Massachusetts]. I would speak with diffidence [modesty] of Mr. Hancock. Common praise would not express his virtues. His character was compounded of mingled gravity [seriousness] and splendor. Accustomed to the luxuries of life, fortune clothed him with her mantle of elegant refinement and poured her gifts upon him in a golden shower. With every prospect of preeminence under the ancient aristocratic system, commanding influence and sure of honors, it was no common strain of patriotism that could put by the glittering bait which courted him. Dignified, graceful, affable, and eloquent, he seemed to win involuntary favor, while to these outward excellencies he added the sterner virtues which the time required. Liberal, charitable, generous, his fortune was his country's and his wealth made for the poor. Generosity was the flower of his life and whether actively exercised in freely bestowing or negatively in giving up emoluments [profits], it bloomed in equal brilliancy. . . . Mr. Hancock was willing to put everything at stake – fortune, honors, safety, life itself were to him worthless in comparison with republican liberty. His soul was comprehensive and his spirit bold as the character which records his signature – and if persevering aid to the right cause in sickness, sorrow, sacrifice are honorable, then is Mr. Hancock's life entitled to our highest panegyric [praise and laud].

While he was thus conspicuous in the front rank of the advocates of liberty and law, beside him stood a Roman patriot. Samuel Adams was certainly an extraordinary character – a man whom few resemble. We should be inclined to think him rather of the school of the younger

Brutus, [†] or bred in the faith of Cato, [††] than an inhabitant of a modern colony; rather taught by the Scottish Covenanters [†††] than by the courtly statesmen in the reign of the third George; contemporary rather with Standish [§] and Carver [§§] than with Bernard [‡] and Hutchinson. [‡‡]

[†] Brutus (circa 85-42 BC) was a Roman patriot, fanatical for liberty, who believed that saving the Roman Republic was the greatest cause for which he could fight. For this reason he helped assassinate Julius Caesar to keep the Republic from falling into degradation and ruin under Caesar's usurped leadership. Because Brutus was an important political figure, when he heard that the Roman army was losing to opponent Marc Antony's army, Brutus committed suicide rather than be captured by the enemy and thus boost their morale. Brutus is sometimes called a "second Cato."

[††] Cato (95-46 BC) was a Roman patriot who refused to make any compromises against the Republic for any reason – he was ardent in his defense of liberty and his country and resisted Greek influence on Rome as decadent and corrupt.

[†††] The Scottish Covenanters (circa 1557-1688) were the Presbyterians of Scotland who formed official covenants to pursue the protection of the Presbyterian religion in England (Presbyterians were a religious minority, and therefore often persecuted and martyred both by Anglicans and Catholics). The Covenanters fought in various civil wars in England, for and against kings (depending on their King's disposition toward presbyterianism, but they were unsuccessful in their quest for the full exercise of their faith until the Glorious Revolution of 1688 restored the Presbyterian church in Scotland. In short, the Covenanters were willing to fight to protect and preserve their faith.

[§] Myles Standish (1584-1656) was the military leader who accompanied the Pilgrims to America and on numerous occasions led successful military defenses of that colony from attack by hostile enemies.

[§§] John Carver (1576-1621) led the Pilgrims to America, arranging for the use of the *Mayflower* and being responsible for the formulation of "The Mayflower Compact" – the first document of self-government written in America. Carver became the first governor of the Plymouth Colony of Pilgrims in Massachusetts.

[‡] Francis Bernard (1712-1779) was a British colonial governor, first of New Jersey and then of Massachusetts; he vigorously enforced the despised Stamp Act and other British measures. (However, when he began to soften and to agree with the colonists' positions, he was recalled to London in 1769 and replaced by the Crown.)

[‡‡] Thomas Hutchinson (1711-1780) became the British colonial governor of Massachusetts in 1771 and served in the tumultuous days leading up to the American Revolution. He was wealthy and was the epitomé of unquestioned loyalty to the British crown, defending the King regardless of which of the colonists' rights might be infringed or violated. He favored the hated Stamp Act and provoked the Boston Tea Party through his unyielding and tyrannical positions. He considered Samuel Adams his bitterest enemy and held a strong personal hatred for him.

There was "a daily beauty in his life" † which calls for our warmest approbation. His public course exhibited a firmness and decision which were indeed remarkable; he was no half way man; reform with him required total, final, essential alteration. Poor as he was, †† it was idle to attempt to bribe such a man – to the allurements of fortune he was blind as her own fabled divinity, but to the real charms of liberty he paid his homage with clear unclouded vision. In private he was conciliating and benevolent, in public strenuous and severe. He could contemplate the gathering clouds with satisfaction, could see a glory in the fearful struggle, could moralize upon the day of battle. . . . Differing widely in character from Mr. Hancock he was equally useful to the cause of American freedom; their names were inscribed together on the same record of proscription and glow with equal grandeur on the same scroll of fame [the Declaration]. . . .

In attempting to award a feeble measure of justice to the memory of these eminent men, it is not designed to assign to them exclusive praise. The results of our Revolution produced a company of patriots unsurpassed in earthly annals – men wise and bold in counsel and the field. The majority of that vigorous race have gone to brighter climes [regions]; a few – alas, how few! – remain to greet this morning: ††† blessed by the wishes of their country – blessed by the sight of na-

---

† This phrase is a line from a famous William Shakespeare (1564-1615) play, *Othello* (Act V, Scene 1).

†† Samuel Adams was indeed poor and in many ways lived what today would be considered a life of poverty. He and his family were often without clothes (except for what his wife sewed for them) and the roof on his house leaked during rains. Nevertheless, Adams was very generous – even to a fault. He often worked for others but required no pay; he freely loaned what little money he had to those in need and more than half the time was never repaid. He was also of a generous spirit in his official position as a collector of taxes for the city. He frequently neglected to collect the taxes of the poor, telling his superiors that the poor needed their belongings more than the town needed the taxes, and that he would resign before he would collect taxes from them. Adams himself was so poor that when he was elected to the Continental Congress, his friends and neighbors were kind enough to arrange to buy him a suit of clothes, shoes, and a hat fitting for his new responsibilities.

††† Only three of the fifty-six signers still remained alive "to greet [that] morning": Thomas Jefferson, John Adams, and Charles Carroll of Carrollton.

tional prosperity beyond their fondest hopes – the rest we trust are joined again with Washington above the reach of time.

The last – the best – effect of this immortal instrument has been upon the nations of the earth. The lessons which it diffuses have not been lost, have not died away unheard. Crushed, trampled on, oppressed, liberty rises by her own resistless energy to renew the struggle for the dearest rights of man. . . . Yes, my fellow citizens, the subtle fluid is at work; the waters are rising and they will pour the great tide of liberty throughout the globe. . . . ■

An Oration by

Noah Webster

1798

AN

ORATION

PRONOUNCED BEFORE THE

CITIZENS of NEW-HAVEN

ON THE

Anniverſary of the Independence of the United States,

JULY 4ᵗʰ 1798;

AND PUBLISHED AT THEIR REQUEST.

By NOAH WEBSTER, jun.

NEW-HAVEN;
Printed by T. and S. GREEN.

Noah Webster

Noah Webster
(1758-1843)

Noah Webster is recognized by most Americans today primarily because of the dictionary that bears his name. However, he also directly impacted the areas of law, politics, government, and especially education (for which he has been titled "America's Schoolmaster").

Noah was raised in rural Connecticut, and in 1774, his father – who had only a limited education – mortgaged the farm to raise the money to send his son to Yale. Noah twice left Yale to join in the fighting of the American Revolution, each time eventually returning to his studies. Upon his graduation, he began teaching school while simultaneously pursuing the study of law. During his three years of legal studies (and while teaching), he lived in the home of attorney Oliver Ellsworth, who later was a delegate to the Constitutional Convention and then a Chief Justice of the US Supreme Court.

Webster's three years of teaching school revealed to him the weaknesses of American education – it was too dependent on British traditions and textbooks. Understanding that a continued attachment to Great Britain in education might lead to a return to her in politics, Webster began to promote a distinctly American system of education.

In 1783, he published his first textbook – a speller that introduced purely American spellings of words – spellings still used today. That first text was followed by dozens of others; over the next six decades Webster authored schoolbooks on history, government, etiquette, medicine, law, agriculture, theology, science, meteorology, and numerous other subjects. Webster's works were praised by many of America's greatest statesmen, including George Washington and Benjamin Franklin.

In the government arena, Noah Webster was one of the first Americans to issue a call to replace the Articles of Confederation with a US Constitution (*Sketches of American Policy*, 1784-1785). When the Constitutional Convention assembled in Philadelphia (where Webster was at that time teaching school), many of the delegates to the Convention dined with or called on Webster at his home (e.g., George Washington, William Livingston, Roger Sherman, Ben Franklin, Abraham Baldwin, James Madison, etc.). In fact, Article I, Section 8 of the Constitution embodied Webster's specific ideas on national copyright protection.

Following the adjournment of the Convention, delegates asked Webster to exert his influence to help secure public acceptance of the new Constitution. He responded enthusiastically and in 1787 published *The Leading Principles of the Federal Constitution* (which he dedicated to Benjamin Franklin) to urge its support and ratification.

Webster's political influence went beyond the formation of the Constitution. For example, when the Jay Treaty was negotiated in 1794 to settle the unresolved difficulties between America and Great Britain following the American Revolution, it was opposed by many well-intentioned Americans. Webster therefore published ten articles explaining the treaty and urging support for it; and according to Rufus King (a signer of the Constitution and a diplomat for four Presidents), Webster's articles caused the public acceptance of that treaty.

Webster served three terms in the Massachusetts legislature and two terms in the Connecticut legislature (as well as a term as a Connecticut judge). He also helped found Amherst College and served as the first president of its board of trustees. Additionally, he established the *American Minerva* – New York City's first daily newspaper.

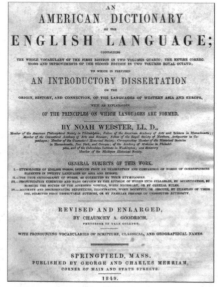

WEBSTER'S 1828 DICTIONARY

Webster's *magnum opus* – and the work for which he is still most famous today – was his masterpiece *Dictionary of the English Language* (1828). In his two-decade long preparation of that dictionary (containing 12,000 words and 40,000 definitions not found in any previous dictionary), Webster learned over twenty languages.

Five years later, Webster applied the knowledge he had gained in his work on the dictionary to produce America's first modern language Bible (*A Revision of the Authorized Version of the English Bible*) in which he updated outmoded English words to their modern meanings (e.g., "bring" for "fetch," "sixty" for "threescore," "perhaps" for "peradventure," etc.).

Webster – like so many others in his day – was thoroughly competent in a wide range of skills and areas of knowledge; throughout all of his diverse endeavors, his Christian faith was apparent – and he applied that faith to all areas of life. For example, in relation to government, Webster declared:

WEBSTER'S 1833 BIBLE

[T]he religion which has introduced civil liberty is the religion of Christ and His apostles, which enjoins humility, piety, and benevolence; which acknowledges in every person a brother or a sister – and a citizen with equal rights. This is genuine Christianity, and to this we owe our free constitutions of government.

And concerning education, Webster declared:

The Christian religion is the most important and one of the first things in which all children under a free government ought to be instructed. . . . No truth is more evident to my mind than that the Christian religion must be the basis of any government intended to secure the rights and privileges of a free people.

In fact, Webster believed that Christianity held the solution to <u>all</u> of the nation's ills. As he explained:

All the miseries and evils which men suffer from vice, crime, ambition, injustice, oppression, slavery, and war, proceed from their despising or neglecting the precepts contained in the Bible.

Webster's lengthy and productive life ended in 1843; his accomplishments prove him to be one of America's most brilliant and well-rounded leaders. In fact, only two years after his death, the publishers of his 1845 *Speller* (a speller first introduced in 1782 and used for over two-centuries in American schools) summarized the belief of earlier generations when it declared:

Webster, "The Schoolmaster of our Republic." . . . grew up with his country and he molded the intellectual character of her people. Not a man has sprung from her soil on whom he has not laid his all-forming hand. His principles of language have tinged every sentence that is now, or will ever be, uttered by an American tongue. . . . Only two men have stood on the New World whose fame is so sure to last – Columbus, its discoverer; and Washington, its savior. Webster is, and will be, its great teacher; and these three make our trinity of fame.

This oration by Webster was delivered in New Haven. Interestingly, New Haven had been started as an independent Colony in 1638. In 1700 a college (Yale) was founded there, and the next year the New Haven Colony merged with the Connecticut Colony. The

NEW HAVEN AT THE TIME OF WEBSTER

two towns of New Haven and Hartford served as the co-capitals of the combined Connecticut Colony until 1873 when Hartford became the sole capital city.

New Haven, with its 3,500 inhabitants, was a center of activity during the American Revolution. Following the Revolution, New Haven became incorporated as a city and Roger Sherman (a signer of both the Declaration of Independence and the Constitution) was elected its first mayor. New Haven was also the site of the controversy over the slave ship *La Amistad* – a case argued and won at the US Supreme Court by anti-slavery advocate John Quincy Adams.

At the time of this oration, Jonathan Trumbull was the State's governor. Trumbull had been an aide-de-camp to General Washington during the Revolution, a framer of the Bill of Rights in the first federal Congress, and a US Senator prior to becoming governor.

On the national scene, John Adams was President and Thomas Jefferson was Vice-President; France was engaged in a war against most of the countries in Europe; the French treachery against America in the XYZ Affair had become public knowledge; and while American leaders were preparing for open war with France, they were still hoping – and striving – to avert it. Simultaneously, American sentiment was growing for an all out war with the Muslim nations terrorizing American interests and shipping overseas. In preparation for that war (which finally commenced under President Jefferson), President Adams organized an independent Department of the Navy and oversaw the construction of a number of American warships, including the *Constitution* ("Old Ironsides"), the *Constellation,* and the *United States.*

Additionally, the 11th Amendment was added to the Constitution; the Marine Corps was officially formed; the first four-man submarine was built; the first American patent for a clock was issued; a side-paddle steamboat had just been built; and John Chapman (known as "Johnny Appleseed") planted his first apple seed nursery in Pennsylvania.

Webster's oration, displaying the depth of his knowledge as well as his abilities with language and words, is an inspiring oration that heralds the uniqueness of American liberty and compares it with that attempted by other nations, explaining why America's succeeded when others' failed. In fact, Webster points out the inherit fallacies of the theories behind other governments and warns against longing after their systems or compromising our own unique system. Webster's oration is a challenge to maintain intact – and preserve from generation to generation – the truly American principles of liberty.

®ration.

FRIENDS AND FELLOW CITIZENS. . . .

Twenty and two years are completed since the fathers of our empire – appealing to God and the impartial world for the purity of their motives – rent asunder the bands that connected the English colonies with their Mother Country and declared them an INDEPENDENT NATION. . . . To a man who believes in the superintendence of Divine Providence over the affairs of this globe, the settlement of America by a civilized people and the establishment of a free government unfold a most splendid and consoling prospect. Secluded as America has been from a knowledge of the Europeans till a late period of the world, may we not consider it as reserved by Heaven for the theatre of important events or as the asylum of persecuted freedom and religion? If we cast our eyes over the other quarters of the earth, where do we find a spot for the retreat of religion, morals, or arts for private peace or public tranquility? In Asia, man is sunk to a brute and so firmly established in the despotism that chains him to the earth that we have no hopes that this condition can be ameliorated [improved] by ordinary means. Africa gives us no better prospect. That portion which was once civilized has been reduced back to barbarism. Europe is in a state of ferment and her future destiny may baffle all our calculations.

So far as history and a knowledge of the human heart will aid our conjectures, we may consider Europe as declining in improvement and reverting back to the darkness and ferocity of the Middle Ages. . . . Improvement arises from competition in a state of society where tranquility fosters taste, and laws secure to every man the fruits of his industry. But under the dominion of a foreign power, all emulation [competition] is destroyed. . . .

A vanquished nation is a debased, a degraded nation. The brave Romans themselves, when they were conquered by the Northern Barbarians, gradually lost their elevation of character and sank to a level with their slaves. With their character and their freedom, the

Romans lost their arts. Europe, by conquest, was reduced to slavery, and under the military system which followed the reduction of the Roman Empire was, for many centuries, overspread with darkness and ferocity. Precisely the same has been the effect of the Saracen and Turkish conquests in all parts of the world where their arms have extended. † And from the uniform tenor of facts we draw the conclusion that the nation which aspires to universal dominion solicits the reign of barbarism.

Indeed, it is a melancholy truth that the progress of civilization and refinement has ever been defeated or retarded by a passion for conquest. An Alexander, †† an Omar, ††† or a Bonaparte, § may in a year destroy the arts and extinguish the genius of a nation. Where is the Italian who will toil for years with his pencil or his chisel if an edict

---

† Both the Saracen and Turkish were Arab Muslims. In the first part of the 8th century AD, the Saracens rampaged through Europe, seized and occupied France (or parts of it) for almost two centuries until expelled by Count William the Liberator in 973 AD. The Saracens and Moors had also taken Sicily and Italy, but those areas were recaptured by the Norman lord Roger de Hauteville in 1071 AD. Webster is charging that during the times when these lands were under these Muslim conquerors, the people were degraded, their character lowered, and their arts debased, just as had been the case in Rome under Barbarian conquerors.

†† Alexander refers to Alexander the Great (356-323 BC), a pupil of the great Aristotle. Alexander, considered one of the greatest military generals in history, literally conquered most of the known world in his lifetime, subduing and ruling areas from Greece to the Persian Empire to India to Asia to northern Africa. He became a harsh and ruthless ruler and even established a worldwide religion requiring that all worship him. He was not greatly mourned upon his premature passing at the age of 32, and his empire crumbled shortly after his death.

††† Omar (circa 634 AD) was a military leader who greatly expanded Muslim rule – named the "Sword of God" for his accomplishments. Among his exploits, he took Jerusalem (638 AD) and led the Arabs in taking the Persian Empire (642 AD).

§ Napoleon Bonaparte (1769-1821) was raised in French military schools – a fit match for his military proclivities. As leader of a French republican military unit, he successfully defeated foreign armies that besieged France and was then promoted and given command of a much larger portion of the army. He next subdued Italy, Austria, Germany, and Egypt, and on his return to France in 1799 was named First Consul and given dictatorial powers over the nation. He began creating his own French empire by systematically conquering most of western Europe, gaining the title, "Master of the Continent." In 1813-1815, Napoleon was finally defeated and exiled, and Europe was freed from his grasp.

from a distant tyrant can at any moment take from him the fruits of his labor and from his country the monuments of his ingenuity? [†] . . . The present war [France v. Europe] is also characterized by circumstances that are more than usually hostile to morality. That species of national piracy (or authorized plunder) which is indulged on the ocean is demoralizing mankind with a rapidity that exceeds all calculation. Should the practice continue a few years longer, we may expect to see revived the condition of man in the tenth century when all commerce was piracy and when the Norwegians and Danes – like modern Algiers [††] – laid Europe under tribute. . . .

[†] That is, Italian renaissance masters such as Leonardo da Vinci (1452-1519) or Michaelangelo (1475-1564) would not have exerted much effort on their masterpieces if there had been no opportunity to enjoy "the fruits of their labor" or view in their own country "the monuments of their ingenuity."

[††] Piracy against America, condoned and encouraged by official governments such as Algiers, placed America in a quasi-war known as the "Barbary Powers Conflict." It began shortly after the Revolutionary War (1784) and continued through the presidencies of George Washington, John Adams, Thomas Jefferson, and James Madison. The Muslim Barbary Powers (Tunis, Morocco, Algiers, Tripoli, and Turkey) were warring against what they called the "Christian" nations (England, France, Spain, Denmark, and the United States). In 1801, Tripoli even declared war against the United States, thus constituting America's first official war as an established independent nation. (In 1787, Morocco had signed a treaty with the United States, and took no further role with the other four Barbary Powers in subsequent actions against America.)

Throughout this long conflict, the Barbary Powers (called "Barbary Pirates" by most Americans) regularly attacked undefended American merchant ships. Not only was the cargo of these unprotected ships easy prey but the Barbary Powers were also capturing and enslaving "Christian" seamen in retaliation for what had been done to Muslims by the "Christians" of previous centuries (e.g., the Crusades, and Ferdinand and Isabella's expulsion of Muslims from Granada). As an indication of the Barbary activity against America, in 1790, Algiers alone captured 11 American ships and enslaved more then 100 sailors, holding them for ransom.

In an attempt to secure a release of captured seamen and a guarantee of unmolested shipping in the Mediterranean, President Washington dispatched envoys to negotiate treaties with the Muslim nations. (Concurrently, he encouraged the construction of American warships to defend the shipping and confront the Barbary government-sponsored pirates – a plan not seriously pursued until President John Adams created a separate Department of the Navy in 1798.) The American envoys negotiated numerous treaties of "Peace and Amity" with the Muslim Barbary nations to ensure "protection" of American commercial ships in the Mediterranean. However, the terms of the treaty frequently were unfavorable to America, either requiring her to pay hundreds of thousands of dollars of "tribute" to each

On the other hand, that condition of man which secures to him freedom in the exercise of all his rational faculties and at the same time places him beyond the reach of demagogues, tyrants, and mobs is best adapted to every species of improvement.

Such a state of society is not to be found in Asia, Africa, or Europe. The two former are overspread with ignorance and despotism; the latter is agitated by an inveterate [stubborn] contest between the advocates of the old systems and the delirious projectors of visionary schemes of reformation. The dove of peace, of virtue, and of religion will for a long time find no rest in that quarter of the globe. America alone seems to be reserved by Heaven as the sequestered region where religion, virtue, and the arts may find a peaceful retirement from the tempests which agitate Europe. And it is a circumstance that ought not to escape our observation that our revolution happened in good time to prepare an empire and a free government for the reception of the wrecks of the little freedom which Europe enjoyed. The Christian and the lover of freedom may consider this continent as destined by Heaven to save and to foster the seeds of a pure church and excellent constitutions of government which may hereafter be transplanted to Europe when the hostile spirit of the present revolution shall have swept away all the old establishments.

After Europe shall have been scourged with the despotism in every shape – the despotism of kings and of mobs, of hierarchies,

---

country to receive a "guarantee" of safety (i.e., official extortion), or else to offer other "considerations" (e.g., providing a warship as a "gift" to Tripoli, a "gift" frigate to Algiers, paying $525,000 to ransom captured American seamen from Algiers, etc.).

Even though President John Adams developed the navy to help protect American shipping and citizens overseas, he pursued a more pacific and less militaristic approach to the Barbary Powers. However, when Thomas Jefferson became President, he utilized the military approach. He appointed General William Eaton as "US Naval Agent to the Barbary States," authorizing him to lead a military expedition against Tripoli. That expedition was successful and freed captured American seamen.

(Incidentally, the US Marines played a large role in that conflict, thus providing the source of the line in the Marine Corp hymn: "From the halls of Montezuma to the shores of *Tripoli* . . ." Interestingly, two centuries later the Marines were ordered into action in the same region of the world – again against Muslim terrorists – in the 2003 war against Saddam Hussein in Iraq.)

of atheists, of visionary theorists, of armies by land and pirates by sea – after the half of her people have been sacrificed to the ambition of men under the different covers of crowns and liberty caps † – the survivors, weary of eternal discord, of error, of faction, of the persecution of princes and private clubs, of war, assassination, and personal danger (the inevitable fruits of atheism and chimerical [fanciful and absurd] systems of government) will recover from their delusion and seek a shelter from their miseries under well-tempered forms of government analogous [similar] to that of the United States, and under the benign [wholesome] influence of that rational system of religion [Christianity] which is the only sure basis of private happiness and public prosperity.

Should this be the destination of the United States, the idea furnishes new and powerful reasons for guarding the independence and government of our country from the arts and the assaults of European nations. If in the Old World men are doomed to sleep away their existence in the torpor [numbness] of slavery or to live in endless hostility, perpetually shedding each others' blood or only enjoying short intervals of repose while resting on their arms, we have the more reason to cling to the Constitution, the laws, to the civil and religious institutions of our country and to cherish the pacific [peaceful] policy which doubles the value of those blessings. If there is a

---

† The liberty cap – a symbol identified primarily with the French Revolution – actually dates back to the time of ancient Rome and Greece when slaves wore liberty caps during their struggle for freedom. The American patriots occasionally used liberty caps (especially in the Northeast) as early as 1765 following the Stamp Act. These caps were knitted stocking caps with the motto "Liberty" or the phrase "Liberty or death" knitted into the cap band. In 1789 the cap received widespread use during the French Revolution as a political statement that individuals wanted to be citizens rather than subjects. By 1792, after the fall of the French monarchy, the liberty cap became a prominent symbol of the Revolution, required to be printed on all official documents and to be worn in the Assemblies. It is therefore associated with the most bloodthirsty French revolutionaries who relied on the indiscriminate use of the guillotine and other brutal measures to silence opponents; and it was in this context that the liberty cap is best known and the context to which Webster is referring. Those with liberty caps became just as repressive and tyrannical as the kings they had opposed, hence his allusion to "half her people sacrificed to . . . crowns _and_ liberty caps," meaning there seemed to be no moral difference between the kings and the alleged freedom fighters.

nation on earth which enjoys the same portion of freedom as the people of this country, a knowledge of that nation has never yet reached us. And the condition of Europe herself demands of us that we should resist with energy and success all attempts to introduce among us the principles and the vices which disturb her repose. [†] . . .

We probably enjoy at this moment more of the blessings of freedom than European nations can acquire, and more than the people in their corrupt and debased condition are capable of enjoying. . . . From these considerations let us learn to estimate the value of the position we hold on the globe, and of our civil and religious institutions. Let us consider them as sacred deposits entrusted to our care by the God of nations, to be guarded with vigilance and to be handed down unimpaired to posterity. . . .

[T]he inevitable consequences of that false philosophy which has been preached in the world by Rousseau, Condorcet, Godwin [††] – and

---

[†] The French Revolution eventually produced such a bloodbath of horrors that it became known as the "Reign of Terror." While America was grateful to France for her assistance during the American Revolution, Americans were unwilling to aid France in her later wars against Britain and the rest of Europe. France, in her anger against America for this lack of assistance, tried "to introduce among us the principles and vices which disturb her repose." For example, in 1793, the French sent to America an ambassador Edmond Charles Genet who attempted to stir up hostile feelings between Americans and President Washington. In 1794, French privateers began to attack and seize American ships on the high seas. President Washington had refused to be drawn into a war with France, and President Adams continued that policy. In fact, Adams dispatched American diplomats to meet with the French in an attempt to resolve the difficulties, but the French refused to receive the American representatives. The French foreign minister Tallyrand made it clear that he would meet with the Americans only if he received $250,000 delivered to him through three French agents designated as X, Y, and Z. Americans, learning of this official extortion (called the XYZ affair), were greatly enraged against the French. This French intrigue was occurring at the time of Webster's oration, and Webster is urging Americans to keep their standards high and not give in to the distasteful "principles and vices" of the French.

[††] These three are political philosophers who held political opinions largely in direct contradiction both to the opinions of the Founding Fathers and of the openly Christian political philosophers on whom the Founders most heavily relied – philosophers such as Baron Secondat de Montesquieu, Sir William Blackstone, John Locke, et al.

The first of the three noted by Webster, Jean Rousseau (1712-1778), was a French political philosopher who openly deplored the influence of both Christians and Christianity on a society. As he explained: "[N]o State has ever been founded without a religious basis [but]

other visionaries who sit down in their closets to frame systems of government – are as unfit for practice as a vessel of paper for the transportation of men on the troubled ocean. In all ages of the world, a political projector or system-monger of popular talents [i.e., an articulate false philosopher] has been a greater scourge to society than a pestilence. While, then, we rejoice that nature has placed our "goodly heritage" [PSALM 16:6; i.e., the lines and boundaries of our country] at an immense distance from the disturbances which harass Europe – and that our citizens have had the fortitude to dissolve our political relation to that quarter of the earth – let us guard our independence, our liberties, our commerce, and our principles with the firmness of freemen and the prudence of enlightened statesmen. Let us remember that force never makes a convert – that no amelioration [improvement] of society can be wrought by violence and that an attempt to reform men by compulsion must produce more calami-

---

the law of Christianity at bottom does more harm by weakening than good by strengthening the constitution of the State." He further declared, "True Christians are made to be slaves."

Marie Jean Antoine Nicolas Caritat Marquis de Condorcet (1743-1794) was a French political philosopher who asserted that man was capable of perfection in this world – an assertion that was anathema to the American belief in the inherent depravity of man, with elevation possible only through the influence of Christ. Condorcet asserted that reason, not God, was the ultimate master – another teaching in direct contradiction to the Founders' declaration of their submission to "the Supreme Judge of the Universe" and their "firm reliance on . . . Divine providence" announced in the Declaration of Independence.

William Godwin (1756-1836), titled the "Father of Philosophical Anarchism," had an intense dislike for religion (he rebelled against everything except "reason") and became an atheist (although he later retreated to a position that he called "vague theism"). Godwin was a student of Rousseau and helped publish Thomas Paine's defense of the French Revolution in his *Rights of Man* – a work vigorously opposed by American Founders, including John Adams, Fisher Ames, *et. al.* Godwin's final work was the fulfillment of his lifelong ambition to refute Christianity and "sweep away the whole fiction of an intelligent former world and a future state."

All three of these philosophers, having rejected religion, embraced the belief that man was perfectible in this world and therefore that a perfect government was achievable – one in which there was no disorder – one in which, according to Godwin, "there will be no war, no crimes, no administration of justice (as it is called), and no government. . . . Every man will seek with ineffable ardor the good of all." Significantly, not one historical account can be invoked to support the thesis of the perfectibility of man, thus causing Webster correctly to label their anti-Christian teachings as "false philosophy" and "chimerical [absurd] systems of government."

ties than benefits. Let us reject the spirit of making proselytes to particular creeds by any other means than persuasion – that fanaticism in politics which (like bigotry in religion) dogmatically arrogates [demands] the exclusive privilege of knowing what is right and denouncing all difference of opinion as damnable heresy. A fanatical [French] republican who imposes his form of government on his neighbors by violence, or silences opposition by the guillotine, is as much a bigot and a tyrant as the Pope who shuts the Bible against investigation and burns heretics at the stake. †

Let us never forget that the cornerstone of all republican governments is that the will of every citizen is controlled by the laws – or supreme will – of the state. The moment in which the regular authorities cease to govern, that moment the principles of our Constitution are prostrated and we are slaves. . . . [L]et us never suffer an external influence unknown to the laws of our country to interpose and warp its administration. How glorious was it for America that her revolution was guided by wise and able men, and that scarcely was its progress disgraced by a popular tumult [mob violence]! If there is a species of despotism more ferocious, more merciless, and inexorable [unyielding] than another, it is the dominion of bullies and ruffians.

---

† Webster condemns fanaticism and extremism whether in politics or religion. The political fanaticism of French Republicanism has already been discussed, and much more will be presented on pp. 84-85. In reference to fanaticism in religion, Webster here specifically cites Papal inquisitions.

Several Catholic Popes over the centuries had practiced or endorsed tyrannical persecution, officially condoning inquisitions that included the killings of dissenters and burnings at the stake – actions that even predated Pope Lucius III's 1184 AD establishment of an official Catholic office of the Inquisition. (It was not until 1962 that Pope John XXIII closed that office.) Not only had Pope Gregory IX and several subsequent Popes declared the Bible off-limits to anyone but priests (i.e., "shuts the Bible against investigation"), but Popes such as Pius V and Sixtus V had even served as chief inquisitors (i.e., "burned heretics at the stake") before their ascension to the papacy. In various centuries, these efforts almost completely eradicated Protestantism in several nations, including Italy, Spain, and France; and in Germany, the Catholic efforts against Protestants led to the Thirty-Years War. However, there were also some atrocities by Protestants as well – such as when John Calvin assisted in having Protestant Michael Servetus burned at the stake for his heterodoxy, or when Henry VIII killed both Catholics and Protestant dissenters in England. In short, Webster is condemning fanaticism, bigotry, and violence whether in politics or religion.

May the illustrious example of the conductors of the American Revolution be sacred to imitation in every period of our history!

Never, my fellow citizens, let us exchange our civil and religious institutions for the wild theories of crazy projectors – or the sober, industrious, moral habits of our country for experiments in atheism and lawless democracy. *Experience* is a safe pilot; but *experiment* is a dangerous ocean, full of rocks and shoals!

Since the establishment of our independence – and more especially since the operation of national government – our growth and prosperity have verified the most sanguine [optimistic] predictions. In the general information of the body of citizens, and in mechanical ingenuity, the American character stands probably unrivalled; in every branch of science it is highly respectable. No nation can boast of more industrious and enterprising citizens. . . . Such advantages of a political, moral, and commercial nature are not to be bartered away for visionary schemes of government or fraternal embraces.

[O]ur fathers were *men* – they were heroes and patriots – they fought – they conquered – and they bequeathed to us a rich inheritance of liberty and empire which we have no right to surrender. . . . Yes, my fellow freemen, we have a rich and growing empire – we have a lucrative commerce to protect – we have indefeasible [inalienable] rights – we have an excellent system of religion and of government – we have wives and children and sisters to defend; and God forbid that the soil of America should sustain the wretch who wants [lacks] the will or the spirit to defend them.

Let us then rally round the independence and Constitution of our country, resolved to a man that we will never lose by folly, disunion, or cowardice what has been planned by wisdom and purchased with blood. ■

An Oration by

George Bancroft

1826

AN

ORATION

DELIVERED ON THE FOURTH OF JULY, 1826,

AT NORTHAMPTON, MASS.

BY

GEORGE BANCROFT.

NORTHAMPTON,

T. WATSON SHEPARD, PRINTER.

1826.

George Bancroft

George Bancroft

(1800-1891)

George Bancroft is one of the nation's foremost historians, titled "The Father of American History" for his herculean and groundbreaking efforts in that field. Bancroft was also a high-ranking and noted political figure, being accorded honors rarely bestowed on any citizen.

George Bancroft was the son of the famous minister, the Rev. Aaron Bancroft, who authored the popular 1807 work, *The Life of Washington*. (Rev. Bancroft was a traditionalist remembered as the last person in his part of Massachusetts to wear the three-cornered hat and the short knee-length pants.) Aaron's regular prayer at family meals had been, "Give us a teachable temper"; his son George epitomized that answered prayer.

At the age of eleven, George went to Phillips Exeter Academy and at thirteen entered Harvard. After graduation, he remained at Harvard for an additional year pursuing the study of divinity and then spent the next four years in Germany, France, Italy, Switzerland (and elsewhere), continuing his studies in Biblical learning and Asian languages. During his time in Europe, he earned both a master's degree and a doctorate.

After his return to Boston, Bancroft pursued a teaching profession and accepted offers to fill pulpits. However, he became dissatisfied with his own efforts both in education and the ministry and instead found his fulfillment in public writing.

In the 1820s and 1830s, he was a frequent contributor to the popular periodical, the *North American Review*, authoring articles on financial, historical, political, and academic topics. In 1834, he began work on his *magnum opus:* the *History of the United States* – a project that spanned four full decades, with the last volume (volume ten) being published in 1874.

During that same time, Bancroft was heavily involved in a number of political endeavors. In 1837, he authored a Thanksgiving proclamation for New York Governor William Marcy and also received a presidential appointment from President Martin Van Buren. In 1844,

as Secretary of the Navy for President James K. Polk, he was responsible for the establishment of the Naval Academy at Annapolis as
well as for advancing the work of the Naval Observatory. And while
serving as Secretary of War, Bancroft oversaw military action in the
early stages of the US-Mexican War of 1845.

Bancroft originally pursued his career as a Democrat and even
delivered the official eulogy following the death of Democratic President Andrew Jackson. However, because Democrats promoted slavery and strongly supported the secession of the South from the
Union during the Civil War, Bancroft supported Republican leaders
and even delivered the official eulogy following the death of Republican President Abraham Lincoln.

This oration by Bancroft was his first in what became a long and
impressive list of public orations and writings. It was delivered in
Northampton, Massachusetts – an historic town with a rich legacy.
Established in 1654 as a Puritan settlement on land purchased from
the Indians, the town was home to famous leaders and the site of
several important historic events. For example, Jonathan Edwards –
a leading minister in America's First Great Awakening – pastored a
church in Northampton; and Northampton was also the area of the
famous Shays' Rebellion following the American Revolution in which
Daniel Shays and a number of farmers revolted against the State
government in protest of tax policies and farm seizures – a rebellion
that was forcefully quelled.

Northampton was also an innovative educational center, housing
schools for girls and for the deaf (two clienteles often neglected in
America during those years). In fact, it was in Northampton that
Bancroft had opened a boy's school three years before this oration.
Even though Northampton was a booming town in those days, it
was still small by today's standards.

On the national scene, the electoral college had been unable to
garner a majority of votes for any one of the four candidates in the
presidential election, so the House of Representatives elected anti-
slavery leader John Quincy Adams as President; his arch-nemesis,

pro-slavery leader John C. Calhoun, had been elected his Vice-President by the Senate. American hero and favorite adopted son Marquis de Lafayette was making a final farewell tour across the United States, being greeted in city after city by massive, cheering crowds.

On the domestic scene, the University of Virginia – the last great work of Thomas Jefferson's hands – had just opened its doors; the steam railroad engine had just been invented; the tin can was patented; Davy Crockett was newly elected to Congress; James Fenimore Cooper had published *Last of the Mohicans*; San Francisco Bay had just been mapped; and the first American warship had visited Hawaii.

Significantly, this oration was delivered on the 50th anniversary of the Declaration of Independence – the day that both John Adams and Thomas Jefferson died (although public knowledge of these events was not yet known at the time of this oration), leaving alive only one remaining signer of the Declaration: Charles Carroll of Maryland.

Bancroft's oration looks first at the powerful influence of liberty throughout the world. He then examines American liberty, noting that the world was being united by the unique ideas of liberty flowing from America. Bancroft's oration is full of thankfulness to God for His blessings upon America. In fact, it opens with the line "Our act of celebration begins with God" and closes with a similar sentiment, challenging Americans to a recognition of the hand of God both in our history and in our future. Bancroft's oration is an uplifting look at the uniqueness of American liberty.

Oration.

Our act of celebration begins with God. To the eternal Providence – on Which states depend and by Whose infinite mercy they are prospered – the nation brings its homage and the tribute of its gratitude. From the omnipotent Power Who dwells in the unclouded serenity of being *without variableness or shadow of change* [JAMES 1:17], we proceed as from the Fountain of Good, the Author of Hope, and the Source of Order and Justice, now that we assemble to commemorate the revolution, the independence, and the advancement of our country!

No sentiments should be encouraged on this occasion but those of patriotism and philanthropy. When the names of our venerated fathers were affixed to the instrument which declared our independence, an impulse and confidence were imparted to all efforts at improvement throughout the world. The festival which we keep is the festival of freedom itself – it belongs not to us only but to man. All the nations of the earth have an interest in it, and humanity proclaims it sacred!

In the name of LIBERTY, therefore, I bid you welcome to the celebration of its jubilee; [†] in the name of our COUNTRY, I bid you welcome to the recollection of its glories and joy in its prosperity; in the name of HUMANITY, I welcome you to a festival which commemorates an improvement in the social condition; in the name of RELIGION, I welcome you to a profession of the principles of public justice which emanate directly from God!

These principles are eternal not only in their truth but in their efficacy [effectiveness]. The world has never been entirely without witnesses to them; they have been safely transmitted through the succession of generations; they have survived the revolutions of individual states and their final success has never been despaired of. Liberty has its foundation in human nature and some portion of it exists wherever there is a sense of honor. Are proofs of its existence demanded? As the mixture of good and evil is the condition of our earthly being,

---

† The Year of Jubilee was established in the Bible in Leviticus 25 to be observed every fifty years; it was a time of national celebration and festivity as well as a time for the restoration of the land to its owners and the freeing of slaves.

the efficient agency of good must be sought for even in the midst of evil – the impulse of free spirits is felt in every state of society and in spite of all constraint! There may have been periods in which the human mind has sunk into slothful indifference, the arm of exertion been paralyzed, and every noble aspiration hushed in the tranquility of universal submission, but even in such periods the world has never been left utterly without hope. And when the breath of tyranny has most effectually concealed the sun of liberty and shrouded in darkness the magnificence of his beams, it has been but for a season.

Tomorrow he repairs the golden flood,
And gilds [adorns] the nations with redoubled ray [rainbow]. [†]

Nature concedes to every people the right of executing whatever plans they may devise for their improvement, and the right of maintaining their independence. Of the exercise of these rights there have always been examples. The innate love of national liberty proceeds from an impulse and waits only for all opportunity to demonstrate its power. It has aroused the brave and generous from the first periods of history to the present moment and has been a principle of action under every form of government. It was this which made Marathon the watchword of those who fight for their country; [††] this pointed the arrows of the Parthian; [†††] this lent an air of romance to the early history of the Swiss and gained the battles of Morgarten and Sempach; [§] this inspired the

---

[†] These lines come from a 1752 poem called "The Bard" by famous English poet Thomas Gray (1716-1771).

[††] The Battle of Marathon (490 BC) is considered one of history's most decisive battles. Some 10,000 Greeks defeated a much larger Persian invading force of 25,000 soldiers and 40,000 sailors, thus preserving Greek independence.

[†††] In 247 BC, the Parthians secured their independence from Greece and defeated Alexander the Great's successors (the Seleucids) to create their own independent empire in ancient Persia, comprised of what is now Iran, Iraq, Turkey, Armenia, Georgia, Azerbaijan, Turkmenistan, Afghanistan, Tajikistan, Pakistan, Syria, Lebanon, Jordan, Palestine, and Israel.

[§] Morgarten is a mountain in central Switzerland where in 1315 AD, a small Swiss force defeated the Austrians to help gain Swiss independence. Sempach is a small town – also in central Switzerland – where the Swiss decisively defeated the Austrians in 1386 AD and preserved Swiss independence.

Dutch when their freedom was endangered by the arms of Louis XIV and could be secured by no smaller sacrifice than to lay the soil of Holland beneath the ocean; [†] this blessed the banners that waved on Bunker Hill and canonized the memory of those who fell as the elect martyrs and witnesses to their country's independence; [††] this made the French republic invincible when it stood alone against the world; [†††] this, which formerly at Pultova had taught the Russians to fight, [§] sacrificed Moscow, a splendid victim, on the altar of national existence; [§§] this united the mangled limbs of Germany, breathed a spirit once more into the long divided members, and led them against the French as if

---

† In 1672, when the French attacked the helplessly overmatched Dutch, the Dutch opened the dikes and flooded their own country, thus saving it from French occupation.

†† The Battle of Bunker Hill (which was actually fought on Breed's Hill) occurred outside of Boston on June 17, 1775 – the first full-fledged battle of the American Revolution. (Although the fight between the Minutemen and the British had occurred several weeks earlier at nearby Lexington and Concord, that action was little more than a skirmish followed by very effective guerilla sniping activity from the Americans as the British returned to Boston.) Five thousand British troops attacked one thousand Americans entrenched on Bunker Hill on three separate occasions. They were repulsed by the Americans on the first two attacks, but by the third attack, the Americans were running so low on powder and ammunition that General Israel Putnam ordered his troops, "Don't fire until you see the whites of their eyes!" The Americans finally ran out of ammunition and withdrew from the hill. While the battle was technically a victory for the British, in reality they suffered a military defeat: the British lost 1,000 soldiers, the Americans only 400 (including General Joseph Warren). Untrained American farmers and merchants fighting for their liberties had effectively defeated the greatest military force in the world at that time.

††† When the French established their republic in 1792 and executed Louis XVI, a coalition of other monarchies joined together to attack France and defeat the republic lest the French independence movement spread to their own nations. That coalition against the French included England, Holland, Spain, Sardinia, Italy, Austria, and Prussia.

§ In 1709, the Swedes attacked the Russians at Pultova and were decisively defeated, thus preserving Russia and resulting in the most famous defeat in Swedish history and ending Sweden's role as a major European power. The battle of Pultova is considered one of the fifteen most decisive battles in world history.

§§ In 1812, Napoleon occupied Moscow. A large fire occurred (probably started by French looters) and consumed the city, made largely of wood. The fire initiated an anti-French uprising that eventually caused the Russians to rise up and drive Napoleon's army out of the country. Thus, without the "sacrifice [of] Moscow . . . on the altar of national existence" by fire, it is questionable whether the French invaders would have been defeated.

impelled by the throbbings of one mighty heart! † What need of many words? This made New Orleans a place of proud recollections, †† and still more recently has raised its boldest standard under the Southern sky and finished a career of victory in the field of Ayacucho. †††. . . The historians, the orators, the philosophers are the natural advocates of civil liberty. From all countries and all ages we have the same testimony – it is the chorus of the whole family of nations.

The events of the last fifty years lead us to hope that liberty – so long militant – is at length triumphant. From our own Revolution the period derives its character. As on the morning of the nativity, the astonished wizards hastened with sweet odors on the Eastern road, § our government had hardly come into being and the star of liberty shed over us its benignant [kindly] light before the nations began to follow its guidance and do homage to its beauty. The French Revolution followed our own, and new principles of action were introduced into the politics of Europe. The melancholy events which ensued must be carefully distinguished from the original resistance to unlimited monarchy. . . . The torch of freedom was in their hands (though it had been seized with profane recklessness). §§ The light

---

† In 1806, French Emperor Napoleon took Germany as part of his conquests and dissolved the loosely knit German confederation. In 1813, the separate German affiliates rose up as one and defeated Napoleon, leading to the establishment of a strong German confederation of over three dozen sovereign states, four of which were republics.

†† The battle of New Orleans – the final battle of the War of 1812 (a battle that actually occurred *after* the peace treaty had been signed) – was a resounding American victory. Under the command of General Andrew Jackson, the American forces defeated the British with what historians describe as the most disparate loss in the history of warfare. The British suffered 700 dead, 1,400 wounded, and 500 taken prisoner while the Americans suffered only eight dead and 13 wounded.

††† Ayacucho is an area in south-central Peru where in 1824 a major battle occurred in the Peruvian struggle for independence from Spain. Outnumbered two to one, the Peruvians prevailed against the superior Spanish forces. Simón Bolivar (the South American liberator, called "the George Washington of South America") declared: "The victory of Ayacucho has affirmed for ever the total independence of the [Peruvian] republic."

§ This refers to the birth of Christ, when the three wise men traveled to see the young babe (MATTHEW 2:1-12).

§§ The "armies of the [French] republic" holding "the torch of freedom" indeed manifested their "profane recklessness" through many gruesome and barbaric acts. The French leaders

did indeed glare with a wild and terrific splendor, yet as it waved round the continent of Europe its beams reached the furthest kingdoms and startled tyranny in its securest recesses. . . . But whatever may be the chances that popular sovereignty will finally prevail in Europe, that continent is no longer to the world

who initially fought to oppose the tyranny of the king ironically came to believe – like the king they had overthrown – that terror was a necessity and that due process was unimportant; the indiscriminate use of the guillotine and other tools of brutality therefore became a regular tool to terrorize the populace.

This eventually resulted in what became known as "The Reign of Terror" – an apt description, for in the course of only nine months, some 16,000 citizens were guillotined (and it is believed that 40,000 died as a result of execution or tortures such as whipping, branding, breaking on the wheel, mutilation, etc.). In fact, on one day, 800 were hacked to death, and on another day, 500 children were taken to a meadow and clubbed to death. Additionally, infants were regularly guillotined and river barges were filled with citizens and sunk, drowning all on board. Notwithstanding these horrific atrocities, the French leaders actually condemned the American Revolution for its violence! (By comparison to the French Revolution, 10,000 British combat deaths were caused by Americans during the eight years of the Revolution; and the British caused 4,435 American deaths in battle, with the deaths of an additional 11,500 Americans in British prisoner of war facilities – a total far below the number of French executions, not of enemies, but of citizens.)

There was a distinct philosophical difference between the American and the French Revolutions. The French Enlightenment thought behind their revolution rejected the presence of religion in public life and asserted that morality was attainable without religion – a philosophy that not only produced a bloodbath and display of horrors in the French Revolution but also engendered widespread condemnation of that philosophy by a number of Founding Fathers (Alexander Hamilton, Gouverneur Morris, Noah Webster, John Jay, Fisher Ames, etc.). In fact, Washington delivered a succinct warning against embracing this French anti-religious philosophy in his "Farewell Address" of September 17, 1789:

> Of all the dispositions and habits which lead to political prosperity, religion and morality are indispensable supports. In vain would that man claim the tribute of patriotism, who should labor to subvert these great pillars of human happiness. . . . The mere politician . . . ought to respect and to cherish them. A volume could not trace all their connections with private and public felicity [happiness]. Let it simply be asked, "Where is the security for property, for reputation, for life, if the sense of religious obligation desert . . . ?" And let us with caution indulge the supposition that morality can be maintained without religion. Whatever may be conceded to the influence of refined education on minds . . . reason and experience both forbid us to expect that national morality can prevail in exclusion of religious principle.

While liberty was sought by all nations throughout the world, the principles of American liberty distinguished America from other nations (such as France) not just in philosophy but especially in behavior.

what she once was. She has fulfilled her high destiny; she has been for many centuries the sole depositary and guardian of all that is most valuable in government, letters [learning], and invention [science] in present enjoyment and religious hope. But human culture has at length been transplanted to other climes [regions of the earth], and already grown to a more beautiful maturity. Whatever destiny may hang over Europe, mankind is safe. Intelligence and religion have found another home. Not only in our own free States, the Cross is planted on each side the Andes; [†] and the rivers which empty into either ocean fertilize the abodes of civilization.

A more admirable and cheering spectacle, therefore, than Europe can offer is exhibiting in our own hemisphere. A family of free states has at once come into being and already flourishes on a soil which till now had been drooping under colonial thralldom. [††] Our happiness is increased by the wide diffusion of the blessings of free institutions. And it is a pleasing consciousness that the example of our fathers taught these new republics what were their rights and how they might assert them. . . . Will you not all coincide with me when I say we feel for man – not for a single race of men; and wherever liberty finds followers (as wherever Christ has disciples), be it that English or Indian, Spanish or African blood pours in their veins, we greet them as brethren! . . .

---

† Planting the cross on each side of the Andes refers to Christian missionary efforts along the Andes mountains. The Andes touch seven nations on the western side of South America: Bolivia, Peru, Ecuador, Colombia, Argentina, Chile, and Venezuela. While Catholic missionaries and missions had been present in all seven nations as early as the 1500s (Catholics established missions in Venezuela in 1516; Bolivia in 1537; Argentina in 1539; Ecuador in 1541; Peru in 1567; Chile in 1593; and Columbia in 1604), Protestant missionaries were much later in coming. Since Bancroft was a Protestant, he understandably was most interested in – and spoke here about – the work of Protestant missionaries. The first Protestant missionary in Argentina arrived in 1818; in Chile in 1821; in Peru in 1822; in Bolivia in 1827; in Venezuela in the 1830s; in Columbia in 1856; and in Ecuador in 1895. Obviously, the missionaries in most of these nations arrived after this oration was delivered, but the Protestant missionary work that had by then occurred in Argentina, Chile, and Peru was sufficient to acknowledge that "the Cross is planted on each side of the Andes."

†† Long under Spanish domination, parts of Central America and the north of South America declared independence in 1813, forming the independent nation of Gran Columbia – comprised of what is now the individual nations of Columbia, Ecuador, Panama, and Venezuela.

[This] age has been fertile in strange contrasts – in unforeseen and unparalleled events. Europe is filled with the shadows of departed states and the graves of ruined republics. In the North, an adventurer of fortune has succeeded to the Swedish throne and the legitimate King lives quietly in exile; † while in the rest of Europe the doctrine of the divine right has been revived. †† Rome was once more made the head of a republic. The secular power of the Pope – annihilated for a season – was restored by the help of Turks, Russians, and English, infidels, Schismatics, and Heretics. ††† An army of Europeans, having in its train a band of scientific men, pitched its victorious camp at the foot of the Pyramids. The solitary banks of the Nile again became the temporary abode of glory and civilization; and again the bands of armed men poured through the hun-

---

† At that time, Jean Baptiste Jules Bernadotte (1763-1844, called Charles XIV) ruled over Sweden. He had been a French general under Napoleon and the minister of war for France. The legitimate king of Sweden had been Gustavus IV (1778-1837), but he had opposed Napoleon; Sweden wanted peace with Napoleon and therefore forced Gustavus' abdication, eventually replacing him with Napoleon's general Bernadotte. The former king Gustavus lived the rest of his life in exile in Switzerland.

†† Nations that for a short period had thrown off monarchy had once more reverted to the system of government they once hated – such as France, which overthrew monarchy in 1789 and reinstated it in 1815 – thus demonstrating that "the doctrine of the divine right has been revived."

††† This refers to the invasion and overthrow by Napoleon – on multiple occasions – of the Papal States (a large land area in Italy). The first occasion was from 1793-1797, when Napoleon originally subdued the Papal States. In 1797, a treaty was reached that restored some powers to the Papal States, but the Pope was deposed of his civil powers and died in exile in 1799. In 1800, Napoleon returned to the area and again overthrew Italy and the Papal States; an 1801 treaty returned limited jurisdiction over some of the land back to papal authorities. In 1809 when Napoleon again took the Papal States, the Pope excommunicated him – an act that enraged Napoleon and caused him to take the Pope prisoner. Napoleon then abolished many of the Papal States and merged them into parts of the existing Italian nation. Eventually, several nations (including England, Turkey, Russia, Austria, Spain, and others) formed coalitions to help free Italy and the Papal States from Napoleonic control; they were finally successful in 1815. It was to this coalition that Bancroft alluded, citing "the help of Turks, Russians, and English, infidels, Schismatics, and Heretics" in restoring "the secular power of the Pope" (that is, restoring the Papal States and the Pope's civil authority over the Papal States) through Napoleon's defeat.

dred gates of the long deserted Thebes. [†] . . . The whole East has been a scene of continued turbulence till at last a corporation of merchants residing in a distant island has reduced seventy millions of people to subjection. [††] And finally, to notice a singular fact in our own history, he whose eloquent pen [Thomas Jefferson] gave freedom its charter . . . [and] whose principles are identified with the character of our government and whose influence is identified with the progress of civil liberty throughout the world – after declining to be a third time elected to the highest station in the service of his country – has not preserved on his retirement (I will not say fortune enough to bury him with honor) – has not saved the means of supporting the decline of life with decency! [†††] . . .

[†] The "army of Europeans" refers to Napoleon's forces that came to Egypt in 1798 and defeated the Egyptians in an area near the Pyramids. Accompanying Napoleon's army were a number of historians, engineers, and scientists. After the military forces conquered the country, this non-military contingency began their work and achieved many major scientific milestones, including the discovery of the Rosetta Stone, deciphering the hieroglyphics, and uncovering much of Egypt's ancient history and civilization. As Napoleon left Egypt to take Palestine, the "army of Europeans" marched up the Nile and "poured through the hundred gates of the long deserted Thebes" where they saw the majesty of that ancient city which – although constructed in 2000 BC and destroyed in 30 BC by the Romans – nevertheless was still home of some of the best preserved ancient monuments in Egypt (e.g., the colossi of King Ramases, the temple of King Tut, etc.). In 1805, following Napoleon's departure from Egypt, an Ottoman (Turkish) army officer (Mohamad Ali) became the Egyptian leader and greatly modernized the nation.

[††] The "corporation of merchants" was the East India Company and the "distant island" was England. The British East India Company literally ruled more than seventy million inhabitants in India with an iron fist, operating a monopoly and successfully eliminating rivals, sometimes by commercial and sometimes by military means. As a result of the efforts of the East India Company, the entire nation of India eventually came under British control. The company was not disbanded until 1858.

[†††] This section is not referring to the death of Jefferson, for although Jefferson died in Virginia on the very day of this oration, that was not yet known in Massachusetts. What Bancroft is commenting on here is that although Jefferson gave so much to America (the Declaration, his Presidency, the Louisiana Purchase, etc.), he did not have enough personal finances left at the end of his life to support his own retirement. In fact, the personal economic difficulties of Jefferson were well known to the nation at that time – he even sold his prized private library to Congress in order to raise funds on which to live. Therefore, Bancroft notes that although Jefferson has enough to be buried should he die, he does not have enough to be "buried with honor" or even to "support the decline of life [his latter years] with decency" – that is, Jefferson gave the nation much and received nothing in return and did not even have enough of his own finances left to live comfortably or securely in his retirement.

While the United States show to what condition a nation is carried by establishing a government strictly national, we have in Russia and in Haiti examples of a military despotism; in England a preponderating [all-powerful] aristocracy; in France a monarchy with partial limitations; in Prussia an absolute monarchy, yet dependent for its strength on the spirit of the people; in Naples, the old-fashioned system of absolute caprice [lawlessness]. Let men reason if they will on the different systems of government; the history of the age is showing from actual experiment which of them best promotes the ends of the social compact.

Thought has been active in our times not with speculative questions but in devising means for improving the social condition. Efforts have been made to diffuse Christianity throughout the world. The cannibal of the South Sea forgets his horrid purpose and listens to the instructions of religion; the light of the Sabbath morn is welcomed by the mild inhabitants of the Pacific islands; and Africa and Australia have not remained unvisited. Colonies which were first established on the Guinea coast for the traffic in slaves have been renewed for the more effectual suppression of that accursed trade. † . . .

I turn from the consideration of foreign revolutions to our own condition and meet with nothing but what may animate our joy and increase our hopes. . . . In whatever direction we turn our eyes, we find one unclouded scene of prosperity – everywhere marks of advancement and increasing opulence [affluency]. . . . I will ask you to look around at your own fields and firesides, your own business and prospects. There is not one desirable privilege which we do not

---

† Some of the lands along the Guinea coast from which so many had been enslaved and exported in the slave trade subsequently became colonies to help reverse that evil and repatriate African slaves (and their descendants) to their homeland. For example, in 1822 the American Colonization Society founded Liberia on the Guinea coast to receive free blacks from America who wanted to return to their own continent (Liberia's capitol was named "Monrovia" in honor of President James Monroe, who helped found the colony). Similarly, Sierra Leone (also along the Guinea coast) became a British colony to which slaves from England could return (founded largely through the efforts of British abolitionist Thomas Clarkson, it was originally called the "Province of Freedom" and its main settlement was "Freetown"); and Ghana (another site on the Guinea coast originally used for slave trading) eventually became used by the British as a base to suppress slavery and the slave trade.

enjoy – there is not one social advantage that reason can covet which is not ours. I speak not merely of our equal rights to engage in any pursuit that promises emolument [profit] or honor, I speak also of the advantages which we are always enjoying – security in our occupations, liberty of conscience, the certain rewards of labor; … moral order pervades an industrious population, intelligence is diffused among our yeomanry [average citizens], the plow is in the hands of its owner, and the neat aspect of our farmhouses proves them the abode of contentment and successful diligence!

Nor are we without our recollections. I never can think without reverence of the spirited veteran who, on the morning of the seventeenth of June, in the seventieth year of his age, was hastening on horseback as a volunteer to Bunker Hill; but coming to Charlestown Neck and finding the fire from the British ships so severe that crossing was extremely dangerous, coolly sent back the animal which he had borrowed of a friend and shouldering his musket, marched over on foot! When the Americans saw him approach, they raised a shout and the name of Pomeroy ran along the lines. † Since the ashes of the gallant soldier do not rest among us, let us the more do honor to his

---

† Seth Pomeroy (1706-1777) was a gunsmith who early in his life had entered the military and became distinguished as a soldier and officer. At the time of this incident in the American Revolution, he had already seen over thirty years of close-quarter combat experience. Pomeroy was so recognized for his bravery and patriotism that he was elected to the Provincial Congress even though he was nearly 70 years old at the time. After it was evident that a war with Great Britain would occur, Pomeroy – a distinguished officer of many previous battles – went to General Artemas Ward in 1775 to enlist as a volunteer. When Pomeroy heard the sound of cannon fire from Bunker Hill, he borrowed a horse from General Ward and rode at breakneck speed toward the battle. The closer he came to the battle, the more dangerous the area became with flying bullets – and the more Pomeroy feared for the safety of the General's horse. He therefore dismounted, left the horse in the care of a sentry, shouldered the musket he had made for himself, and marched the rest of the way on foot. When he reached the scene of fighting, the other soldiers instantly recognized the great hero, his name being shouted in joy along the front line by the soldiers. He knelt down with those soldiers – soldiers the age of his grandchildren – behind a rail fence to defend the area. As a volunteer private, he and the others stood their ground until ordered to withdraw. Five days later, he received an appointment as a senior brigadier-general (one of only eight named by Congress), but he declined the appointment and headed home. However, the next year when Pomeroy heard that Washington was in trouble, he led a force of militia to aid Washington in New Jersey; he never returned from that march.

memory! We have raised a simple monument to his name in our graveyard but his body reposes where he breathed out life on his country's service, in the maturity of years and yet a martyr!

Even before that time and before the hour of immediate danger when the boldest spirits might have wavered in gloomy uncertainty and precious moments were wasting in indecision, one of our own citizens, my friends – his memory is still fresh among us – had been the first to cry in a voice which was heard beyond the Potomac, "We must fight!" And when some alternative was desired and reconciliation hoped from inactivity and delay, clearly saw the absolute necessity of the case and did but repeat, "We must fight!" It was in front of the very place where we are now assembled that the hearts of our fathers were cheered and their resolution confirmed by the eloquence of Hawley. †

And what is the cause and the guarantee of our happiness? What but the principles of our Constitution! When our fathers assembled to prepare it, the genius of history admitted them to the secrets of destiny and taught them by the failures of the past to provide for the happiness of future generations. No model was offered them which it seemed safe to imitate; the Constitution established a government on entirely liberal principles [unselfish principles that benefit the general public rather than a few elite] such as the world had never beheld in practice. The sovereignty of the people is the basis of the system. With the people the power resides – both theoreti-

---

† Joseph Hawley (1723-1788) was a patriot from Northampton, Massachusetts (the site where this oration was delivered). He early embraced the cause of American liberty (perhaps even more ardently than John Adams or James Otis) and organized pre-Revolutionary activities in the western part of the State. In the summer of 1774, Hawley addressed the Massachusetts delegates to Congress in a written paper called "Broken Hints" in which he proffered his advice to that group. In that writing, Hawley forcefully declared: "_We must fight_ if we cannot otherwise rid ourselves of British taxation. The form of government enacted for us by the British parliament is evil – against right – utterly intolerable to every man who has any idea or feeling of right or liberty. There is not heat [public intensity] enough yet for battle; constant and negative resistance will increase it. There is not military skill enough; that is improving and must be encouraged. _Fight we must_, finally, unless Britain retreats." Hawley's words were so widely circulated and his voice was indeed "heard beyond [south of] the Potomac." In fact, when John Adams later read Hawley's words to Virginian Patrick Henry, Henry warmly responded, "I am of that man's mind."

cally and practically. The government is a democracy – a determined, uncompromising democracy – administered immediately by the people or by the people's responsible agents. In all the European treatises on political economy – and even in the state-papers of the Holy Alliance – the welfare of the people is acknowledged to be the object of government. We believe so too. But as each man's interests are safest in his own keeping, so in like manner the interests of the people can best be guarded by themselves. . . .

We believe the sovereign power should reside equally among the people. We acknowledge no hereditary distinctions and we confer on no man prerogatives [superiority] or peculiar privileges. Even the best services rendered the state cannot destroy this original and essential equality. Legislation and justice are not hereditary offices – no one is born to power, no one dandled [pampered] into political greatness! Our government – as it rests for support on reason and our interests – needs no protection from a nobility. And the strength and ornament of the land consist in its industry and morality, its justice and intelligence.

The states of Europe are all intimately allied with the church and fortified by religious sanctions. We approve of the influence of the religious principle on public not less than on private life, but we hold religion to be an affair between each individual conscience and God, superior to all political institutions and independent of them. Christianity was neither introduced nor reformed by the civil power. And with us the modes of worship are in no wise prescribed by the state.

Thus, then, the people governs – and solely; it does not divide its power with a hierarchy, a nobility, or a king. The popular voice is all powerful with us. This is our oracle; this we acknowledge is the voice of God! . . . The interests of the people are the interests of the individuals who compose the people. . . . We give the power to the many [the people] in the hope and to the end that they may use it for their own benefit – that they may always so legislate as to open the fairest career to industry and promote an equality founded on the safe and equitable influence of the laws. We do not fear – we rather invite – the operation of the common motives which influence humanity. . . .

The laws of the land are sacred – they are established by the majority for the general good. Private rights are sacred – the protection of them is the end of law and government. When the rules of justice are trampled on, or the power of maintaining it wrested from the hands of its appointed guardians, there is tyranny – let it be done where and by whom it may, in the Old World or in the New, by a monarch or by a mob. Liberty frowns on such deeds as attacks on her safety, for liberty knows nothing of passion. She is the daughter of God and dwells in unchanging tranquility beside His throne; her serene countenance is never ruffled by excitement; reason and justice are the pillars of her seat, and truth and virtue the angels that minister unto her. When you come with violence and angry fury, do you pretend to come in her name? In vain; she is not there; even now she has escaped from among you!

Thus, then, our government is strictly national, having its origin in the will of the people, its object in their happiness, its guarantee in their morality. [Our] government [is] essentially radical (in so far as it aims to facilitate the prompt reform of abuses) and essentially leveling (as it prohibits hereditary distinctions and tends to diminish artificial ones). . . .

And that our glory as a nation might in nothing be wanting, the men to whom the people first confided their interests – they whose names stand highest in the annals of our glory – the statesmen by whose voice the pure spirit of the country expressed its desires – the leaders by whose bravery and skill our citizens were conducted to success in the contest for their rights – were of undoubted integrity and spotless patriotism, men in whom the elements of human greatness were so happily mixed that as their principles were generous and elevated, so their lives were distinguished by a course of honorable action and the sacrifice of private advantage to the public good! . . . [And t]he political privileges of the people correspond with the moral greatness of our illustrious men. . . .

In possession of complete personal independence, our religious liberty is entire; our press without restrictions; the channels of wealth and honor alike open to all; the cause of intelligence asserted and advanced by the people! In our houses, our churches, our halls of justice, our legislatures – everywhere there is liberty! . . . Soul is breathed into the public administration by the suffrages [votes] of the people, and the aspect of our policy on the world is favorable to universal improvement.

The dearest interests of mankind were entrusted to our country. It was for her to show that the aspirations of former ages were not visionary – that freedom is something more than a name – that the patriots and the States that have been martyrs in its defense were struggling in a sacred cause and fell in the pursuit of a real good. The great spirits of former times looked down from their celestial abodes to cheer and encourage her in the hour of danger [c.f., HEBREWS 12:1]. The nations of the earth turned towards her as to their last hope. And the country has not deceived them. . . .

Liberty is her device [banner]; liberty is her glory; liberty is the American policy! This diffuses its blessings throughout all our land; this is cherished in our hearts, dearer than life and dear as honor; this is imbedded in our soil more firmly than the ancient granite in our mountains! This has been bequeathed to us by our fathers – and whatever may befall us, we will transmit the heritage unimpaired to the coming generation!

Our service began with God. May we not believe that He Who promises assistance to the humblest of us in our efforts to do His will regards with complacency the advancement of the nation and now from His high abode smiles on us with favoring benignity [kindness]? Trusting in the Providence of Him, the Universal Father, let the country advance to the glory and prosperity to which – mindful of its exalted privileges – it aspires! Wherever its voice is heard, let it proclaim the message of liberty and speak with the divine energy of truth [and let] the principles of moral goodness [be] consistently followed in its actions! And while the centuries – as they pass – multiply its population and its resources, let it manifest in its whole history a devoted attachment to public virtue, a dear affection for mankind, and the consciousness of its responsibility to the God of nations! ■

An Oration by

John Lathrop, Jr.

1796

AN

O R A T I O N,

PRONOUNCED

J U L Y 4, 1796,

AT THE

REQUEST OF THE INHABITANTS

OF THE

TOWN OF *B O S T O N.*

IN

COMMEMORATION

OF THE

ANNIVERSARY

OF

AMERICAN INDEPENDENCE,

BY JOHN LATHROP, JUN.

B O S T O N,
PRINTED AND SOLD BY BENJAMIN EDES,
*Kilby Street.—*1796.

John Lathrop, Jr.
(1772-1820)

John Lathrop, Jr., was a famous writer and educator from a long line of distinguished ministers bearing the same name. In fact, his early ancestor, the Rev. John Lathrop (1584-1653), was the founder of several towns in Massachusetts and is considered one of the four most influential ministers in colonial America.

His father (also a John Lathrop) was a famous patriot minister; at his side, John Jr., had personally experienced some of the darker aspects of the American Revolution when his father's church in Boston was destroyed by the British. His father had been so intimately involved in the Revolution that in 1815 he authored a famous history of that conflict: *A Compendious History of the Late War*. Clearly, the younger Lathrop was raised with a full appreciation of the cost and responsibilities of liberty as well as an intimate knowledge of the principal actors in the conflict.

Lathrop – like many of his forebears – graduated from Harvard; but unlike many of his ancestors, he did not enter the ministry, becoming instead a poet and an attorney. He became associated with some of the leading American writers (such as Robert Treat Paine) and prominent statesmen of his day (e.g., Fisher Ames – a leader in framing the Bill of Rights).

In 1799, Lathrop traveled to the British colonial possession of India, where he started a school in which he infused the ideas of liberty and independence in his lessons. As an unforeseen result, the school was largely unsuccessful: he encountered official resistance to his school because he taught the ideas of freedom. In fact, the famous British statesman Lord Wellesley directly opposed Lathrop's teaching of liberty in India's education system because he felt such teachings would increase the difficulty of keeping India a conquered nation. After a decade of largely futile efforts as a missionary of liberty, Lathrop returned to the United States where he continued his teaching, directing a school in Boston.

Lathrop's endeavors were not limited to education; he also received political appointments, edited almanacs, delivered scientific lectures, and became a recognized speaker delivering numerous public addresses – including this Fourth of July oration.

At the time of this oration, Boston was one of America's largest and most historic towns. Founded in 1630 by Puritan elder John

EARLY BOSTON – A PORT CITY FILLED WITH SHIPS AND CHURCHES

Winthrop, it soon became New England's center of religion, politics, and commerce. A century and a half later, Boston was still a recognized center – but this time as a hotbed of opposition to Great Britain and home to leading "Sons of Liberty" such as John Hancock, Samuel Adams, James Otis, and Paul Revere. Consequently, some of the harshest early British actions against American independence occurred around the Boston area (e.g., the attack on Lexington and Concord, the battle of Bunker Hill, the burning of Charlestown, etc.).

At the time of this oration in 1796, the State's governor was Samuel Adams ("Father of the American Revolution"), and Boston had grown to 18,000 inhabitants, making it one of America's largest cities.

WITH 18,000 INHABITANTS, BOSTON WAS ONE OF AMERICA'S LARGEST CITIES

On the world scene, the French Revolution – at first applauded by Americans as an attempt to overthrow a tyrannical monarchy – had degenerated into the bloody "Reign of Terror," and the French were at war against almost every country in Europe; they even directly intruded into American internal affairs and almost brought America into a war against them. Elsewhere, American ships in the Mediterranean were being attacked regularly by Muslim terrorists.

On the national scene, George Washington was in his second term as President; the bank of the United States and the US Mint had just been created; Washington, DC was selected as the new capital city; and construction was authorized on both the Capitol and the White House. Vermont, Kentucky, and Tennessee had also been added as new States to the Union.

Science and technology were making revolutionary strides. African-American astronomer Benjamin Banneker was becoming famous for his almanacs; a helium-filled balloon had carried a passenger a mile high over Philadelphia (which President George Washington looking on); and African-Americans Absalom Jones and Richard Allen were working with signer of the Declaration Dr. Benjamin Rush to deliver medical treatment during what was at that time the nation's worst-ever plague: the yellow-fever epidemic in Philadelphia. The nation's first steam engine, first cotton gin, and first primitive wooden railroad had just been built.

On the cultural front, the first national abolition movement had been started by Benjamin Rush, joining individual State abolition societies into a national working group, and Richard Allen founded the first African Methodist Episcopal (AME) Church and was ordained its first bishop.

Lathrop begins his oration with a look at the causes of the American Revolution. He next expounds on the blessings of America's liberty and extols those who played a prominent role in her revolution. He then traces the development of American government after the Revolution and finishes by comparing our liberties with that in other nations across the world. Lathrop not only identifies the reasons for America's success but he also challenges future generations to preserve our unique freedoms.

Oration.

It is now acknowledged as a fact in political biography that liberty descended from Heaven on the 4th of July, 1776. We are assembled on this day, the twentieth anniversary of her advent, to sympathize in those pleasures which none but freemen can enjoy – to exchange those mutual congratulations which none but freemen can express.

The first promulgation of the Gospel of Liberty was the declaration of American independence. Her apostles – the venerable Congress, whose mode of evangelizing made many a *Felix tremble* [ACTS 24:25] – sealed the doom and issued the death-warrant of despotism. The measure of *her iniquity was filled up* [c.f., GENESIS 15:16] – the decree was gone forth: the Americans were elected by God to redeem from bondage the miserable victims of arbitrary power.

But it would have been of no avail for them to publish to the enslaved the beauties of freedom, describe her charms, and urge the duty of possessing her while they themselves were declared by an act of the British legislature liable to be bounden by the will and laws of that overbearing kingdom, *"In All Cases Whatsoever."*[†] They disdained an inconsistency of character; they presented the world with a glorious example by effecting their own emancipation. Yes, my fellow countrymen, you indignantly refused a base submission to the usurpation of Great Britain – to the impositions of her Parliament and the insolence of her ministry. After opposing reasoning and argument to her absurd pretensions, and dignified remonstrance [petition] to her unjustifiable encroachments, the solemn appeal was made to Heaven, the sword was drawn, and the once inseparable tie of connection between the two countries severed in twain. The mighty blow re-

---

† When the British Parliament finally repealed the odious Stamp Act of 1765, they replaced it with the Declaratory Act of 1766. This Act asserted that America had no right to choose representatives either to make the laws under which she would be governed or to impose the taxes under which she would live. According to the 1766 Declaratory Act, the King and the Parliament – containing no American representatives – "had, hath, and of right ought to have, full power and authority to make laws and statutes of sufficient force and validity to bind the colonies and people of America, subjects of the crown of Great Britain, *in all cases whatsoever.*" In other words, self-government was not allowed in America.

sounded through the universe. The nations of the earth were astonished. . . . The Bastilles of tyranny – driven by the shock – reluctantly
admitted the rays of hope to gladden the desponding hearts of their
wretched tenants and opened to their view a distant prospect of scenes
illumined with Liberty's full and perfect day. [†]

What were the feelings, manners, and principles which produced
the great national event, the subject of our anniversary commemoration? Sprung from an ancestry ennobled by their virtue and their
bravery, . . . Americans could not disguise their abhorrence of that
system of policy [government] which had for its object the increase
of regal prerogative [royal privileges] and consequent diminution
[reduction] of the privileges of the people. They had learned the
nature of the rights of man among the earliest rudiments of their
education. That God never created a human being to be a slave was,
in their opinion, an axiom so self-evident – so sacred an article of
natural and revealed religion – that it would have been blasphemy
to have deemed it problematical. . . .

What, then, were their feelings when they were declared slaves by
the most insolent of all the decrees that ever emanated from the pol-
luted source of usurped authority? What were their feelings when
the advice of a Camden was rejected [††] – when the eloquence of a
Chatham, their immortal advocate, was unregarded by the infatu-

---

[†] The Bastille was the prison used by the kings of France both to torture dissident
subjects into obedience and to terrorize the populous in general (for this reason, it was
called by Lathrop "the Bastilles *of tyranny*"). In 1789 at the commencement of the French
effort to throw off monarchy, French citizens stormed the Bastille and freed its prisoners.
In 1790, General Marquis de Lafayette, the young French general so crucial to America's
victory in the Revolution (and a close and devoted personal friend of George Washington),
obtained one of the keys from the dreaded west portal of the Bastille and sent it to Washington as a memento of the freedom that they both richly cherished. (The key now hangs
at Washington's home in Mount Vernon, Virginia.) Lathrop is noting that America's independence directly affected other nations around the world (such as France), spurring them
to seek their own independence.

[††] Camden was Charles Pratt (1714-1794), the 1st Earl of Camden, and a chief justice in
England. Following the imposition of the Stamp Act upon the Americans (1765), Pratt
(Camden) became a strong advocate for the Americans and boldly denounced the British
policies against them.

ated projectors [schemers] of American subjugation?[†] Such their feelings (as those which inspired the patriots of ancient days and the heroes of former times) impelled them to vengeance against tyrants and urged them to godlike achievements. Such as glowed in the authors of Roman and Grecian, of Belgic [Belgian] and Helvetic [Swiss] liberty in the Catos, the Tells, the Nassaus, the Hampdens, the Adamses, and the Washingtons who have maintained and supported the rights of the people;[††] and by preserving their freedom, given life its best grace and existence its brightest charm.

Their manners, Americans! – may those manners and those feelings which inspired the actions and were expressed in the conduct of the patriots of 1776 be exhibited in the deportment of our latest posterity! They were incapable of dissimulation [hypocrisy] – they could not conceal their thoughts nor did they blush to communicate to their sovereign their sorrows and their fears. . . . They petitioned, they argued, they remonstrated [reasoned]. Their petitions were treated with silent contempt; their arguments were addressed to the deaf ears of pride and obstinacy; their remonstrances were construed into overt acts of treason for which they were sentenced to suffer the severest punishment that cruelty could devise or despotism inflict. . . . They unequivocally demonstrated their determined courage and were dignified as the resolutions of their enthusiastic souls. Enthusiastic? Yes! And it was a glorious enthusiasm which inspired with one sen-

---

[†] Chatham was William Pitt (1708-1778), the 1st Earl of Chatham, titled "The Great Commoner" for his advocacy of the common man. Pitt served twice as the Prime Minister of Great Britain; he was an ardent friend to the American Colonies and a vocal critic of the harsh British policies leveled against them. In fact, he collapsed and died in the House of Lords in 1778 while denouncing an anti-American policy.

[††] This list refers to patriots from various nations who led efforts for liberty in their own countries. The "Catos" were Roman patriots who fought political corruption and the rising forces of tyranny and autocracy; the "Tells" refers to William Tell, a patriot fighting for Swiss liberty; the "Nassaus" included William of Nassau, patriot in Belgium, called "The Father of Belgic Liberty"; the "Hampdens" were an English family who resisted King Charles and brought about the English Civil War by fighting unjust taxes and monarchal powers; the "Adams and the Washingtons" were the American patriot leaders, John and Samuel Adams and George Washington.

timent and one intent more than three millions of brave men and kindled those unquenchable flames which melted the manacles of tyranny and illumined with luster divine an emancipated world! . . .

It is my pleasing duty, my fellow citizens, to felicitate you on the establishment of our national sovereignty. . . . Thank God! Uniting in the celebration of this anniversary, I behold many of the illustrious remnant of that band of patriots who – despising danger and death – determined to be free or gloriously perish in the cause. Their countenances [faces] beam inexpressible delight; our joys are increased by their presence – our raptures are heightened by their participation. †

The feeling which inspired them in the "times which tried men's souls" †† are communicated to our bosoms. We catch the Divine spirit which impelled them to bid defiance to the congregated host of despots – which enabled them to dart the lightnings and hurl the bolts which their Franklin had wrested from Jove's right hand at their proud oppressors and ruthless foes. ††† We swear to preserve the blessings

---

† Many of the Massachusetts patriots still alive at that time included notable signers of the Declaration such as Samuel Adams, John Adams, Elbridge Gerry, and Robert Treat Paine; military heroes such as Gen. Artemas Ward, Gen. Benjamin Lincoln, Gen. William Heath, Gen. Rufus Putnam, and Gen. Timothy Pickering; and leaders such as Paul Revere and William Cushing.

†† This phrase is taken from Thomas Paine's famous revolutionary pamphlet, *The Crisis* (1776). Its first paragraph declares:

> These are the times that try men's souls. The summer soldier and the sunshine patriot will, in this crisis, shrink from the service of their country; but he that stands by it now deserves the love and thanks of man and woman. Tyranny, like hell, is not easily conquered; yet we have this consolation with us, that the harder the conflict, the more glorious the triumph. What we obtain too cheap, we esteem too lightly: it is dearness only that gives everything its value. Heaven knows how to put a proper price upon its goods and it would be strange indeed if so celestial an article as freedom should not be highly rated. Britain – with an army to enforce her tyranny – has declared that she has a right (not only to tax) but "to bind us in all cases whatsoever," and if being bound in that manner is not slavery, then is there not such a thing as slavery upon earth. Even the expression is impious, for so unlimited a power can belong only to God.

††† Jove was an allusion to the Greek god "Zeus" (also known as the Roman god "Jupiter") who wielded bolts of thunder and hurled them from heaven to earth; Franklin "wrested" lightning from "Jove's right hand" in his experiments converting lightning to electricity in 1752.

they toiled to gain (which they obtained by the incessant labors of eight distressful years) – to transmit to our posterity our rights undiminished, our honor untarnished, and our freedom unimpaired.

After encountering the combined force of European tyrants in the field in 1783, the claims of America were acknowledged. . . . Britain, humbled and exhausted, worn down with the burden of an unsuccessful war and bleeding with unnumbered wounds, yielded to the imperious [pressing] control of necessity and declared the thirteen United States to be free, sovereign, and independent. Columbia [the United States] reclined at her ease beneath the shade of her laurels. The roses of peace were interwoven with the wreath of glory that encircled her brows. The sword which she had wielded in the cause of Liberty was committed to the hands of Agriculture and furrowed the soil she had fertilized with the blood of her enemies.

But the work was not accomplished; other labors were yet to be performed, other difficulties to be vanquished. During the critical time when harmony of sentiment united the different States – when they were all engaged in the attainment of their freedom – when all their interests were involved in the event of the conflict and the success of their arms – the old system of confederation was adequate to the purposes for which it was instituted. But when danger was over and the ardent passions which inspired every bosom with the generous glow of sympathy and affection of manly courage and fraternal solicitude had subsided, the situation of our country was discovered to be truly alarming. . . . But I will not enlarge on the scenes which followed on that disastrous state of America which was remedied alone by a political revolution more wonderful than the sanguinary [bloody] one which effected her separation from Britain. . . . †

---

† The "political revolution more wonderful" than the "one which effected [America's] separation from Britain" was the replacement of the Articles of Confederation by the US Constitution. At the outset of the Revolution, the thirteen States operated more like thirteen independent nations than like States within the same nation. Each State was zealous to protect its own rights and powers, and each sought to strengthen itself rather than the nation as a whole. Despite the jealous and often petty quarrels between the States, they nevertheless recognized that they had a common enemy (the British), and that it behooved them to

The debilitated [weak] confederation of the States – the inefficacy
[ineffectiveness] of a recommendatory [chosen] system where the obstinacy or envy of one inferior department of government could "put a

---

cooperate together for the common defense of them all. To this end, shortly after approving
the Declaration of Independence, they pursued the formation of some sort of national government – a "firm league of friendship" as the Articles of Confederation later described it.

The Articles of Confederation were approved by Congress in November, 1777, but it was
not until March, 1781 (when the American Revolution was almost over) that they were
finally ratified by the States. Under the Articles of Confederation, a national Congress was
established and each State was allotted delegates to Congress, with the number of delegates
from each State depending on the size of the State and its population. While this caused the
size of a State's delegation to vary from two to seven representatives, each State had only
one vote in the Congress. Neither a judicial nor an executive branch was established.

The weakness of this system soon became apparent to all in five important areas. First,
although the national Congress had power to pass legislation, it had no power to enforce its
laws – and its laws pertained only to States and not citizens. Second, Congress had no
power to tax and therefore no manner in which to raise funds either for the prosecution of
the Revolution or for the common defense of the Colonies. Instead, each State was assigned
a portion of the total expenses of the War (the amount was based on the value of the land
each State possessed); each State was to tax its own citizens in whatever manner it saw fit to
raise the amount due, and then turn the tax receipts over to the national Congress. But
because the States could not be forced to pay their allotted amount, most States rarely met
their obligations. Therefore, a few industrious and energetic States carried the burden of the
others. For example, the tiny State of Connecticut, under Governor Jonathan Trumbull,
contributed more in money, supplies, men, materials, and munitions than larger and more
populated States. Third, Congress had no authority over commerce; and since the treaties
made by one nation with another usually dealt with trade, Congress therefore had no power
to work with foreign countries for the benefit of the nation's commerce. Fourth, decisions
could be made by the national Congress only if two-thirds of the States agreed, thereby
effectively giving to five States the ability to block any measure agreed to by the other eight.
The system therefore empowered a small block of States to create a paralysis of the rest
(which often happened). Fifth, the internal provisions of the Articles made it almost impossible to correct any of its inherent weaknesses, for amendments to the Articles required
unanimous approval by all thirteen State legislatures.

It was fortunate – rather, Providential – that the Articles were ratified so late in the
contest, for had Congress been required to operate under them during the Revolution, it
would have been completely powerless and ineffective during the crucial periods of the
War. Prior to the official adoption of the Articles in 1781, Congress generally operated
upon the majority vote principle rather than the two-thirds standard finally adopted a few
months before the British surrender at Yorktown. Nevertheless, in the short time that the
Articles were in effect, it quickly became apparent that a new form of a national government was needed – eventually resulting in the Constitutional Convention of 1787 that
produced the Constitution.

negative upon the collected wisdom of the Union"[†] – the absolute weakness and nominal supremacy of Congress – were productive of uncounted evils, of continual jargon, and perpetual feuds. And upon minute inspection, the whole structure of our national sovereignty – the temple where were to reside the power and dignity of the United States – appeared so feeble, built of such slight materials, so disproportioned in its form and incompetent to the design of its erection, that it was pronounced unworthy the trouble and expense of alteration or repair.

The decaying edifice was peaceably taken down by consent of the people and the majestic fabric of the Federal Constitution reared in its stead. Sublimely towering to the heavens, its high dome concentrates the admiration and applause of all the kingdoms and dominions of the earth. Supported by its massive columns, it shall stand unshaken and uninjured until in one general conflagration [blaze of fire] the great globe that we inhabit shall be dissolved in the undistinguishable ruin of suns and of worlds [i.e., until the end of the world]!

Americans could not hesitate in their choice of a chief magistrate. From the calm shades of Mount Vernon – called by the voice of his country – he who was our cloud and pillar during our pilgrimage and warfare [c.f., EXODUS 13:21-22] arose to govern and guard

---

[†] This quote is taken from a February 4, 1788, speech made by the Rev. Mr. Thomas Thacher in the Massachusetts State Convention to ratify the US Constitution (a convention presided over by John Hancock). Mr. Thatcher rose to explain why the national government under the Articles of Confederation was too weak and why the Articles should be replaced with the Constitution. His argument was straightforward:

> At the conclusion of the late war, two thirds of the Continental army were from Massachusetts; their provision and their clothing proceeded also – in a great measure – from our extraordinary exertions. The people did this in the fullest confidence that when peace and tranquillity were restored, from the honor and justice of our sister States, our [Massachusetts'] supernumerary expenses would be abundantly repaid. But, alas! how much hath our expectation been blasted! The Congress, though willing, yet had no power to do us justice. The small district of Rhode Island *put a negative upon the collected wisdom of the continent.* (RECORDED IN JONATHAN ELLIOT, *THE DEBATES IN THE SEVERAL STATE CONVENTIONS ON THE ADOPTION OF THE FEDERAL CONSTITUTION* (WASHINGTON, 1836), VOL. II, pp. 141-143.)

In short, the objection of one small State (Rhode Island) was sufficient to prevent another State (Massachusetts) from receiving justice at the hands of the national Congress.

us in peace. Every heart beat with transports [strong emotions], every tongue hailed him welcome – thrice welcome! † Under his wise and unequalled administration, all ranks and degrees of our fellow citizens have been happy and prosperous. The lofty pyramid of American glory has been completed. As our struggles for freedom were unparalleled in their force and success, so our sense of its value has been estimated and proportioned. We have secured it by the best constitution that ever was devised by the wisdom of man; we have defended it as well from foreign invasion as from the more dangerous attacks of domestic ambition. . . .

As Americans we should be jealous of our national character; let us not present it to the world colored with the mottled [mixed] appearance which will be given by division of feelings, difference of manners, and a servile submission to any foreign influence. We have a right – a right dearly purchased – a right which we ought sooner die than relinquish – to act, speak, and think for ourselves. . . .

Intelligence is the soul of liberty. Impressed with a due sense of this important truth, our ancestors instituted seminaries of learning and engrafted the scions [seeds] of literature on their political constitutions. The venerable walls of Harvard are monuments to their eternal honor. An American who can neither read nor write is as rare a phenomenon as the visit of a comet to our hemisphere. Enlightened, honest, and independent, the citizens of our populous towns – the inhabitants of our villages and hamlets – act, reason, and determine for themselves on subjects of the greatest moment [consequence] with such propriety [justness] that the voice of the American people may with justice be termed the voice of God. Let us, then, be Americans!

Our alliance [relationship through treaty] will be courted so long as we behave with that dignified reserve which refuses alike to urge foreign intimacies [agreements] when they are unnecessary and the

---

† Although Washington was asked to serve a third presidential term, he declined and retired; however, at the time of this oration, that decision had not yet been made public. It was four months after this oration that he issued his "Farewell Address," declining a third term by announcing: "I should now apprise you of the resolution I have formed, to decline being considered among the number of those out of whom a choice [for President] is to be made."

adoption of foreign principles and habits. . . . No one member of
the great family of nations has a right to interfere in our domestic
concerns or to impose upon us partial and particular obligations.
To France we owe unbounded gratitude. When assailed by the
tempests and tossed by the rough billows of war, she burst in all the
radiance of her power upon our dreary situation and illumined our
passage to the haven of freedom. Ah! Do we not pay the tributary
sigh to the memories of those Gallic [French] heroes who fell in
our cause or have been sacrificed the victims of revolutionary rage
in that country for which they would have cheerfully shed the last
drop of their blood? † Can we check the tear that gratitude claims
when in mournful idea we visit the dark dungeon of Fayette and
listen to the clanking of his chains? †† . . .

To preserve – to perpetuate – the independence of our country is
the duty not only of our civil rulers but of every individual. Much
depends, frequently, upon the exertions and designs of a single mem-

---

† The "Gallic [French] heroes who fell in our cause or have been sacrificed" in their own
country (that is, who died in America, fighting for Americans, or who were killed when
they returned to France) included Admiral Comte D'Estaing, who twice brought the French
fleet to America to fight the British during our Revolution but who was executed in the
French Revolution in 1794; Pierre Francois-Vernier, who died in combat against the British
while leading American forces in South Carolina; Johann "Baron" de Kalb, a Major-General in the American Army who also died leading American troops in battle in South Carolina; Louis Le B gue de Presle du Portail, who headed the American engineering corps but
who – as Minister of War in France – was forced to flee to America during the "Reign of
Terror," dying at sea on his subsequent return to France; Franois-Louis Teiss dre de Fleury,
who commanded a battalion in the American Revolution and was awarded a Congressional
Medal but who was executed in 1794 during the French Revolution; Jean Baptiste Gouvion,
a colonel in the American Engineer Corps later killed in action during the French Revolution in 1792; and Thomas Conway, an Irish-born Frenchman who served as a Major-General during the American Revolution, later fled France in 1793 during the French Revolution, and died in exile seven years later. These were some of the many "Gallic heroes who fell
in our cause or have been sacrificed [as] the victims of revolutionary rage in that country
[France] for which they would have cheerfully shed the last drop of their blood."

†† Lafayette, the young 19 year-old Frenchman who was a Major-General in the American Revolution (and given an American citizenship at the end of the Revolution), was
imprisoned five years (1792-1797) because of his views of liberty, first in Germany and then
in Austria. At the time of this oration, Lafayette was still in prison – a fact that greatly
angered Americans since he was an American citizen as well as an American hero.

ber of society. The fate of empires has been decided by an aspiring demagogue [†] or an ambitious hero!

Intrigue [secret scheming] and faction [seeking special interests rather than the common good] are the instruments which designing and artful men employ to produce the destruction of good government and the consequent annihilation of order and of law. When those infernal agents [evil influences] are at work, he who bellows loudest for liberty intends to be the tyrant-in-chief. Let us be jealous [suspicious] of those Sempronii [††] – unmantle their nefarious [wicked] intentions and convince them of the fallacy of their hopes to effect their purposes in the midst of an enlightened people.

That a well-regulated militia is necessary to protect our freedom and our happiness – to guard the temple of justice from the outrages of the lawless and abandoned, and to wreak the vengeance of an insulted and powerful nation upon the insolent invaders of our soil – is a truth too generally acknowledged to require any support from argument or from eloquence. Our brave and hardy yeomanry [average citizens], strong and vigorous, compose an army whose force would be as irresistible as their hatred of tyrants is unconquerable. Disciplined and patriotic, their soldierly appearance would make the slaves of Hesse or Waldeck tremble [†††] (though those wretched hirelings have not sense to discern or respect the ardent virtue of their dauntless bosoms).

America – the birth place of Liberty, the trophied abode of victory, the only and fairest residence of Peace, the asylum of the oppressed –

---

† An 1830s educational maxim offers this definition of a demagogue:

A demagogue would like a people half educated; enough to read what he says, but not enough to know whether it is true or not.

†† The Sempronii were two Roman brothers (one died in 133 BC and the other in 131 BC) who – as civil leaders – helped destroy the Roman Republic while allegedly attempting to better the country.

††† Hesse was a German province, and Waldeck was a part of Hesse; from this area came the hated Hessians – the German mercenaries hired by the British to fight the Americans during the Revolution. The Hessians were the "wretched hirelings" of Great Britain who had committed brutal barbarities and atrocities against the Americans. Lathrop is noting that our armed citizens would make even the murderous Hessians tremble.

presents to the world an object for admiration, to superior [civilized] beings a subject for applause. Independent and free, she is subject to no extraneous [foreign] control. . . . May her peace – like her glory and freedom – be perpetual!

On the last page of fate's eventful volume, with the raptured ken [spiritual insight] of prophesy, I behold Columbia's [the United States'] name recorded – her future honors and happiness inscribed. In the same important book, the approaching end of tyranny and the triumph of right and justice are written in indelible characters. The struggle will soon be over; the tottering thrones of despots will quickly fall and bury their proud incumbents in their mass ruins!

Then peace on earth shall hold her easy sway tried source
And man forget his brother man to slay.
To martial [military] arts shall milder arts succeed
Who blesses most shall gain the immortal meed [reward].
The eye of pity shall be pained no more
With victory's crimson banners stained with gore.
Thou glorious aera [era] come! Hail blessed time!
When full-orb'd [uneclipsed] Freedom shall unclouded shine,
When the chaste muses cherished by her rays,
In olive groves shall tune their sweetest lays –
When bounteous Ceres † shall direct her car [chariot]
O'er fields now blasted by the fires of war –
And angels view with joy and wonder join'd
The golden age return'd to bless mankind! ∎

---

† Ceres is Mother-Earth, the Roman goddess of Agriculture.

✶ ✶ ✶ ✶ ✶ ✶ ✶

An Oration by

Elias Boudinot

1793

1793

A N
O R A T I O N,

DELIVERED AT ELIZABETH-TOWN,

N E W - J E R S E Y,

AGREEABLY TO A RESOLUTION

OF THE

STATE SOCIETY OF CINCINNATI,

ON THE

FOURTH OF JULY,
M.DCC.XCIII.

BEING THE

SEVENTEENTH ANNIVERSARY

OF THE

INDEPENDENCE OF AMERICA.

By ELIAS BOUDINOT, *L.L.D.*

Deus enim, qui homines generat et inspirat, omnes æquos, id est pares, esse voluit: eandem conditionem vivendi omnibus posuit. Omnes ad sapientiam genuit: omnibus immortalitatem spopondit. Nemo apud Deum servus est, nemo Dominus.
LACTANT. Lib. 5. Cap. 14. Fol. 501.

ELIZABETH-TOWN:
PRINTED BY SHEPARD KOLLOCK, AT HIS PRINTING-OFFICE AND BOOK-STORE, 1793.

Elias Boudinot

Elias Boudinot

(1740-1821)

Elias Boudinot, a name unknown to most Americans today, was a leading light in the American Revolution – a name as recognizable in his generation as Samuel Adams, Patrick Henry, or Paul Revere. Elias Boudinot was a member of the Continental Congress and played an invaluable role during the fight for independence. In fact, Commander-in-Chief George Washington relied heavily on Boudinot not only for military intelligence about the British but also for advice on military tactics. Congress even vested Boudinot with the individual authority to change the instructions of the congressional Board of War that directed the Revolution. Additionally, Boudinot was appointed by Congress to secure the release of captured American soldiers, and he even expended $30,000 of his own money to help secure their release – an amount that today would equate to over $500,000.

So respected was Boudinot by his peers, that in 1782 he was elected as President of the Continental Congress – one of only fourteen Founders to hold that position. As President of Congress, Boudinot signed the final treaty of peace with Great Britain to end the Revolution, issued the congressional proclamation for a national thanksgiving following the peace, and authorized the orders for disbanding the Continental Army.

Following the Revolution, Boudinot was a member of the New Jersey convention to ratify the US Constitution; he was then elected to the first federal Congress where he helped frame the Bill of Rights. It was Boudinot who initiated the 1789 congressional request to President George Washington that resulted in America's first national day of prayer and thanksgiving being declared under the new Constitution. In 1790, Boudinot became the first attorney officially recognized by the US Supreme Court and admitted to the Supreme Court bar; and in 1795, President Washington appointed Boudinot as Director of the US Mint – a position he also held under Presidents John Adams and Thomas Jefferson. (Some of the rules he implemented in the mint two centuries ago are still in force today.)

Boudinot clearly was dedicated to helping his country; however, he was just as firmly committed to helping those in need. For example, he provided assistance for the education of deaf-mutes, helped fund a hospital to provide medical care for foreigners, gave wooded land to the city of Philadelphia so that the poor could be provided with firewood at low prices, purchased spectacles for the aged poor, and assisted in several other philanthropic endeavors.

Boudinot was reknowned for his Christian commitment – a commitment begun early in his life when he was baptized by the famous Rev. George Whitefield during the First Great Awakening. His Christian convictions remained unwavering throughout his life; in fact, nearly half a century after his baptism, Boudinot left public life and his position at the mint in order to dedicate more time to the study of the Bible.

Over the course of his life, Boudinot authored a number of major religious and theological works, the first of which was his *Age of Revelation* (1795) – a direct rebuttal of Thomas Paine's attack on Christianity and religion in *The Age of Reason*. Boudinot also authored *The Second Advent, or Coming of the Messiah in Glory, Shown to be a Scripture Doctrine and Taught by Divine Revelation from the Beginning of the World* (1815) and *A Star in the West, or An Attempt to Discover the Long-Lost Tribes of Israel* (1816). Additionally, he was a founder and the first President of the American Bible Society (as well as president of the New Jersey Bible Society), served on the American Board of Commissioners for Foreign Missions, encouraged persecuted Jews to come to America to find freedom to worship God, and was active in efforts to train both Indians and young men for the Gospel ministry.

Boudinot delivered this oration in Elizabethtown, New Jersey – an historic town founded by the Puritan fathers and also the site of the State's first legislative meeting in 1668. During the Revolution, many battles were fought in or around the city; and it was the home of one of the States more fiery – and famous – Revolutionary patriots: the Rev. James Caldwell, a Presbyterian minister who led military forces in the State.

Boudinot's oration was delivered in 1793 before the New Jersey Society of the Cincinnati. The Society of the Cincinnati had been founded over a decade earlier (in May 1783) to maintain the bonds of friendship forged among the officers during the Revolution and to provide benevolent care for needy officers and their families. The feelings behind the formation of the society were clearly visible six months after its formation during the emotion-laden disbanding of the army by Washington in December 1783.

During the war, ties of close comradeship had been formed between the officers: men from different States who had never before seen each other were now fighting side by side in their common quest for national independence, losing their new-found friends to British bullets, and binding up the wounds of their injured brethren. With the war over and the soldiers returning home to their farms and businesses, they knew that they would probably never see each other again. At their final meeting, the usually well-controlled emotions of those brave and seasoned veteran officers gave way to kindlier impulses.

Perhaps the best account of that moving scene was given by Col. Benjamin Tallmadge, [†] who reported:

> On Tuesday the 4th of December, it was made known to the officers then in New York that General Washington intended to commence his journey on that day [homeward to Mt. Vernon]. At 12 o'clock the officers repaired to Fraunces Tavern [††]

[†] Benjamin Tallmadge (1754-1835) was a distinguished officer during the American Revolution. He took his orders directly from Washington, who kept him and his cavalry close at hand to perform special assignments during key battles. Tallmadge was an intimate part of Washington's military family, and after the war became the President of the Connecticut Society of the Cincinnati. Tallmadge was later elected to Congress where he served during the presidencies of Thomas Jefferson and James Madison.

[††] Fraunces Tavern was owned by black patriot Samuel Fraunces (1722-1795). Before and during the Revolution, the tavern had been a center of patriot meetings and activities. Washington delivered his military farewell at the tavern in 1783; in 1785 the tavern was sold and later served as offices for the Continental Congress. After the Constitution was ratified and New York City became the temporary federal capital, Washington returned to the city in 1789 as President. Samuel Fraunces became the steward of Washington's household and Fraunces Tavern became home to several federal government agencies, including the Department of Foreign Affairs (which today is the State Department).

in Pearl Street where General Washington had appointed to meet them and to take his final leave of them. We had been assembled but a few moments when his excellency entered the room. His emotions were too strong to be concealed, which seemed to be reciprocated by every officer present. After partaking of a slight refreshment in almost breathless silence, the General filled his glass with wine and turning to the officers said, "With a heart full of love and gratitude I now take leave of you. I most devoutly wish that your latter days may be as prosperous and happy as your former ones have been glorious and honorable." After the officers had taken a glass of wine, General Washington said, "I cannot come to each of you but shall feel obliged if each of you will come and take me by the hand." General Knox being nearest to him turned to the Commander-in-chief who, suffused [bathed] in tears, was incapable of utterance but grasped his hand when they embraced each other in silence. In the same affectionate manner every officer

WASHINGTON TAKING LEAVE OF HIS OFFICERS IN NEW YORK

in the room marched up and parted with his general in chief. Such a scene of sorrow and weeping I had never before witnessed and fondly hope I may never be called to witness again.

Following the tearful farewell, the officers escorted Washington to the river where he boarded a barge to begin his journey to Mt. Vernon by way of Annapolis, where he would resign his commission before the Continental Congress then assembled in that city.

It was to maintain their friendship and preserve an indissoluble union among the officers that General Henry Knox had proposed that a society of perpetual friendship be formed. The name chosen was Society of the Cincinnati – a name based on the account of Cincinnatus, a 5th century BC Roman patriot. Cincinnatus was a farmer who, when Rome was threatened, left his farm and led the citizens in victorious defense of their country against the attacking enemies. After his duties were completed, he retired from public service and returned to his farm. In the minds of the American patriots, Cincinnatus was the epitomé of the citizen-soldier model in which they viewed themselves. The seal of their Society was a medal suspended on a ribbon, and on the medal was an engraving of Cincinnatus at his plow receiving three Roman senators who came to seek his assistance. †

GENERAL HENRY KNOX

Not surprisingly, Washington was chosen the first national president of the organization, and General Henry Knox its first secretary general.

MEDAL OF THE
SOCIETY OF THE CINCINNATI

† Cincinnatus (519-430 BC) was actually called to lead Rome on two occasions about twenty years apart. He declined further service after the second occasion. Washington has been referred to as "The American Cincinnatus" because he declined further service beyond his second term as President.

Chapters were formed in each of the thirteen States so that Revolutionary veterans periodically could gather together in their various geographic regions. (Additionally, a fourteenth chapter was formed in France so that the numerous French officers who fought in the Revolution – officers such as Louís du Portial, Francóis Fleury, Marquis de Lafayette, Marquis de Tuffin, Baron de Kalb, Pierré la Enfant, Count de Rochambeau, and others – could also gather together in their homeland.)

To perpetuate the membership of the Society, it was determined that the eldest male descendant of original officers would always be members – as well as any other worthy individuals voted into the Society by the members themselves. The Society of the Cincinnati (America's first veterans' organization) still exists today.

Given Boudinot's direct assistance to the military during the Revolution, it is easy to understand why he was invited to address the Society. He dedicated his oration to his close friend:

To George Washington,
President of the United States of America.

Sir,

The great respect due to your public character as the first servant of a nation of free men, greatly heightened by a knowledge of the amiableness of your deportment [conduct] in private life, have been additional arguments with me to dedicate an oration to you which – however inadequate to the purpose – was designed to promote a reverence for

GEORGE WASHINGTON

that happy revolution in which Divine Providence has been pleased to make you so peculiar an instrument.

A frequent recurrence to the first principles of our Constitution – and from thence to inculcate the necessity of a free, firm, and energetic government in which liberty shall rise superior to licentiousness [contempt for law and morality], and obedience to the laws become the best evidence of attachment to the independence of our common country — cannot but meet with your approbation [approval].

This is the great object designed by instituting the anniversary of the Fourth of July, 1776, as a festival to be sacredly observed by every true American. This is the day chosen by the Defenders of our Country — your friends and companions in arms — to meet together and rejoice in the recollection of past labors while they receive the glorious reward of their services by looking forward to the increasing prosperity of the Union secured by their united exertions. . . .

You, sir, as their head, must enjoy — in a very peculiar [special] manner — the contemplation of these blessings; and to you every attempt in this important service will be most properly dedicated.

Long may you personally experience their benign [healthy and wholesome] effects. Long may you live to testify — by a successful practice — the truth of the theory established by your struggles in the cause of universal liberty.

I have the honor to be, with every proper expression of respect and esteem, Sir,

Your affectionate Friend and Fellow Citizen,
The Orator.

As would be expected by someone of Boudinot's background, this oration is overflowing first with thankfulness to God and then to the patriotic veterans who gave so much in the cause of American liberty. Boudinot invokes numerous Biblical references and Scriptural citations and presents a glowing picture of American liberty and of what it will mean for ages to come — if Americans remain faithful guardians of the liberties entrusted to them by previous generations.

⫯𝔒𝔯𝔞𝔱𝔦𝔬𝔫⫯

GENTLEMEN, BRETHREN, AND FELLOW CITIZENS:

Having devoutly paid the sacrifice of prayer and praise to that Almighty Being by Whose favor and mercy this day is peculiarly dedicated to the commemoration of events which fill our minds with joy and gladness, it now becomes me – in obedience to the resolutions of our Society – to aim at a further improvement of this Festival by leading your reflections to the contemplation of those special privileges which attend the happy and important situation you now enjoy among the nations of the earth. . . .

The history of the world – as well sacred as profane [secular] – bears witness to the use and importance of setting apart a day as a memorial of great events, whether of a religious or political nature.

No sooner had the great Creator of the heavens and the earth finished His almighty work and pronounced all very good, He set apart (not an anniversary, or one day in a year, but) one day in seven for the commemoration of His inimitable [unrivaled] power in producing all things out of nothing.

The deliverance of the children of Israel from a state of bondage to an unreasonable tyrant was perpetuated by the eating of the Paschal Lamb and enjoining it on their posterity as an annual festival forever [the Passover], with a *remember this day* in which ye came out of Egypt, out of the house of bondage [EXODUS 13:3].

The resurrection of the Savior of mankind is commemorated by keeping the first day of the week not only as a certain memorial of His first coming in a state of humiliation but the positive evidence of His future coming in glory.

Let us then, my friends and fellow citizens, unite all our endeavors this day to remember with reverential gratitude to our Supreme Benefactor all the wonderful things He has done for us in our miraculous deliverance from a second Egypt – another "house of bondage." And thou *shalt show thy son on this day, saying, this day is kept* as a day of joy and gladness because of the great things *the Lord hath done for us when we were delivered from* the threatening power of an invading foe. And it shall *be a sign unto thee upon thine hand, and for a memorial between thine eyes, that the law of the Lord may be in thy mouth, for with a strong hand hast thou been delivered from thine enemies: Thou shalt therefore keep this ordinance in its season, from year to year forever* [EXODUS 13:8-10].

When great events are to be produced in this our world, great exertions generally become necessary; men are therefore usually raised up with talents and powers peculiarly adapted to the purpose intended by Providence, who often – by their disinterested [selfless] services and extreme sufferings – become the wonder as well as the examples of their generation. The obligations of mankind to these worthy characters increase in proportion to the importance of the blessings purchased by their labors.

It is not, then, an unreasonable expectation (which I well know generally prevails) that this day should be usually devoted to the perpetuating and respectfully remembering the dignified characters of those great men with whom it has been our honor to claim the intimate connection of *Fellow Citizens* – men who have purchased our present joyful circumstances at the invaluable price of their blood.

But you must also acknowledge with me that this subject has been so fully considered and so ably handled by those eloquent and enlightened men who have gone before me in this honorable path that had their superior abilities fallen to my lot, I could do but little more than repeat the substance of their observations and vary their language.

Forgive me, ye spirits of my worthy departed Fellow Citizens! † Patriots of the first magnitude whose integrity no subtle arts of bribery and corruption could successfully assail, and whose fortitude and perseverance no difficulties or dangers could intimidate – whose labors and sufferings in the common cause of our country – whose exploits in

---

† By 1793 – the time of this oration – many of the "worthy departed fellow citizens" of the military arena to which he spoke included beloved heroes such as Gen. Ethan Allen, Gen. Nathanael Greene, Gen. Israel Putnam, Gen. Joseph Reed, Gen. Mordecai Gist, and dozens of other generals – not to mention such conspicuous patriots as John Hancock, Stephen Hopkins, and Jonathan Trumbull.

the field and wisdom in the cabinet I have often been witness to during a cruel and distressing war! – Forgive, O Warren! [†] O Montgomery! [††]

[†] Joseph Warren (1741-1775) was a distinguished Massachusetts physician in charge of the local militia and a friend and compatriot of leaders such as Samuel Adams, James Otis, and John Hancock. It was Warren who dispatched Paul Revere and William Dawes on their famous midnight ride to warn the citizens of Lexington and Concord. As a Major-General of

DEATH OF JOSEPH WARREN AT BUNKER HILL

the Massachusetts militia, Warren fought at the Battle of Bunker Hill and was killed by the British early in the battle, being the first officer to lose his life in that conflict.

[††] Richard Montgomery (1736-1775) was a seasoned British veteran soldier who, during the French and Indian War, fought in a number of important battles in America, Canada, and elsewhere (Martinique, Havana, West Indies, etc.). In 1773, he retired from the British army, left England, and moved to New York where he purchased an estate and began a family.

As tensions between Great Britain and the Colonies mounted, he sided with the Americans. He was sent as a New York delegate to the First Provincial Congress and later appointed as a general in the Continental Army. Since American leaders feared a British invasion from Canada into New York, it was believed that America therefore should attempt to neutralize the British in Canada by a preemptive strike. It was hoped that such an American assault would keep the British in Canada from joining the British in America to mass their joint forces against Boston or some other key American area.

Congress placed Montgomery in command of an expedition to Canada where he conducted a brilliant campaign with untrained soldiers and insufficient equipage, taking

– and all the nameless heroes of your illustrious group! Forgive that I omit on the present occasion to follow the steps of those compatriots who have preceded me but had rather spend this sacred hour in contemplating those great purposes which animated your souls in the severe conflict – and for which you fought and bled!

Were you present to direct this day's meditations, would you not point to your scarred limbs and bleeding breasts and loudly call upon us to reward your toils and sufferings by forcibly inculcating and improving those patriotic principles and practices which led you to those noble achievements that secured the blessings we now enjoy?

Yes, ye martyrs to liberty – ye band of heroes – ye once worthy compatriots and fellow citizens – we will obey your friendly sugges-

---

Montreal. He was promoted to Major-General and joined forces with American General Benedict Arnold, already in Canada, to take Quebec (the last remaining British stronghold in Canada) with the hope that the French Canadians there would join with the Americans against the British. On December 31, 1775, during a heavy snowstorm, Montgomery began the attack on Quebec. Courageously leading at the front of the charge and urging his soldiers to follow, he was shot down in the first volley from the British,

DEATH OF GEN. RICHARD MONTGOMERY AT QUEBEC

causing his soldiers to panic and flee. This left Arnold exposed and resulted in Arnold's defeat and the capture of nearly two-thirds of his men.

Following Montgomery's death, all – including his enemies – paid tribute to his bravery. Congress erected a statue to him in front of St. Paul's church in his home of New York City, and a monument in Canada marks the place where he fell.

tion and greatly prize that freedom and independence purchased by your united exertions as the most invaluable gem of our earthly crown!

The late revolution, my respected audience, in which we this day rejoice, is big with events that are daily unfolding themselves and pressing in thick succession to the astonishment of a wondering world!

It has been marked with the certain characteristic of a Divine overruling hand in that it was brought about and perfected against all human reasoning and apparently against all human hope – and that in the very moment of time when all Europe seemed ready to be plunged into commotion and distress.

Divine Providence, throughout the government of this world, appears to have impressed many great events with the undoubted evidence of His own almighty arm. He *putteth down* kingdoms and he *setteth up* whom he pleaseth [c.f., PSALM 75:7], and it has been literally verified to us that *no king prevaileth by the power of his own strength* [PSALM 33:16-17].

The first great principle established and secured by our revolution – and which since seems to be pervading all the nations of the earth and which should be most zealously and carefully improved and gloried in by us – is the rational equality and rights of men, as men and citizens.

I do not mean to hold up the absurd idea charged upon us by the enemies of this valuable principle (and which contains in it inevitable destruction to every government), "that all men are equal as to acquired or adventitious [self-achieved] rights." Men must and do continually differ in their genius, knowledge, industry, integrity, and activity.

Their natural and moral characters, their virtues and vices, their abilities, natural and acquired – together with favorable opportunities for exertion – will always make men different among themselves and, of course, create a preeminency and superiority one over another. But the equality and rights of men here contemplated are natural, essential, and unalienable, such as the security of life, liberty, and property. These should be the firm foundation of every good government as they will apply to all nations at all times and may properly be called a universal law. It is apparent that every man is born with the same right to improve the talent committed to him for the use and benefit of society, and to be respected accordingly.

We are all the workmanship of the same Divine hand. With our Creator, abstractly considered, there are neither kings nor subjects, masters nor servants (otherwise than stewards of His appointments, to serve each other according to our different opportunities and abilities, and of course accountable for the manner in which we perform our duty) – *He is no respecter of persons* [ACTS 10:34; ROMANS 2:11] – He beholds all with an equal eye. . . . It is our duty, then, as a people acting on principles of universal application, to convince mankind of the truth and practicability of them by carrying them into actual exercise for the happiness of our fellow men without suffering them to be perverted to oppression or licentiousness.

The eyes of the nations of the earth are fast opening, and the inhabitants of this globe – notwithstanding it is 3,000 years since the promulgation of that invaluable precept *thou shalt love thy neighbor as thyself* [LEVITICUS 19:18] – are but just beginning to discover their brotherhood to each other, and that all men – however different with regard to nation or color – have an essential interest in each other's welfare.

Let this be our peculiar, constant care and vigilant attention to inculcate this sacred principle and to hand it down to posterity improved by every generous and liberal [benevolent] practice, that while we are rejoicing in our own political and religious privileges, we may with pleasure contemplate the happy period when all the nations of the earth shall join in the triumph of this day and one universal anthem of praise shall arise to the Universal Creator in return for the general joy.

Another essential ingredient in the happiness we enjoy as a nation – and which arises from the principles of our revolution – is the right that every people have to govern themselves in such manner as they judge best calculated for the common benefit.

It is a principle interwoven with our Constitution – and not one of the least blessings purchased by that glorious struggle to the commemoration of which this day is specially devoted – that every man has a natural right to be governed by laws of his own making either in person or by his representative, and that no authority ought justly to be exercised over him that is not derived from the people of whom he is one.

This, fellow citizens, is a most important practical principle first carried into complete execution by the United States of America.

I tremble for the event while I glory in the subject.

To you, ye citizens of America, do the inhabitants of the earth look with eager attention for the success of a measure on which their happiness and prosperity so manifestly depend. . . . On your virtue, patriotism, integrity, and submission to the laws of your own making (and the government of your own choice) do the hopes of men rest with prayers and supplications for a happy issue. Be not therefore careless, indolent, or inattentive in the exercise of any right of citizenship. Let no duty, however small or seemingly of little importance, be neglected by you.

Ever keep in mind that it is parts that form the whole, and fractions constitute the unit. Good government generally begins in the family and if the moral character of a people once degenerate, their political character must soon follow. . . . These considerations should lead to an attentive solicitude to keep the pure unadulterated principles of our Constitution always in view – to be religiously careful in our choice of all public officers; and as they are again in our power at very short periods, lend not too easily a patient ear to every invidious [slanderous] insinuation or improbable story but prudently mark the effects of their public measures and judge of the tree by its fruits [MATTHEW 12:33; LUKE 6:44 – i.e., don't listen only to what is said about them, look at what they do].

I do not wish to discourage a constant and lively attention to the conduct of our rulers. A prudent suspicion of public measures is a great security to a republican government; but a line should be drawn between a careful and critical examination into the principles and effects of regular systems after a fair and candid trial, and a captious [nitpicking and hypercritical], discontented, and censorious [complaining] temper [attitude] which leads to find fault with every proposition in which we have not an immediate hand, and raise obstacles to rational plans of government without waiting a fair experiment. It is generally characteristic of this disposition to find fault without proposing a better plan for consideration.

We should not forget that our country is large and our fellow citizens of different manners, interests, and habits. That our laws to be right must be combined [consistent and even-handed], and brotherly conciliation and forbearance continually exercised if we will judge with propriety of those measures that respect a nation at large. . . .

I can no longer deny myself the felicity, my beloved friends and fellow citizens – members of a Society founded in these humane and benevolent principles – of addressing myself more particularly to you on a day which in so peculiar a manner shines with increasing luster on you, refreshing and brightening your hard-earned laurels by renewing the honorable reward of your laborious services in the gratitude of your rejoicing fellow citizens.

Methinks I behold you on the victorious banks of Hudson, [†] bowed down with the fatigues of an active campaign and the sufferings of an inclement winter, receiving the welcome news of approaching peace and your country's political salvation with all that joy of heart and serenity of mind that became citizens who flew to their arms merely at their country's call in a time of common danger.

The war-worn soldiers, reduced to the calamities of a seven-year's arduous service, now solemnly pause and reflect on the peculiarity of their critical situation. The ravages of war had been extended through

---

† The American Army was on the banks of the Hudson River in New York City when the American Revolution came to an end. The Revolution had culminated with a rapid series of momentous events: British General Lord Cornwallis surrendered to Washington at Yorktown in October 1781; in February 1783, Great Britain officially declared an end to hostilities in America; and in September 1783 the peace treaty to end the Revolution was signed. In November 1783 on the banks of the Hudson, Washington bid his officers a final farewell, thus signifying the official military end of the Revolution. (A month later in Annapolis, Maryland, on December 23, 1783, Washington resigned his military commission given by the Continental Congress, thus closing the civilian side of his military efforts.)

a country dearer to them than life and thereby prevented that ample provision in service or reasonable recompense on their return to private life that prudence required and gratitude powerfully dictated. They thought that the distresses of the army had before been brought to a point – "That they had borne all that men could bear; their property expended, their private resources at an end, their friends wearied out and disgusted with incessant applications." But another trial, severer than all, still awaits them: they are now to be disbanded and a separation to take place more distressing than every former scene! Till now the severe conflict was unseen, or unattended to. Poverty and the gratitude of their country are their only reward. . . . Their country's exhausted treasury cannot yield them even the hard-earned pittance of a soldier's pay. . . .

Some guardian angel – perhaps the happy genius of America ever attendant on the object of her care – raises the drooping head, wipes the indignant falling tear from the hardy soldier's eye, and suggests the happy expedient!

Brotherly affection produces brotherly relief – the victorious bands unite together – they despise the infamous idea † – they refuse to

---

† When the Revolution was successfully won, a seven-page unsigned letter circulated among George Washington's officers on May 22, 1782, advancing the idea that Washington should be made king. On hearing of this, Washington immediately quashed the move, writing to its author – on the very day the letter was circulated – declaring that "*nothing* in the course of the War has given me more painful sensations." Washington told him that the idea of being made king was an idea that "I must view with abhorrence and reprehend with severity." In fact, Washington was mystified as to what could have caused anyone to believe that he would even consider such an idea:

> I am much at a loss to conceive what part of my conduct could have given encouragement to an address which to me seems big with the greatest mischiefs that can befall my country. If I am not deceived in the knowledge of myself, you could not have found a person to whom your schemes are more disagreeable. . . . Let me conjure you, then, if you have any regard for your country, concern for yourself or posterity, or respect for me, to banish these thoughts from your mind and never communicate – as from yourself or anyone else – a sentiment of the like nature.

Washington's words had their intended effect; the movement was stopped. In fact, the author of the letter profusely apologized to Washington on several subsequent occasions for having ever made the suggestion.

listen to the Siren's song [†] – they form the social tie – they cast in the remaining fragment of their scanty pay and instead of seizing their arms and demanding their right by menace and violence, they refuse "to lessen the dignity or fully the glory they had hitherto maintained. They determine to give one more proof of unexampled patriotism and patient virtue, rising superior to the pressure of their complicated sufferings and thereby afford an occasion to posterity to say, had that day been wanting, the world had not seen the last stage of political perfection to which human nature is capable of attaining." [††]

[†] The "Siren's song" is an allusion to Homer's *Odyssey* (800 BC) in which Odysseus was warned against listening to the songs of the Sirens who would attempt to lure him and his sailors to their deaths on the rocks. Quoting from the *Odyssey* (Book XII):

> First you will come to the Sirens who enchant all who come near them. If anyone unwarily draws in too close and hears the singing of the Sirens, his wife and children will never welcome him home again, for they sit in a green field and warble him to death with the sweetness of their song. There is a great heap of dead men's bones lying all around with the flesh still rotting off them. Therefore pass these Sirens by, and stop your men's ears with wax that none of them may hear . . .

As Odysseus and his ship drew near to the home of the Sirens, he did indeed plug all his sailors ears with wax and then he had them tie him to the mast. He became curious as to what the Sirens sounded like and when he heard their beautiful music, he ordered the sailors to untie him but they ignored him until they were safely out of earshot. Thus Odysseus and his ship were saved.

[††] This lengthy quote came from a speech given by George Washington (1732-1799) shortly after the successful conclusion of the American Revolution. At that point in American history, the national government (the Articles of Confederation) was too weak and inadequate to govern the nation, and Congress was unable to pay either its debts or the soldiers' pay. On March 10, 1783, an anonymous letter was circulated at Washington's military camp calling for an unscheduled meeting of the officers to consider an armed military show of force and even a coup as a means of forcing Congress to address the soldier's needs since it appeared that Congress had neither the power nor the will to address the problems facing the military. When Washington discovered the plans, he forbade any special meeting and instead instructed that the officers preserve their regular meeting already scheduled for March 15th – a meeting to be conducted under the direction of General Horatio Gates (who had helped foment and circulate the letter). Following Washington's order to keep the regularly scheduled meeting with General Gates, additional letters and rumors were circulated suggesting that Washington was sympathetic to the goals and desires of the discontented officers.

On March 15, 1783, the officers gathered for their meeting in a church building in Newburgh, New York, and much to their surprise, Washington himself was present (the regularly scheduled officers' meetings usually were conducted by a subordinate officer such

The glorious certainty of peace, purchased by their sufferings and perseverance, now rouses the patriotic fire. They again rejoice in the event: they unite in a firm indissoluble bond . . . "to continue their mutual friendship which commenced under the pressure of common danger and to effectuate [complete] every act of beneficence [charity] dictated by a spirit of brotherly kindness to any of their number and their families who might unfortunately be under the necessity of receiving them," and by this unanimous act, establish their sacred truth "that the glory of soldiers cannot be completed without acting well the part of citizens." †

This, gentlemen, is your origin as a Society – the source from whence you sprang – and this day we are carrying on the work first begun in these social principles.

With a heart filled with unfeigned gratitude to the Author of all our mercies, and overflowing with the most affectionate friendship towards you, suffer me to congratulate you on this seventeenth anniversary of our happy independence. Long! – long! – even to the remotest ages! – may the citizens of this rising empire enjoy the triumph of this day – may they never forget the invaluable price which

---

as General Gates, and Washington very rarely attended). Washington personally addressed the officers and denounced their plans, observing that it was a plan better concocted by British agents rather than by true Americans (the above excerpt is taken from Washington's speech to the group). He then proceeded to read a letter from a Member of Congress to demonstrate the good will of that body and its desire to provide relief for the soldiers. He had read just one paragraph in that letter when he unexpectedly paused, and to the shock of them all, put on eyeglasses that he had only recently received from Ben Franklin (no one had ever seen him wear eyeglasses before on any occasion). By way of explanation, he commented, "I have grown gray in your service – and now find myself growing blind!" – a comment that pierced the soul of every officer present, reminding them that he had personally suffered no less sacrifice and loss then they. Washington finished the letter setting forth Congress' resolve to address the problems facing the military and then withdrew from the officers. The officers then passed a unanimous resolution – much to General Gates' chagrin – "that the officers of the American army view with abhorrence and reject with disdain the infamous propositions contained in a late anonymous address to them" and thus quashed the attempted military insurrection.

† The Society of the Cincinnati was officially formed on May 10, 1783. On May 13th, its "Institution" was penned, setting forth both the purposes and operations of the Society. The quotations in this paragraph are taken from the "Institution."

it cost as well as the great purposes for which it was instituted, and may a frequent recurrence to the first principles of our Constitution on this anniversary be a constant source of security and permanence to the rising fabric. . . . May the remembrance of those worthy heroes – once our beloved companions whose lives they did not hold dear when required for their country's safety – animate us to preserve inviolate [intact] what they purchased at so high a rate! . . .

If we turn our attention to the strong hope of every community – the rising generation – the world has yet enjoyed nothing equal to their advantages and future prospects.

The road to honors, riches, usefulness, and fame in this happy country is open equally to all. . . . The meanest [lowliest or poorest] citizen of America educates his beloved child with a well-founded hope that if he should become equal to the task, he may rationally aspire to the command of our armies, a place in the cabinet, or even to the filling of the presidential chair; he stands on equal ground in regard to the first honors of the state with the riches of his fellow citizens.

The child of the poorest laborer, by enjoying the means of education (afforded in almost every corner of this happy land), is trained up for and is encouraged to look forward to a share in the legislation of the Union or of a particular State with as much confidence as the noblest subject of an established monarchy. This is a peculiar happiness of our highly favored republic among the nations of the earth, proceeding from the successful revolution in which we this day rejoice.

Suffer me, ye fair daughters of New Jersey, to call on you also in a special manner to add your invigorating smiles to the mirth and festivity of this day. . . . The rights of women are no longer strange sounds to an American ear; they are now heard as familiar terms in every part of the United States, and I devoutly hope that the day is not far distant when we shall find them dignifying, in a distinguishing code, the jurisprudence of the several States in the Union.

But in your domestic character, do you not also enjoy the most delightful contemplations arising from the Revolution of 1776? Can you look on the children of your tenderest care and reflect on the cheerful prospects opening upon them through life without feeling the most lively emotions of gratitude for the inestimable privileges conferred on the citizens of America? Are not your resolutions strengthened and your endeavors redoubled to furnish them with every qualification, both mental and personal, for the future service of a country thus rendered dear to you?. . . To whom are we more indebted for the origin of our present happiness than to your delicate and discerning sex? . . .

To your sex, then, ladies, are we obliged to yield the palm † – had this great event depended altogether on our sex, it is not easy to guess what our united fate had been at this moment. Instead of our present agreeable employment, we might have been hewers of wood and drawers of water to some mighty Pharaoh whose tender mercies would have been cruelty [c.f., PROVERBS 12:10]. Your right then, my fair auditory [female listeners], to a large portion of the general joy must be acknowledged to be of a superior kind.

Do you, my worthy fellow citizens of every description, wish for more lasting matter of pleasure and satisfaction in contemplating the great events brought to your minds this day? Extend, then, your views to a different period of future time. Look forward a few years and behold our extended forests (now a pathetic wilderness) converted into fruitful fields and busy towns. Take into view the pleasing shores of our immense lakes, united to the Atlantic States by a thousand winding canals and beautified with rising cities, crowded with innumerable, peaceful fleets, transporting the rich produce from one coast to another.

Add to all this what must most please every humane and benevolent mind: the ample provision thus made by the God of all flesh for the reception of the nations of the earth flying from the tyranny and oppression of despots of the Old World †† and say if the prophecies

---

† The palm leaf was an emblem of victory dating from ancient days (for example, the Greek goddess of victory is always depicted with a palm-leaf in her hand). To "yield the palm" is giving honor to one who excels and surpasses others and is declaring them the victor.

†† America was indeed an "ample provision made by the God of all flesh" to receive the persecuted from across the world who were "flying from the tyranny and oppression of the despots of the Old World." The Pilgrims came to America in 1620 to escape the hounding persecution of England's King James, and a decade later the Puritans (some 20,000) also came to America after Puritan laymen in England received life sentences (as well as hav-

of ancient times are not hastening to a fulfillment when this *wilderness shall blossom as a rose* [ISAIAH 35:1] and *the heathen be given* to the Great Redeemer as His *inheritance and these uttermost parts of the earth for His possession* [PSALM 2:8].

Who knows but the country for which we have fought and bled may hereafter become a theatre of greater events than yet have been known to mankind?

May these invigorating prospects lead us to the exercise of every virtue – religious, moral, and political. May we be roused to a circumspect conduct – to an exact obedience to the laws of our own making – to the preservation of the spirit and principles of our truly invaluable Constitution – to respect and attention to magistrates of our own choice – and finally, by our example as well as precept, add to the real happiness of our fellow men and the particular glory of our common country.

And may these great principles in the end become instrumental in bringing about that happy state of the world when – from every human breast joined by the grand chorus of the skies – shall arise with the profoundest reverence that divinely celestial anthem of universal praise: *"Glory to God in the highest – Peace on earth – Good will towards men"* [LUKE 2:14]. ∎

---

ing their noses slit, ears cut off, and a brand placed on their foreheads). Similarly, in 1632, Catholics persecuted in England fled to America; in 1654 Jews persecuted by Catholics and facing the Inquisition in Portugal fled to America; in 1680, Quakers fled to America after some 10,000 had been imprisoned or tortured in England for their faith; in 1683, persecuted German Anabaptists (Mennonites, Moravians, Dunkers, etc.) fled to America; in 1685, Huguenots fled France (eventually some 400,000) to avoid death and persecution; in 1731, 20,000 Lutherans fled to America after being expelled from Austria; and the story has been often repeated across the pages of America's history. America indeed was (and is) a place of asylum chosen by the Almighty for the benefit of those in the rest of the world who were persecuted for their faith in God.

An Oration by

Daniel Webster

1851

MR. WEBSTER'S ADDRESS

AT THE

LAYING OF THE CORNER STONE

OF THE

ADDITION TO THE CAPITOL;

JULY 4TH, 1851.

"STET CAPITOLIUM
FULGENS;
LATE NOMEN IN ULTIMAS
EXTENDAT ORAS."

WASHINGTON:
GIDEON AND CO., PRINTERS.
1851.

Daniel Webster

Daniel Webster
(1782-1852)

Daniel Webster was part of the second generation of American patriots. His father served as an officer during the American Revolution, a member of the New Hampshire legislature, and was a ratifier of the US Constitution. Daniel not only grew up in a patriotic family but he grew up in an era where he could listen to the speeches of George Washington, John Adams, Thomas Jefferson, and James Madison.

Daniel was a young man with a delicate health and was very swarthy and dark skinned (nicknamed "Black Dan" and often mistaken for an Indian). His father, determined to give Daniel the education he never had, made provision for him to attend Exeter Academy and then Dartmouth College. Webster's speaking skills developed quickly, and by the age of eighteen, he had been selected by the city of Hanover to deliver its Fourth of July oration.

Following graduation, Webster began the study of law. To provide income during his legal studies, he accepted a position as a teacher in an academy. He was admitted to the Boston bar in 1805 and shortly thereafter married Grace Fletcher, the daughter of a New Hampshire clergyman.

In 1812, Webster was elected to Congress as a Representative under President Madison, where he opposed the war of 1812. By his second term, his remarkable ability as an attorney and public speaker caused him to be retained to represent three cases before the US Supreme Court. His success in these efforts led to additional cases, and eventually he was involved in several landmark constitutional decisions. Webster became known as the foremost lawyer of his time, and so great were his skills that legal opponents actually withdrew from cases after learning they would have to face Webster.

Webster was an ardent opponent of slavery and in 1819 delivered a superb speech strongly opposing the admission of Missouri as a slave State. That speech was the first of what rapidly became a lengthy string of brilliant orations, including one in commemoration of the 200th anniversary of the arrival of the Pilgrims (1820) and another at the laying of the cornerstone of the Bunker Hill monument (1825) on the 50th anniversary of the famous battle.

Webster – known as one of the greatest orators in American history – asserted that no one could be a good orator unless he practiced reading aloud from the Bible. So accomplished was Webster at this task that crowds actually would gather just to listen to him read lengthy passages aloud from the Bible. The love for the Bible that characterized his entire life was first demonstrated at an early age: in 1788 when only six years old, he won a Bible memorization contest at his school. As explained by his teacher, Charles Tappan:

> Daniel was always the brightest boy in the school. . . . He would learn more in five minutes than any other boy in five hours. . . . One Saturday, I remember, I held up a handsome new jackknife to the scholars and said the boy who would commit to memory the greatest number of verses in the Bible by Monday morning should have it. Many of the boys did well; but when it came to Daniel's turn to recite, I found that he had committed so much [to memory] that after hearing him repeat some sixty or seventy verses, I was obliged to give up, he telling me that there were several chapters [still] that he had learned. Daniel got that jackknife.

In 1827, Webster was elected a US Senator from Massachusetts under President John Quincy Adams. During this period, Webster suffered a series of personal losses and tragedies (including the unexpected deaths of his wife and his brother), but he nonetheless continued his powerful leadership in behalf of the nation. In fact, in 1832 he ably rebutted the doctrine of nullification – the twin sister of the doctrine of secession that eventually split the nation during the Civil War. In renouncing the idea of breaking up the Union, Webster declared that he spoke, "not as a Massachusetts man, nor as a Northern man, but as an American," and proclaimed

"Liberty and Union – now and forever – one and inseparable!" Because he opposed every effort to weaken the Constitution, he was titled, "The Defender of the Constitution."

Webster's political career spanned several years, including a decade of service in the US House, two decades in the US Senate, and Secretary of State for three Presidents: William Henry Harrison, John Tyler, and Millard Fillmore. In fact, this oration was delivered as part of Webster's official duties as President Fillmore's Secretary of State on the occasion of the laying of the cornerstones for major additions to the US Capitol. This oration came at a time of rapid and almost incomprehensible progress in the nation.

For example, in medicine, the first surgery had just been performed using an anesthetic (ether), cough drops had been invented, and the American Medical Association had been formed.

In athletics, baseball had been officially organized as an independent sport, its rules set, and a baseball club (the New York Knickerbocker) formed.

In technology, the sewing machine, the safety pin, and an ice-making machine had been patented; the first rotary printing press was in use; a public building was being heated with steam; Samuel Colt was mass-producing revolvers; chewing gum had been manufactured; and the world's longest suspension bridge had just been built across the Ohio River.

A number of new States had recently been added to the Union, including Texas, California, Florida, and Iowa. The Oregon Territory had been acquired from Great Britain and travel along the Oregon Trail was in full swing; Mormons were migrating to Utah; gold had been discovered in California; and news in the West was being carried by Pony Express, while in the East every State had the telegraph.

In the political rights arena, women had just rallied at the famous Seneca Falls Convention, demanding that they be recognized with equal rights; and the first woman to receive a medical degree had just graduated. African American anti-slavery leaders such as Frederick Douglass, Sojourner Truth, and Harriet Tubman were becoming prominent, and Harriet Beecher Stowe had just written *Uncle Tom's Cabin* exposing the mistreatment of slaves to the nation.

In Washington, DC, Congress had set the first Tuesday in November as the day for national presidential elections, and war hero Zachary Taylor had become the first President to be elected by all the States on the same day. Taylor died in office shortly thereafter and his Vice-President Millard Fillmore became President (and was President at the time of this oration). The US Capitol grounds were being illuminated at night by gas lights, and both the Smithsonian Institution and the Washington Monument were under construction. It was indeed a time of rapid modernization throughout the nation.

Webster's oration – delivered to a crowd of 10,000 on the east side of the Capitol a year before his death – was actually a dual oration. Since the public ceremony for the laying of the cornerstone occurred on the

WEBSTER SPOKE TO A CROWD OF 10,000 GATHERED AT THE CAPITOL

4ᵗʰ of July, the first part of his oration was a patriotic address; the second part was directed to the specific ceremony at hand and what the growth of the Capitol symbolically represented for the nation.

Webster's address surveys the remarkable changes in America since the laying of the first cornerstone at the Capitol 58 years earlier in 1793 by President Washington. His oration is a wonderful review of the growth of the country and its increasing abundant prosperity and includes a direct rebuke of those who were criticizing America and trying to undermine the Union. Webster reminded his listeners of what had caused America to become – and would cause her to remain – a world leader.

Oration.

FELLOW CITIZENS:

I greet you well! I give you joy on the return of this anniversary and I felicitate you also on the more particular purpose of which this ever-memorable day has been chosen to witness the fulfillment. Hail! All hail! I see before and around me a mass of faces glowing with cheerfulness and patriotic pride. I see thousands of eyes turned towards other eyes, all sparkling with gratification and delight. This is the New World! This is America! This is Washington! And this the Capitol of the United States! And where else among the nations can the seat of government be surrounded on any day of any year by those who have more reason to rejoice in the blessings which they possess? Nowhere, fellow-citizens, assuredly nowhere! Let us, then, meet this rising sun with joy and thanksgiving!

This is that day of the year which announced to mankind the great fact of American Independence! This fresh and brilliant morning blesses our vision with another beholding of the birthday of our nation, and we see that nation of recent origin now among the most considerable and powerful and spreading over the continent from sea to sea. . . .

On the 4th of July, 1776, the Representatives of the United States of America in Congress assembled declared that these United Colonies are, and of right ought to be, free and independent States. This declaration – made by most patriotic and resolute men trusting in the justice of their cause and the protection of Heaven, and yet made not without deep solicitude [concern] and anxiety – has now stood for seventy-five years, and still stands. It was sealed in blood. It has met dangers and overcome them; it has had enemies and conquered them; it has had detractors and abashed [silenced] them all; it has had doubting friends but it has cleared all doubts away; and now, today, raising its august [majestic] form higher than the clouds, twenty millions of people contemplate it with hallowed love and the world beholds it and the consequences which have followed from it with profound admiration.

This anniversary animates and gladdens and unites all American hearts. On other days of the year we may be party men [political partisans], indulging in controversies more or less important to the public good; we may have likes and dislikes; and we may maintain our political differences often with warm and sometimes with angry feelings. But today we are Americans all, and all nothing but Americans. . . . [and] this inheritance which we enjoy today is not only an inheritance of liberty but of our own peculiar American liberty.

Liberty has existed in other times, in other countries, and in other forms. There has been a Grecian liberty, bold and powerful, full of spirit, eloquence, and fire – a liberty which produced multitudes of great men and has transmitted one immortal name (the name of Demosthenes) to posterity. † But still it was a liberty of disconnected states, sometimes united (indeed, by temporary leagues and confederacies) but often involved in wars between themselves. The sword of Sparta turned its sharpest edge against Athens, enslaved her, and devastated Greece; and in her turn, Sparta was compelled to bend before the power of Thebes. †† And let it ever be remembered – especially let the truth sink deep into all American minds – that it was

---

† Demosthenes (384-322 BC) became the greatest of Greek orators. He had a severe speech impediment as a youth but overcame it by an arduous regimen of self-imposed exercises – speaking with pebbles in his mouth, reciting verses while running, and delivering practice speeches on the seashore over the noise of the waves. Demosthenes entered public life at the age of 25, and when Greece was invaded by Philip of Macedon, Demosthenes used his oratorical skills in an attempt to rally his countrymen to unite in defense of their liberty, but they responded to his passionate pleas too late. He was later imprisoned and exiled, and when his final attempt to achieve liberty for Greece failed, he committed suicide.

†† Athens, Sparta, and Thebes were each powerful city-states in Greece. After a nearly three-decade long conflict between Athens and Sparta (the two greatest city-states) in the Peloponnesian War (431-404 BC), Sparta eventually defeated Athens and became the greatest force in Greece. Sparta was in turn subdued by Thebes (which used Sparta's own military tactics against her in the Battle of Leuctra (371 BC); Thebes then became the greatest city-state. During this period, Greece was unwilling to unify, and the city-states attacked each other. This lack of national unity enabled first Phillip of Macedon and then his son, Alexander the Great, to subdue Greece.

the want of union among her several states which finally gave the mastery of all Greece to Philip of Macedon. †

And there has also been a Roman liberty – a proud, ambitious, domineering spirit professing free and popular principles in Rome itself – but even in the best days of the republic, [it was] ready to carry slavery and chains into her provinces and through every country over which her eagles could be borne. What was the liberty of Spain, or Gaul [France], or Germany, or Britain in the days of Rome? Did true constitutional liberty then exist? As the Roman empire declined, her provinces – not instructed in the principles of free popular government – one after another declined also; and when Rome herself fell in the end, all fell together.

I have said, gentlemen, that our inheritance is an inheritance of American liberty. That liberty is characteristic, peculiar, and altogether our own. Nothing like it existed in former times nor was known in the most enlightened states of antiquity; while with us its principles have become interwoven into the minds of individual men, connected with our daily opinions and our daily habits until it is – if I may so say – an element of social as well as of political life. And the consequence is that to whatever region an American citizen carries himself, he takes with him – fully developed in his own understanding and experience – our American principles and opinions and becomes ready at once, in cooperation with others, to apply them to the formation of new governments. . . .

Now, fellow-citizens, if your patience will hold out, I will venture – before proceeding to the more appropriate and particular duties of the day – to state in a few words what I take these American political principles in substance to be.

---

† Philip of Macedon (father of Alexander the Great) had taken control of all Greece by about 338 BC and conquered each individual city-state (*polis*), bringing them under his exclusive rule. Although Philip described the conquered area as a federal union, it was far from any modern type of federalism: Philip was the sole authority and dictator over them all. The city-states conquered by Philip had been too weak to resist him individually and had refused to cooperate with each other in their own mutual defense, thus ensuring their defeat. Since the South was at that moment making much noise about seceding from the Union, Webster is reminding secessionists about the consequences resulting from a lack of national unity.

They consist, as I think in the first place, in the establishment of popular governments on the basis of representation, for it is plain that a pure democracy (like that which existed in some of the states of Greece in which every individual had a direct vote in the enactment of all laws) cannot possibly exist in a country of wide extent. This representation is to be made as equal as circumstances will allow. Now, this principle of popular representation (prevailing either in all the branches of government or in some of them), has existed in these States almost from the days of the settlements at Jamestown and Plymouth [†] – borrowed, no doubt, from the example of the popular branch of the British legislature. . . . [O]ur ancestors, acting upon this example, introduced more equality of representation – the idea assumed a more rational and distinct shape. At any rate, this manner of exercising popular power was familiar to our fathers when they settled on this continent. They adopted it and generation has risen up after generation, all acknowledging it and all learning its practice and its forms.

The next fundamental principle in our system is that the will of the majority – fairly expressed through the means of representation – shall have the force of law; and it is quite evident that in a country without thrones or aristocracies or privileged castes or classes, there can be no other foundation for law to stand upon.

And as the necessary result of this, the third element is that the law is the supreme rule for the government of all. . . .

[A] most important part of the great fabric of American liberty is that there shall be written constitutions founded on the immediate authority of the people themselves and regulating and restraining all the powers conferred upon government, whether legislative, executive, or judicial.

---

† Webster's allusion to the "principle of popular representation" that had "existed in these States almost from the day of the settlements of Jamestown and Plymouth" refers to a deeply-rooted tradition of self-government that had early been planted into America by its first colonists. In 1619, America's first representative assembly met in Virginia (the House of Burgesses). Representative government was similarly introduced into Massachusetts, Plymouth, and Maryland in 1634; in Connecticut in 1639; etc. When Great Britain began to restrict the principles of representation and to dissolve representative assemblies prior to the American Revolution, she was attacking principles firmly embedded in the country for more than 150 years and was therefore met by fierce resistance on the part of the Americans.

This, fellow-citizens, I suppose to be a just summary of our American principles, and I have on this occasion sought to express them in the plainest and in the fewest words. The summary may not be entirely exact, but I hope it may be sufficiently so to make manifest to the rising generation among ourselves (and to those elsewhere who may choose to inquire into the nature of our political institutions) the general theory upon which they are founded.

And I now proceed to add that the strong and deep-settled conviction of all intelligent persons amongst us is that in order to support a useful and wise government upon these popular principles, the general education of the people and the wide diffusion of pure morality and true religion are indispensable. Individual virtue is a part of public virtue. It is difficult to conceive how there can remain morality in the government when it shall cease to exist among the people, or how the aggregate of the political institutions – all the organs [agents] of which consist only of men – should be wise and beneficent and competent to inspire confidence if the opposite qualities belong to the individuals who constitute those organs and make up that aggregate.

And now, fellow-citizens, I take leave of this part of the duty which I proposed to perform; and once more felicitating you and myself that our eyes have seen the light of this blessed morning and that our ears have heard the shouts with which joyous thousands welcome its return, and joining with you in the hope that every revolving year may renew these rejoicings to the end of time, I proceed to address you, shortly, upon the particular occasion of our assembling here today. . . .

— — — • • • — — —

Having finished his remarks about the 4th of July and our government, Webster then turned his focus to the main-event of the gathering: the laying of the cornerstone to expand the Capitol and the growth of the nation that it represented.

The anniversary of national independence appeared to afford an auspicious occasion for laying the foundation stone of the additional building. That ceremony has now been performed by the President himself, in the presence and view of this multitude. He has thought that the day and the occasion made a united and imperative [necessary] call for some short address to the people here assembled, and it is at his request that I have appeared before you to perform that part of the duty which was deemed incumbent on us.

Beneath the stone is deposited, among other things (a list of which will be published), the following brief account of the proceedings of this day in my handwriting:

On the morning of the first day of the seventy-sixth year of the Independence of the United States of America, in the city of Washington, being the 4th day of July, 1851, this stone, designed as the cornerstone of the extension of the Capitol according to a plan approved by the President in pursuance of an act of Congress, was laid by

Millard Fillmore,
President of the United States,

assisted by . . . a few surviving gentlemen who witnessed the laying of the cornerstone of the Capitol by President Washington, on the 18th day of September, A.D. 1793.

PRESIDENT MILLARD FILLMORE

If, therefore, it shall be hereafter the will of God that this structure shall fall from its base – that its foundation be upturned and this deposit brought to the eyes of men – be it then known that on this day the Union of the United States of America stands firm – that their Constitution still exists unimpaired and with all its original usefulness and glory growing every day stronger and stronger in the affections of the great body of the American people and attracting more and more the admiration of the world. And all here assembled – whether belonging to public life or to private life, with hearts devoutly thankful to Almighty God for the preservation of the liberty and happiness of the country – unite in sincere and fervent prayers that this deposit, and the walls and arches, the domes and towers, the columns and entablatures [ornaments atop the columns], now to be erected over it may endure for ever! †

God Save the United States of America!
Daniel Webster,
Secretary of State of the United States.

Fellow-citizens, fifty-eight years ago Washington stood on this spot

to execute a duty like that which has now been performed. He then laid the corner-stone of the original Capitol. He was at the head of the govern-ment – at that time weak in resources, burdened with debt, just struggling into

WASHINGTON LAYING THE CORNERSTONE IN 1793

political existence and respectability, and agitated by the heaving waves which were overturning European thrones. But even then, in many important respects, the government was strong. It was strong in Washington's own great character; it was strong in the wisdom and patriotism of other eminent public men – his political associates and fellow-laborers; and it was strong in the affections of the people.

---

† This prayer apparently was answered not only during the Civil War but again on September 11, 2001, when a plane hijacked by terrorists and aimed at the US Capitol building was prematurely and intentionally crashed by heroic citizens into a field in Pennsylvania, thus saving the Capitol building. That act not only proved that our government "still exists unimpaired and with all its original usefulness and glory, growing every day stronger and stronger in the affections of the great body of the American people," but that act of bravery also ensured that "the walls and the arches, the domes and towers, the columns and entab-latures" of the US Capitol still endure and stand firm today – just as prayed by Daniel Webster a century-and-a-half ago.

Since that time, astonishing changes have been wrought in the
condition and prospects of the American people and a degree of
progress witnessed with which the world can furnish no parallel.
As we review the course of that progress, wonder and amazement
arrest our attention at every step. The present occasion – although
allowing of no lengthened remarks – may yet, perhaps, admit of a
short comparative statement of important subjects of national interest as they existed at that day and as they now exist. I have adopted
for this purpose the tabular form of statement as being the most
brief and significant.

Comparative Table

	Year 1793	Year 1851
Number of States	15	31
Representatives and Senators in Congress	135	295
Population of the United States . . .	3,929,328	23,267,498
Amount of receipts into the Treasury	$5,720,624	$52,312,980
Amount of expenditures . . .	$7,529,575	$48,005,879
Area of the United States in square miles . . .	805,461	3,314,365
Rank and file of the army	5,120	10,000
Militia (enrolled)		2,006,456
Navy of the United States (vessels) . . .	0	76
Treaties and conventions with foreign powers	9	90
Lighthouses and light-boats . . .	12	372
Area of the Capitol	1/2 acre	4 1/3 acres
Number of miles of railroad in operation . . .		10,287
Lines of electric telegraph, in miles		15,000
Number of post-offices	209	21,551
Number of miles of post route . . .	5,642	196,290
Number of colleges	19	121
Public libraries . . .	35	694
Emigrants from Europe to the United States	10,000	299,610
Coinage at the Mint	$9,664	$52,019,465

... And now, fellow-citizens, having stated to you this infallible proof of the growth and prosperity of the nation, I ask you – and I would ask every man – whether the government which has been over us has proved itself an affliction or a curse to the country, or any part of it? Ye men of the South, of all the original Southern States, what say you to all this? † Are you – or any of you – ashamed of this great work of your fathers? Your fathers were not they who stoned the prophets and killed them [c.f., MATTHEW 23:37; LUKE 13:34]. They were among the prophets; they were of the prophets; they were themselves the prophets.

Ye men of Virginia, what do you say to all this? Ye men of the Potomac, dwelling along the shores of that river on which Washington lived and died and where his remains now rest, ye – so many of whom may see the domes of the Capitol from your own homes – what say ye?

---

† Webster here directed his remarks toward the South because they were at that very instant talking secession. In fact, only nine months later, in April 1852, South Carolina proceeded beyond talk and actually held a secession convention, determining that she had the right to secede (although she refrained from doing so until nine years later when the other Southern States joined her). Webster was an ardent opponent of secession. In fact, in January 1830, during the nullification and secession crisis that culminated in 1832 (again centered around South Carolina), Webster had delivered his famous speech, "Liberty and Union, Now and Forever, One and Inseparable." His closing of that speech accurately summarized both his feelings, and those of much of the rest of the nation at that time:

> While the Union lasts, we have high, exciting, gratifying prospects spread out before us – for us and our children. Beyond that I seek not to penetrate the veil. God grant that in my day, at least, that curtain may not rise! God grant that on my vision never may be opened what lies behind! When my eyes shall be turned to behold for the last time the sun in heaven, may I not see him shining on the broken and dishonored fragments of a once glorious Union – on States dissevered, discordant, belligerent – on a land rent with civil feuds, or drenched (it may be!) in fraternal blood [the blood of brothers]! Let their last feeble and lingering glance rather behold the gorgeous ensign [flag] of the republic – now known and honored throughout the earth – still full high advanced, its arms and trophies streaming in their original luster, not a stripe erased or polluted, nor a single star obscured, bearing for its motto no such miserable interrogatory as "What is all this worth?'" nor those other words of delusion and folly, "Liberty first and Union afterwards"; but everywhere, spread all over in characters of living light, blazing on all its ample folds as they float over the sea and over the land and in every wind under the whole heavens, that other sentiment – dear to every true American heart: Liberty and Union, now and forever, one and inseparable!

Ye men of James River and the Bay – places consecrated by the early settlement of your Commonwealth – what do you say? Do you desire from the soil of your State, or as you travel to the North, to see these halls vacated – their beauty and ornaments destroyed and their national usefulness gone for ever?

Ye men beyond the Blue Ridge, many thousands of whom are nearer to this Capitol than to the seat of government of your own State – what do you think of breaking this great association into fragments of States and of people? I know that some of you – and I believe that you all – would be almost as much shocked at the announcement of such a catastrophe as if you were to be informed that the Blue Ridge itself would soon totter from its base.

And ye men of Western Virginia who occupy the great slope from the top of the Alleghanies to Ohio and Kentucky, what benefit do you propose to yourselves by disunion? If you "secede," what do you "secede" from – and what do you "accede" to? Do you look for the current of the Ohio to change and to bring you and your commerce to the tidewaters of Eastern rivers? What man in his senses can suppose that you would remain part and parcel of Virginia a month after Virginia should have ceased to be part and parcel of the United States?

The secession of Virginia! The secession of Virginia – whether alone or in company – is most improbable – the greatest of all improbabilities. Virginia, to her everlasting honor, acted a great part in framing and establishing the present Constitution. She has had her reward and her distinction. Seven of her noble sons have each filled the Presidency and enjoyed the highest honors of the country. [†]

Dolorous [regretful] complaints come up to us from the South that Virginia will not head the march of secession and lead the other Southern States out of the Union [that is, some Southern States are complaining that Virginia has not taken the lead in the secession move-

---

† The seven Virginia Presidents included George Washington (1st), Thomas Jefferson (3rd), James Madison (4th), James Monroe (5th), William Henry Harrison (9th), John Tyler (10th), and Zachary Taylor (12th).

ment]. This, if it should happen, would be something of a marvel –
certainly considering how much pains Virginia took to lead these same
States into the Union and considering, too, that she has partaken as
largely of its benefits and its government as any other State.

And ye men of the other Southern States – members of the Old
Thirteen; yes, members of the Old Thirteen that always touches my
regard and my sympathies: North Carolina, Georgia, South Carolina! What page in your history – or in the history of any one of you
– is brighter than those which have been recorded since the Union
was formed? Or through what period has your prosperity been greater
or your peace and happiness better secured? What names even has
South Carolina – now so much dissatisfied – what names has she of
which her intelligent sons are more proud than those which have
been connected with the government of the United States? In Revolutionary times and in the earliest days of this Constitution, there
was no State more honored or more deserving of honor. † Where is
she now? And what a fall is there, my countrymen! †† But I leave her
to her own reflections, commending to her with all my heart the due
consideration of her own example in times now gone by.

Fellow-citizens, there are some diseases of the mind as well as of
the body – diseases of communities as well as diseases of individuals
– that must be left to their own cure; at least it is wise to leave them
so until the last critical moment shall arrive.

I hope it is not irreverent – and certainly it is not intended as reproach – when I say that I know no stronger expression in our lan-

---

† Early heroes of South Carolina who received national acclaim and were almost universally recognizable names throughout the nation included <u>revolutionary generals</u> such as
Francis Marion (the "Swamp Fox"), Nathanael Greene, Christopher Gadsden, William
Moultrie, and Andrew Pickens; <u>signers of the Declaration</u> Thomas Lynch, Arthur Middle-
ton, Thomas Heyward, and Edward Rutledge; <u>signers of the Constitution</u> Charles Pinckney, John Rutledge, Pierce Butler, and Charles Cotesworth Pinckney; and other notables.

†† Webster is noting that South Carolina had few national heroes after her efforts for
American Independence and the establishment of the Constitution – that is, her glory days
were when she was fighting for union, not against it.

guage than that which describes the restoration of the wayward son: *he came to himself* [LUKE 15:17]. He had broken away from all the ties of love, family, and friendship – he had forsaken everything which he had once regarded in his father's house – he had forsworn [renounced] his natural sympathies, affections, and habits, and taken his journey into a far country. He had gone away from himself and out of himself. But misfortunes overtook him and famine threatened him with starvation and death; no entreaties from home followed him to beckon him back; no admonition from others warned him of his fate. But the hour of reflection had come, and nature and conscience wrought within him until at length *"he came to himself."* †

And now, ye men of the new States of the South! †† You are not of the original thirteen. The battle had been fought and won, the Revolution achieved, and the Constitution established before your States had any existence as States. You came to a prepared banquet and had seats assigned you at table just as honorable as those which were filled by older guests [c.f., LUKE 14: 7-9]. You have been and are singularly prosperous; and if anyone should deny this, you would at once contradict his assertion. You have bought vast quantities of choice and excellent land at the lowest price – and if the public domain has not been lavished upon you, you yourself will admit that it has been appropriated to your own uses by a very liberal hand. And yet in some of these States (not in all) persons are found in favor of a dissolution of the Union or of secession from it. Such opinions are expressed even where the general prosperity of the community has been the most rapidly advanced.

In the flourishing and interesting State of Mississippi, for example, there is a large party which insists that her grievances are intolerable – that the whole body politic is in a state of suffering; and all along

---

† Webster has taken this entire analogy and its language from the account of the prodigal son in Luke 15:11-32.

†† The "new States of the South" (i.e., the southern States admitted subsequent to the original thirteen) included Kentucky (1792), Tennessee (1796), Louisiana (1812), Mississippi (1817), Alabama (1819), Missouri (1821), Arkansas (1836), Florida (1845), and Texas (1845).

and through her whole extent on the Mississippi, a loud cry rings that her only remedy is "Secession," "Secession." Now, gentlemen, what infliction does the State of Mississippi suffer under? What oppression prostrates her strength or destroys her happiness? Before we can judge of the proper remedy, we must know something of the disease and – for my part – I confess that the real evil existing in the case appears to me to be a certain inquietude or uneasiness growing out of a high degree of prosperity and consciousness of wealth and power which sometimes lead men to be ready for changes and to push on unreasonably to still higher elevation. If this be the truth of the matter, her political doctors are about right – if the complaint spring from overwrought prosperity, for that disease I have no doubt that secession would prove a sovereign remedy.

But I return to the leading topic on which I was engaged. In the department of invention there have been wonderful applications of science to arts within the last sixty years. The spacious hall of the Patent Office is at once the repository [storehouse] and proof of American inventive art and genius. Their results are seen in the numerous improvements by which human labor is abridged [made easier]. . . . But we have not confined our attention to the immediate application of science to the useful arts. We have entered the field of original research and have enlarged the bounds of scientific knowledge. †

Sixty years ago, besides the brilliant discoveries of Franklin in electricity, scarcely anything had been done among us in the way of original

---

† The areas of "original research" into which Americans had entered by 1851 were indeed impressive; no where else in the world came close in comparison. For example, in 1831 Samuel Guthrie (1782-1848) discovered chloroform and Cyrus McCormick (1809-1884) patented his famous grain reaper; in 1836, Samuel Colt (1814-1862) patented the revolver; in 1839, Charles Goodyear (1800-1860) discovered the vulcanization of rubber and Alexander Simon Wolcott (?-1844) took the first photographic portrait; in 1840, John William Draper (1811-1882) took the first photograph of the moon and Samuel F. B. Morse (1791-1872) patented the telegraph; in 1842, Crawford Long (1815-1878) first used ether in a surgery; in 1844, dentist Horace Wells (1815-1848) first used an anesthetic in the removal of teeth and Morse sent the first overland telegraphic message; in 1846, Elias Howe (1819-1867) patented the first sewing machine; and there were numbers of other equally impressive life-changing discoveries and inventions rendered in diverse fields ranging from geology to botany to medicine to agriculture.

discovery. Our men of science were content with repeating the experiments and diffusing a knowledge of the discoveries of the learned
of the Old World without attempting to add a single new fact or
principle to the existing stock. Within the last twenty-five or thirty
years a remarkable improvement has taken place in this respect. Our
natural history has been explored in all its branches; our geology has
been investigated with results of the highest interest to practical and
theoretical science. † Discoveries have been made in pure chemistry
and electricity which have received the approbation [praise] of the
world. †† The advance which has been made in meteorology in this
country within the last twenty years is equal to that made during the
same period in all the world besides. †††

In 1793, there was not in the United States an instrument with
which a good observation of the heavenly bodies could be made. There

---

† American geological advances included the first geological survey of an entire State
(North Carolina, 1822); the use of geology to correlate the strata of the American Atlantic
costal plain with that of the Cretaceous in Europe (1827); the first geologist employed by
the US government (1834) completed the first mineralogical and geological survey of the
Ozark Mountains (1835); the first significant American original work on geologic theory
(1841); and numerous other achievements.

†† Advances made in chemistry included the establishment in Boston of the first chemical analysis laboratory in the United States (1836); the establishment in Philadelphia of
America's first student chemistry laboratory (1836); the advancement of the revolutionary
thesis that only the rays that are absorbed can produce chemical change (1841); the hiring in
Baltimore of America's first full-time chemist in an industrial business – a chemical manu-
facturing company (1850); the discovery and identification of certain crystallized salts ad-
joined to the cobalt family (1851); and other advances.

Progress in electricity included machinery for the production of high levels of electric
current (1821); the discovery of the relationship between magnetic fields and electricity –
i.e., electromagnetic induction (1831); the use of electricity to send America's first telegraphic message: "What hath God wrought?" from Washington to Baltimore by Samuel F.
B. Morse (1844); and other notable electrical inventions and applications.

††† American advances in meteorology included the discovery that winds blow counter-
clockwise around the direction of prevailing winds (1831); the use of graphing in relation to
barometric readings (1843); the hiring by the federal government of a paid meteorologist
who issued numerous meteorological reports (1843, 1850, 1851, etc.); the establishment of a
national center for the collection of regional meteorological data via telegraph stations (1849);
and other significant advances.

are now instruments at Washington, Cambridge, and Cincinnati [†] equal to those at the best European observatories; and the original discoveries in astronomy within the last five years in this country are among the most brilliant of the age. [††] . . .

These facts conclusively prove that a great advance has been made among us not only in the application of science to the wants of ordinary life but in science itself, in its highest branches, in its adaptation to satisfy the cravings of the immortal mind.

In respect to literature, with the exception of some books of elementary education and some theological treatises of which scarcely any but those of Jonathan Edwards have any permanent value, and some works on local history and politics like Hutchinson's *Massachusetts*, Jefferson's *Notes on Virginia*, the *Federalist*, Belknap's *New Hampshire*, and Morse's *Geography*, and a few others, America had not produced a single work of any repute in literature. [†††] We were

---

[†] In 1842, the US Naval Observatory had been founded in Washington to study the stars and the heavens; in 1847, a 15-inch telescope was installed in Cambridge (at the time of this oration, it was America's largest telescope – and one of the best in the world – and remained the world's largest until 1867); in 1842 an observatory was built in Cincinnati (with the cornerstone laid by John Quincy Adams) that housed the largest refracting telescope in America, and it continues today as the oldest operational telescope in the world.

[††] In the five years preceding this oration, a number of significant astronomical discoveries had been made. For example, in 1847, Maria Mitchell (1818-1899) discovered a new comet; in 1847, George Phillips Bond (1825-1865) began work on early photography of stars, resulting in the first stellar photograph in 1850; in 1848 George Bond had discovered the eighth moon of Saturn and William Cranch Bond (1789-1859) discovered the dusty ring around Saturn; and in 1850, George Bond made the first clear photographic image of the moon. Indeed, much had occurred in the field of astronomy in the five years preceding Webster's oration.

[†††] Webster listed five impressive American literary works beyond those of Jonathan Edwards (1703-1758). Edwards – the president of Princeton – was a theologian and scientist who authored a number of works of great importance widely read for generations.

Of the other five works cited by Webster, Hutchinson's *Massachusetts* was a three-volume history of the State written by Thomas Hutchinson (1711-1780), the last royal governor of Massachusetts; Jefferson's *Notes on the State of Virginia* was written by Thomas Jefferson (1743-1826) in 1781 as a work to acquaint French citizens with the State of Virginia; the *Federalist Papers* were written by Alexander Hamilton (1755-1804), James Madison (1751-1836), and John Jay (1745-1829) and published in 1788 to explain to the American public the

almost wholly dependent on imported books. Even our Bibles and Testaments were, for the most part, printed abroad. The book trade is now one of the greatest branches of business, and many works of standard value and of high reputation in Europe as well as at home have been produced by American authors in every department of literary composition.

While the country has been expanding in dimensions, in numbers, and in wealth, the government has applied a wise forecast in the adoption of measures necessary (when the world shall no longer be at peace) to maintain the national honor, whether by appropriate displays of vigor abroad or by well-adapted means of defense at home. A navy – which has so often illustrated our history by heroic achievements (though in peaceful times restrained in its operations to narrow limit) – possesses in its admirable elements the means of great and sudden expansion and is justly looked upon by the nation as the right arm of its power. An army – still smaller but not less perfect in its detail – has on many a field exhibited the military aptitudes and prowess of the race and demonstrated the wisdom which has presided over its organization and government. . . .

The navy is the active and aggressive element of national defense, and let loose from our own seacoast must display its power in the seas and channels of the enemy. To do this, it need not be large, and it can never be large enough to defend by its presence at home all our ports and harbors. But in the absence of the navy, what can the regular army or the volunteer militia do against the enemy's line-of-battle ships and steamers falling without notice upon our coast? What will guard our cities from tribute, our merchant-vessels and our navy-yards from conflagration [attack and burning]? . . . In this connection, one most important facility in the defense of the country is not to be overlooked: it is the extreme rapidity with which the soldiers of the army

various aspects of the newly proposed US Constitution and to gain public support for its ratification; Belknap's *New Hampshire* was written by Dr. Jeremy Belknap (1744-1798) and was a three-volume history of the State published from 1784-1792; and Morse's *Geography* was written by Jedediah Morse (1761-1826) – titled "The Father of American Geography" – who published his first comprehensive geography book (of North America) in 1796.

and any number of the militia corps may be brought to any point where a hostile attack shall at any time be made or threatened. And this extension of territory embraced within the United States, increase of its population, commerce, and manufactures, development of its resources by canals and railroads, and rapidity of intercommunication by means of steam and electricity have all been accomplished without overthrow of, or danger to, the public liberties by any assumption of military power. . . .

I now do declare – in the face of all the intelligent of the age – that for the period which has elapsed from the day that Washington laid the foundation of this Capitol to the present time, there has been no country upon earth in which life, liberty, and property have been more amply and steadily secured or more freely enjoyed than in these United States of America. Who is there that will deny this? Who is there prepared with a greater or a better example? Who is there that can stand upon the foundation of facts – acknowledged or proved – and assert that these our republican institutions have not answered the true ends of government beyond all precedent in human history?

There is yet another view. There are still higher considerations. Man is an intellectual being, destined to immortality. *There is a spirit in him, and the breath of the Almighty hath given him understanding* [JOB 32:8; 33:4]. Then only is he tending toward his own destiny while he seeks for knowledge and virtue, for the will of his Maker, and for just conceptions of his own duty. Of all important questions, therefore, let this – the most important of all – be first asked and first answered: In what country of the habitable globe of great extent and large population are the means of knowledge the most generally diffused and enjoyed among the people? This question admits of one and only one answer: it is here in these United States – it is among the descendants of those who settled at Jamestown – of those who were Pilgrims on the shore of Plymouth – and of those other races of men who in subsequent times have become joined in this great American family. . . .

But there is something even more than this. Man is not only an intellectual but he is also a religious being, and his religious feelings and habits require cultivation. Let the religious element in man's nature be neglected – let him be influenced by no higher motives than low self-interest and subjected to no stronger restraint than the limits of civil authority – and he becomes the creature of selfish passion or blind fanaticism.

The spectacle of a nation [France] powerful and enlightened, but without Christian faith, has been presented, almost within our own day, as a warning beacon for the nations.

On the other hand, the cultivation of the religious sentiment represses licentiousness, incites to general benevolence and the practical acknowledgment of the brotherhood of man, inspires respect for law and order, and gives strength to the whole social fabric at the same time that it conducts the human soul upward to the Author of its being.

Now I think it may be stated with truth that in no country in proportion to its population are there so many benevolent establishments connected with religious instruction – Bible, Missionary, and Tract Societies, supported by public and private contributions – as in our own. There are also institutions for the education of the blind, of idiots [mentally retarded], of the deaf and dumb; for the reception of orphan and destitute children and the insane; for moral reform, designed for children and females respectively; and institutions for the reformation of criminals – not to speak of those numerous establishments in almost every county and town in the United States for the reception of the aged, infirm, and destitute poor, many of whom have fled to our shores to escape the poverty and wretchedness of their condition at home.

In the United States there is no church establishment or ecclesiastical authority founded by government. Public worship is maintained either by voluntary associations and contributions or by trusts and donations of a charitable origin.

Now, I think it safe to say that a greater portion of the people of the United States attend public worship decently clad, well-behaved, and well-seated [well-accommodated] than of any other country of the civilized world. Edifices of religion are seen everywhere. Their aggregate cost would amount to an immense sum of money. They are, in general, kept in good repair and consecrated to the purposes of public worship. In these edifices the people regularly assemble on the Sabbath day, which by all classes is sacredly set apart for rest from secular employment and for religious meditation and worship, to listen to the reading of the Holy Scriptures and discourses from pious ministers of the several denominations.

This attention to the wants of the intellect and of the soul as manifested by the voluntary support of schools and colleges, of churches and benevolent institutions, is one of the most remarkable characteristics of the American people – not less strikingly exhibited in the new than in the older settlements of the country. On the spot where the first trees of the forest were felled (near the log cabins of the pioneers) are to be seen rising together the church and the schoolhouse. So has it been from the beginning – and God grant that it may thus continue! . . .

Who does not admit that this unparalleled growth in prosperity and renown is the result – under Providence – of the union of these States under a general Constitution which guarantees to each State a republican form of government [†] and to every man the enjoy-

---

[†] This is required by the US Constitution in Art. IV, Sec. IV. Today, however, we have grown accustomed to hearing that we are a democracy, but we are not; such was never intended and the Constitution does not allow it. While many Americans today do not understand the difference between a democratic and a republican form of government, previous generations did – especially our Founders. They had an opportunity to establish a democracy in America and chose not to. In fact, they made clear that we were *not* – and were *never* to become – a democracy:

> [D]emocracies have ever been spectacles of turbulence and contention; have ever been found incompatible with personal security, or the rights of property; and have, in general, been as short in their lives as they have been violent in their deaths. JAMES MADISON

> Remember, democracy never lasts long. It soon wastes, exhausts, and murders itself. There never was a democracy yet that did not commit suicide. JOHN ADAMS

> A democracy is a volcano which conceals the fiery materials of its own destruction. These will produce an eruption and carry desolation in their way. The known propensity of a democracy is to licentiousness [lack of restraint by law or morality]

ment of life, liberty, and the pursuit of happiness free from civil tyranny or ecclesiastical domination? And to bring home this idea to the present occasion, who does not feel that when President Washington laid his hand on the foundation of the first Capitol, he performed a great work of perpetuation of the Union and the Constitution? . . .

Before us is the broad and beautiful river, separating two of the original thirteen States [Virginia and Maryland] which a late Presi-

---

which the ambitious call, and ignorant believe to be, liberty. FISHER AMES, A FRAMER OF THE BILL OF RIGHTS

We have seen the tumult of democracy terminate . . . as [it has] everywhere terminated, in despotism. . . . Democracy! savage and wild. Thou who wouldst bring down the virtuous and wise to thy level of folly and guilt. GOUVERNEUR MORRIS, PENMAN AND SIGNER OF THE CONSTITUTION

[T]he experience of all former ages had shown that of all human governments, democracy was the most unstable, fluctuating and short-lived. JOHN QUINCY ADAMS

A simple democracy . . . is one of the greatest of evils. BENJAMIN RUSH, SIGNER OF THE DECLARATION

In democracy . . . there are commonly tumults and disorders. . . . Therefore a pure democracy is generally a very bad government. It is often the most tyrannical government on earth. NOAH WEBSTER

Pure democracy cannot subsist long nor be carried far into the departments of state – it is very subject to caprice [whim] and the madness of popular rage. JOHN WITHERSPOON, SIGNER OF THE DECLARATION

It may generally be remarked that the more a government resembles a pure democracy, the more they abound with disorder and confusion. ZEPHANIAH SWIFT, AUTHOR OF AMERICA'S FIRST LEGAL TEXT

Because the Founders understood the inherent weaknesses of a democracy, Article IV in the Constitution required that every State have a republican – and not a democratic – form of government.

While many Americans today seem unable to define the difference between a republic and a democracy, there is a difference – a big difference. Although "the people" is the source of authority in both, the difference rests on how the power from the people is exercised. A pure democracy operates by direct majority vote of the people. When an issue is to be decided, the entire population votes on it; the majority wins and rules. A republic differs in that the people elect representatives who then pass laws to govern the nation. A democracy is rule by the majority feeling at that moment (what the Founders described as a "mobocracy"); a republic is rule under a written constitution and fixed laws that govern both the people and their government. And who will deny the success of the American system that forbids democracy but preserves republicanism?

dent – a man of determined purpose and inflexible will but patriotic heart – desired to span with arches of ever-enduring granite, symbolical of the firmly cemented union of the North and the South. That President was General Jackson.

On its banks repose the ashes of the Father of his Country and at our side – by a singular felicity [unique blessing] of position, overlooking the city which he designed and which bears his name – rises to his memory the marble column, sublime in its simple grandeur and fitly intended to reach a loftier height than any similar structure on the surface of the whole earth. Let the votive [dedicated] offerings of his grateful countrymen be freely contributed to carry this monument higher and still higher. † May I say, as on another occasion, "Let it rise; let it rise till it meet the sun in his coming; let the earliest light of the morning gild it, and parting day linger and play on its summit!" ††

Fellow-citizens, what contemplations are awakened in our minds as we assemble here to reenact a scene like that performed by Washington! Methinks I see his venerable form now before me as pre-

---

† This is a reference to the Washington Monument. In 1833, the Washington National Monument Society was formed to build a "great National Monument to the memory of Washington at the seat of the Federal Government." By 1847, $87,000 had been collected by public contributions and an architectural design had been selected. On July 4, 1848, the cornerstone was laid for the monument and at the time of this oration, work was progressing nicely. However, in 1854 the funds ran out, political squabbles set in, and the work ceased. At the time, the column was only about 150 feet high (of its final 555 feet) and it remained incomplete until 1876 when President Ulysses S. Grant provided federal funds for its completion. Work was resumed in 1880; the monument was completed in 1884, dedicated in 1885, and opened to the public in 1888.

†† This quotation is from an 1825 speech by Daniel Webster given at the laying of the cornerstone of the Bunker Hill Monument outside Boston – a monument similar in design to the Washington Monument. In that speech, Webster had declared:

> We wish that this column, rising towards Heaven among the pointed spires of so many temples [churches] dedicated to God, may contribute also to produce in all minds a pious feeling of dependence and gratitude. We wish, finally, that the last object to the sight of him who leaves his native shore, and the first to gladden his who revisits it, may be something which shall remind him of the liberty and the glory of his country. Let it rise! Let it rise, till it meet the sun in his coming; let the earliest light of the morning gild [illuminate] it, and the parting day linger and play on its summit!

sented in the glorious statue by Houdon
now in the Capitol of Virginia. † He is
dignified and grave, but concern and
anxiety seem to soften the lineaments of
his countenance. The government over
which he presides is yet in the crisis of
experiment. Not free from troubles at
home, he sees the world in commotion
and in arms all around him. He sees that
imposing foreign powers are half disposed to try the strength of the recently
established American government. We
perceive that mighty thoughts, mingled
with fears as well as with hopes, are
struggling within him. He heads a short
procession over these then–naked fields;
he crosses yonder stream on a fallen tree;
he ascends to the top of this eminence,

HOUDON'S STATUE OF WASHINGTON

whose original oaks of the forest stand as thick around him as if the
spot had been devoted to Druidical worship; †† and here he per-
forms the appointed duty of the day.

---

† In 1784, the Virginia Assembly commissioned a statue of Washington. Thomas Jefferson
– then the American Ambassador to France – recommended that Jean-Antoine Houdon
(1741-1828), the most famous sculptor of that day, execute the work. (In 1780, Houdon had
painted a portrait of Lafayette on display in the Virginia State Capitol.) Houdon came to Mt.
Vernon in 1785 and took complete measurements of Washington and a mold of his face. He
returned to France to begin work on the statue; in 1796, it was completed, shipped to America,
and placed in the Virginia Capitol in Richmond, where it still stands today. (A casting was
made from that original statue and the replica now stands in the US Capitol Rotunda.)

†† Druidical worship refers to the religious practices of Celtic Britain in the 3rd century
BC. Druids were considered not only priests but magicians (or "wizards") able to control
weather, predict the future, and change themselves into various animals. Their religious
rituals and sacrifices were performed in remote and largely inaccessible groves of oak trees
adjoining rivers and lakes. Hence, Webster is saying that when Washington laid the cornerstone at the Capitol, the area was still so remote and the forest so thick that it would have
been acceptable for use by the ancient Druids.

And now, fellow-citizens, if this vision were a reality – if Washington actually were now amongst us and if he could draw around him the shades of the great public men of his own day, patriots and warriors, orators and statesmen, and were to address us in their presence – would he not say to us: "Ye men of this generation, I rejoice and thank God for being able to see that our labors and toils and sacrifices were not in vain. You are prosperous, you are happy, you are grateful; the fire of liberty burns brightly and steadily in your hearts while duty and the law restrain it from bursting forth in wild and destructive conflagration [consuming flames]. Cherish liberty as you love it; cherish its securities as you wish to preserve it. Maintain the Constitution which we labored so painfully to establish and which has been to you such a source of inestimable blessings. Preserve the union of the States, cemented as it was by our prayers, our tears, and our blood. Be true to God, to your country, and to your duty. So shall the whole Eastern world follow the morning sun to contemplate you as a nation; so shall all generations honor you as they honor us; and so shall that Almighty Power which so graciously protected us – and which now protects you – shower its everlasting blessings upon you and your posterity."

Great Father of your Country! We heed your words – we feel their force as if you now uttered them with lips of flesh and blood. Your example teaches us   your affectionate addresses teach us – your public life teaches us – your sense of the value of the blessings of the Union. Those blessings our fathers have tasted and we have tasted – and still taste. Nor do we intend that those who come after us shall be denied the same high fruition [fulfillment]. Our honor as well as our happiness is concerned. We cannot – we dare not – we will not – betray our sacred trust. We will not filch [steal] from posterity the treasure placed in our hands to be transmitted to other generations. The [rain]bow that gilds [adorns] the clouds in the heavens, the pillars that uphold the firmament may disappear and fall away in the hour appointed by the will of God; but until that day comes – or so long as our lives may last – no ruthless hand shall undermine that bright arch of Union and Liberty which spans the continent from Washington to California. . . .

Fellow-citizens, take courage – be of good cheer. We shall come to no such ignoble [shameful] end. We *shall live and not die* [PSALM 118:17; GENESIS 42:2]. During the period allotted to our several lives, we shall continue to rejoice in the return of this anniversary. The ill-omened sounds of fanaticism will be hushed; the ghastly specters [demons] of secession and disunion will disappear; and the enemies of united con-stitutional liberty – if their hatred cannot be appeased – may prepare to have their eyeballs seared as they behold the steady flight of the Ameri-can eagle on his burnished [shining] wings for years and years to come.

Fellow-citizens, I now bring this address to a close by expressing to you in the words of the great Roman orator [Cicero] the deepest wish of my heart – and which I know dwells deeply in the hearts of all who hear me: "Duo modo haec opto; unum, ut moriens populum romanum liberum relinquam; hoc mihi majus a diis immortalibus dari nihil potest: alterum, ut ita cuique eveniat, ut de republica quisque mereatur." †

And now, fellow-citizens, with hearts void of hatred, envy, and malice towards our own countrymen, or any of them – or towards the subjects or citizens of other governments, or towards any member of the great family of man – but exulting, nevertheless, in our own peace, security, and happiness, in the grateful remembrance of the past and the glorious hopes of the future, let us return to our homes and with all humility and devotion, offer our thanks to the Father of all our mercies – political, social, and religious. ■

---

† This quotation is from Cicero's (106-43 BC) "Second Philippic," delivered as a response to Marc Antony's furious attack upon Cicero after Cicero had called for the death of Antony in the Roman Senate because of Antony's desire to replace the Roman Republic with a military dictatorship. As a result of his speech, Cicero was added to the "hit list" of Antony. Cicero realized that he would probably soon die (which he did, assassinated while trying to flee the area), and his quotation in that speech (cited by Webster) was essentially Cicero's last spoken wish for the Republic, and would be translated: "I desire these two things: one, that dying I may leave the Roman people free; no greater boon [gift] than this can be granted me by the immortal gods. The other, that everyone may meet with a fate suitable to his deserts and conduct toward the republic."

An Oration by

John Quincy Adams

1837

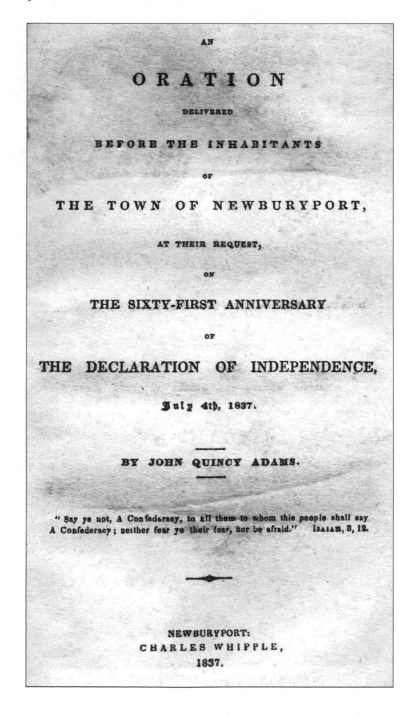

AN

ORATION

DELIVERED

BEFORE THE INHABITANTS

OF

THE TOWN OF NEWBURYPORT,

AT THEIR REQUEST,

ON

THE SIXTY-FIRST ANNIVERSARY

OF

THE DECLARATION OF INDEPENDENCE,

July 4th, 1837.

BY JOHN QUINCY ADAMS.

" Say ye not, A Confederacy, to all them to whom this people shall say A Confederacy; neither fear ye their fear, nor be afraid." ISAIAH, 8, 12.

NEWBURYPORT:
CHARLES WHIPPLE,
1837.

John Quincy Adams

John Quincy Adams
(1767 - 1848)

John Quincy Adams, sixth President of the United States, had one of the most brilliant political careers in American history. Fortunately for Americans today, we can enjoy his career with insights unavailable from many other leaders and statesmen because he kept extensive diary and memoirs, candidly recording many of his innermost thoughts and most personal experiences. (Adams began keeping a diary at the age of 11 and continued that practice until his death almost seven decades later. In one twenty-four year period, he never missed a day's entry in his diary – despite his extensive political and professional involvements – and those entries were not abbreviated but often included several pages of detailed information for each day.)

Adams' love for liberty was instilled in him from his earliest years by his parents, John (a signer of the Declaration, a signer of the Bill of Rights, and the 2nd US President) and Abigail (a remarkably courageous woman, the daughter of a minister, and the first First Lady to live in the White House).

In 1775 when John Quincy was just seven, the American Revolution was underway with the battles of Lexington and Concord, Bunker Hill, and the bombardment and burning of Charlestown by the British. The young Adams was directly impacted by these events and they produced in him vivid and indelible memories – memories still uneffaced decades later. In fact, in a conversation with a legendary Minuteman some fifty-years after the original event:

> Mr. Cary. . . . asked me if I remembered a company of militia who, about the time of the battle of Lexington in 1775, came down from Bridgewater and passed the night at my father's house and barn at the foot of Penn's Hill, and in the midst of whom my father placed me (then a boy between seven and eight years) and I went through the manual exercise of the musket by word of command from one of them. I told him I remembered it as distinctly as if it had been last week. He said he was one of that company.

The young JQA watched his parents sacrifice much for the cause of liberty during that period – even in the realm of sentimental keepsakes. As he explained:

> In 1775, the Minutemen from a hundred towns in the province were marching – at a moment's warning – to the scene of opening war. Many of them called at my father's house in Quincy and received the hospitality of John Adams. All were lodged in the house which the house would contain; others in the barns and wherever they could find a place. There were, then, in my father's kitchen some dozen or two of pewter spoons; and I well recollect going into the kitchen and seeing some of the men engaged in running [melting] those spoons into bullets for the use of the troops! Do you wonder that a boy of seven years of age who witnessed this scene should be a patriot?

JQA personally experienced the earliest and some of the most dreadful scenes of the Revolution – including the loss of his family physician, Dr. Joseph Warren, at the 1775 Battle of Bunker Hill. He later recounted:

> My father was separated from his family, on his way to attend the Continental Congress; and there my mother with her children lived in unintermitted danger of being consumed with them all in a conflagration [blaze of fire] kindled by a torch in the same hands which on the 17th of June lighted the fires of Charlestown. I saw with my own eyes those fires – and heard Britannia's thunders in the battle of Bunker's Hill – and witnessed the tears of my mother (and mingled with them my own) at the fall of Warren, a dear friend of my father and a beloved physician to me. He had been our family physician and surgeon, and had saved my forefinger from amputation under a very bad fracture.

Throughout that entire time, Abigail faithfully instilled in her young son both patriotism and a love for God – and he never forgot those early lessons. According to JQA:

In that same spring and summer of 1775, she taught me to repeat daily after the Lord's Prayer (before rising from bed) the
Ode of Collins on the patriot warriors who fell in the war. † . . .
Of the impression made upon my heart by the sentiments inculcated in these beautiful effusions [outpourings] of patriotism and poetry, you may form an estimate by the fact that now
– seventy-one years after they were thus taught me – I repeat
them from memory without reference to the book.

In 1778 at the age of 11, JQA's own distinguished political service
began when he became the official secretary to his father, America's
diplomat to France. After a voyage of several weeks, he arrived in
France. His mother, concerned for the welfare of his soul and the
maintenance of his private character, wrote him and succinctly reminded him of his duties to God and to his training, forcefully declaring to him:

> I would much rather you should have found your grave in the
> ocean you have crossed – or that an untimely death crop you
> [mow you down prematurely] in your infant years – than see
> you an immoral, profligate [wicked and unprincipled], or
> graceless child.

At the age of 14, John Quincy received a congressional appointment as secretary to Francis Dana, Ambassador to Russia. He traveled alone (by horse and carriage) across the Continent from France
to Russia. (Imagine a fourteen-year old overcoming the various language barriers and arranging food, lodging, and financial needs for
that lengthy journey of weeks!) When the Revolution was finally
over, Adams returned to America where he attended and graduated
from Harvard, and then pursued his training as an attorney.

---

† English poet William Collins (1721-1759) penned "Ode Written in the Beginning of the
Year 1746" to commemorate brave British troops who fell during the Jacobite Insurrections of
1745-1746. (The Jacobites sought to restore full hereditary monarchies in Great Britain and to
remove from Parliament and the people the power that had been gained first under Cromwell
and then during the Glorious Revolution of 1688.) Collins is considered the second most
influential English poet, behind only Thomas Gray (1716-1771).

President George Washington placed him in the State Department, declaring him to be one of the most effective of American diplomats. At George Washington's strong recommendation, John Quincy continued his foreign diplomacy under President John Adams.

Under President Jefferson, Adams became a US Senator and a professor of oratory and rhetoric at Harvard.

Under President Madison, he was nominated and confirmed to the US Supreme Court but declined that appointment to serve as Ambassador to Russia. (Over his lengthy diplomatic career, Adams served as diplomat to the Netherlands, Portugal, Germany, Russia, and Great Britain). Adams also helped negotiate the peace treaty with Britain to end the War of 1812.

Under President Monroe, Adams was Secretary of State and the main instrument in constructing the famous "Monroe Doctrine," declaring America off-limits to any foreign power seeking to own or establish colonies here, thus halting further European intervention in America. He also negotiated the treaty to obtain the Florida Territory from Spain.

Following Monroe's presidency, Adams became President – elected by the US House because none of the four presidential candidates garnered a majority from the electoral college. John C. Calhoun (Adams' ardent political enemy) was selected as Adam's Vice-President by the US Senate under the provisions of the 12th Amendment of the Constitution. During his administration, Adams focused on internal improvements in America, including efforts to establish the Smithsonian Institution as well as celestial observatories and other scientific improvements.

Following his presidency, Adams was elected to the US House of Representatives where he served until his death 17 years later. (Adams is the only President to serve in the House *following* his presidency; six Presidents served in the House before they became President.)

John Quincy Adams was known throughout his life for his strong humanitarian and religious convictions. He became the leading anti-slavery voice of his day (his opponents called him "The Hell Hound of Abolition") and he argued the noted *La Amistad* case before the

US Supreme Court, winning the release of African slaves in a near unanimous decision from a pro-slavery Supreme Court. Adams also was a vice-president of the American Bible Society and the author of several religious works, including *Letters of John Quincy Adams to his Son on the Bible and its Teachings* and *Poems of Religion and Society*. Adams was one of the greatest orators of his – or any – age, and even today his writings remain inspiring.

At the time of this oration, he was 70 years old and serving in the House of Representatives, having finished his term as President nearly a decade earlier.

The years immediately preceding this oration had been a time of serious domestic difficulties across America: in New York City a cholera epidemic had killed 4,000 citizens, and a smallpox outbreak in the West had killed 15,000 Indians in three tribes; South Carolina was threatening secession from the Union over the nullification crisis and President Andrew Jackson was threatening to invade the State with the US military and put down the rebellion.

Although slavery had finally been abolished in the British Empire, not so in America. Slavery in the South was becoming stronger and more entrenched, thus fomenting stronger anti-slavery sentiments in the predominantly slave-free North. In fact, the American Anti-Slavery Society mailed 75,000 anti-slavery tracts to southern slave owners, greatly outraging the South and causing her to become more hardened in her pro-slavery positions and even more aggressively pro-slavery.

War had occurred between Texas and Mexico, fanned on first by tyrannical Mexican ultimatums (e.g., Mexico had mandated the secularization of all missions, forcing them to drop their religious affiliations) and then by atrocities such as the famous massacre of Texans at Goliad. The Alamo had already fallen; Santa Anna subsequently had been defeated at the Battle of San Jacinto, thus establishing Texas as an independent republic with Sam Houston as its President at the time of this oration.

Following the revelation that Daniel Morgan of New York apparently had been murdered by Masons to prevent his exposing the

AT THE TIME OF ADAM'S ORATION, NEWBURYPORT WAS STILL A MAJOR SEAPORT

"secrets" of Freemasonry, the anti-Masonic movement was sweeping the country. Masonic membership was plummeting; not only were anti-Masonic parties being formed in most New England States but Anti-masons were winning seats in numerous State legislatures. In fact, John Quincy Adams had written a book against Masonry and had been an anti-Masonic party nominee for Congress. The national Anti-Masonic Party had even run a candidate for President: US Attorney General William Wirt.

This oration by Adams was delivered in Newburyport, a town of 7,000 inhabitants whose commerce centered around shipping and shipbuilding. Newburyport was the burial place of the Rev. George Whitefield (the most popular and best known evangelist of the First Great Awakening) and Matthew Thornton (signer of the Declaration). It was also where the first Coast Guard ship was built and launched, and was the birthplace of abolition leader William Lloyd Garrison. Newburyport had been visited by many distinguished leaders, including Presidents George Washington, James Monroe, John Quincy Adams, and American hero, General Marquis de Lafayette.

Adams – who delivered this oration in the largest meeting house in town (the Presbyterian church) – recorded that day's events in his diary:

I delivered an oration before the inhabitants of the town of Newburyport (at their request) on the anniversary of our national independence. . . .

The firing of guns began at midnight, and continued all night, together with squibs [firecrackers] and crackers [rockets] almost without intermission.

At nine this morning, Colonel Coleman came and took me in a chaise [carriage] down to Water Street, where I found Mr. Cushing standing upon a platform and delivering an address to the eminent members of the fire department, drawn up in a line in front of him. . . . I gave them a toast in lemonade: "The Fire Department of Newburyport: always prepared for duty; may they never be needed to perform it!"

I then returned to Mr. Cushing's and shortly proceeded to join the procession formed in High Street. . . . The procession was very large and with it were several hundreds of children of the public schools, male and female. The march and counter march [parade], traversing many streets of the town, took a long hour.

The meetinghouse. . . . was crowded with auditors [listeners] as full as it could hold; hundreds could not obtain admission. There was music, instrumental and vocal; four stanzas . . . of *Adams and Liberty* were sung; prayer; . . . then an anthem; next the Declaration of Independence was read . . . [and] the 194th hymn of Dr. Belknap's collection: "O'er mountain tops the mount of God in latter days shall rise." This was performed at my request, and immediately preceded the delivery of my oration, which

THE PRESBYTERIAN CHURCH IN WHICH
ADAMS DELIVERED HIS ORATION

occupied an hour and a half – listened to with deep attention and occasional applause. The *Hallelujah Chorus, Anthem Chorus*, and the *Benediction Chorus* closed the performances at half past two o'clock.

As I descended the pulpit, in a small room adjoining the church an old lady came to me and shook hands with me, saying she was now satisfied that I was a Christian – of which she had entertained doubts. . . . [I] closed the evening by going . . . on the Mall, where there were fireworks. Passed by T. Parson's house. † The office taken away.

In his oration, Adams first chronicled what led up to the Declaration of Independence and expounded on the subsequent development of American government, including the Articles of Confederation and then the Constitution. He reminded Americans of fundamental principles: of how liberty was a gift from God and therefore why the Founders intended for slavery eventually to be abolished; and of how union was a first principle and therefore why secession and disunion were abhorrent to the Founders and should be repugnant to every generation. Adams' oration is an inspiring look at the reason that the Fourth of July had become such a celebrated day in America – a day on which we looked into our past history, and also a day when we looked at our present responsibilities and renewed our pledge to preserve the trust that had been given us by God and by our Founders.

---

† Theophilus Parsons (1750-1813) was a brilliant attorney, influential in framing Massachusetts' first State constitution (1780) and in securing the ratification of the US Constitution in Massachusetts (1788). He served as the Chief Justice of the State Supreme Court and by 1800 was considered the leading lawyer in America. John Quincy Adams – himself an attorney – studied law under Parsons from 1787 to 1790.

𝕺𝖗𝖆𝖙𝖎𝖔𝖓.

Say ye not, "A Confederacy," to all them to whom this people shall say
"A Confederacy"; neither fear ye their fear nor be afraid." ISAIAH 8:12

Why is it, friends and fellow citizens, that you are here assembled?
Why is it that entering upon the sixty-second year of our national
existence, you have honored with an invitation to address you from
this place a fellow citizen of a former age, [†] bearing in the records of
his memory the warm and vivid affections which attached him – at
the distance of a full half century – to your town and to your forefathers, then the cherished associates of his youthful days? Why is it
that next to the birthday of the Savior of the world, your most joyous and most venerated festival returns on this day? And why is it
that among the swarming myriads [countless numbers] of our population [that] thousands and tens of thousands among us (abstaining
under the dictate of religious principle – from the commemoration
of that birthday of Him Who *brought life and immortality to light*
[II TIMOTHY 1:10]) [††] yet unite with all their brethren of this community
year after year in celebrating this, the birthday of the nation?

[†] Adams – who had played an active role during the American Revolution – was now
speaking at a celebration six decades later, thus making him "a fellow citizen of a *former* age."

[††] It seems unimaginable today that "tens of thousands" in the then extremely religious
New England region would abstain "under the dictate of religious principle" from celebrating Christmas (which today has become such a prominent religious holiday), yet such was
the case. Why? Because the Pilgrims and Puritans of New England found no Biblical precedent for a public celebration of that day (recall that the goal of these groups was to sim-
plify religious worship and to cut away all religious rituals and celebrations not specifically
cited in the Bible); nothing in the Bible established any date for the birth of Christ; the
holiday was instead established by Roman tradition, thus making it – in their view – one of
the many "pagan" holidays that had been inculcated into the corrupt church that had persecuted them, and which they and other religious leaders wished to reform. Consequently,
Christmas in New England remained a regular working day. In fact, Massachusetts passed
an anti-Christmas law in 1659 declaring: "Whosoever shall be found observing any such day
as Christmas, or the like, either by forbearing [ceasing from] labor, feasting, or any other
way upon such account as aforesaid, every such person so offending shall pay for each of-
fense five shillings as a fine to the country." The law was repealed in 1681, but the holiday
still was not celebrated by religious non-conformists or dissenters (i.e., the Puritans and

Is it not that in the chain of human events, the birthday of the nation is indissolubly linked with the birthday of the Savior? – that it forms a leading event in the progress of the gospel dispensation? Is it not that the Declaration of Independence first organized the social compact on the foundation of the Redeemer's mission upon earth? – that it laid the cornerstone of human government upon the first precepts of Christianity and gave to the world the first irrevocable [absolute] pledge of the fulfillment of the prophecies announced directly from Heaven at the birth of the Savior and predicted by the greatest of the Hebrew prophets six hundred years before?

Cast your eyes backwards upon the progress of time sixty-one years from this day, and in the midst of the horrors and desolations of civil war [the American Revolution] you behold an assembly of planters, shopkeepers, and lawyers – the representatives of the people of thirteen English colonies in North America – sitting in the city of Philadelphia. These fifty-five men on that day unanimously adopt and publish to the world a state paper under the simple title of "A Declaration." †

Pilgrims); it usually was celebrated only by a few Anglicans (later Episcopalians), Catholics, and other more formal or high-church-tradition New England families. It was not until the 1830s and 1840s (at the time of this oration) that Christmas celebrations were just beginning to be accepted in New England (primarily due to the influence of large-scale Christmas celebrations in cities such as New York) – although as late as 1870 in Boston public schools, a student missing school on Christmas Day could be punished or expelled. By the 1880s, however, Christmas celebrations had finally become as accepted in New England as they were in other parts of the country.

† To many today who know that there were fifty-six who signed the Declaration of Independence, JQA's reference to fifty-five seems an error; yet it is not. Actually, both fifty-five _and_ fifty-six are correct.

The Declaration of Independence was approved in principle on July 2nd, 1776, and then approved by the full vote of Congress on July 4th, 1776. At that time, the Declaration was signed only by John Hancock (President of Congress) and Charles Thomson (Secretary of Congress). On July 19th, Congress agreed to prepare a beautifully engrossed copy of the Declaration to be signed by all the members. On August 2nd, the proposed Declaration was signed in a formal ceremony by fifty delegates of Congress. Among the signers were several who originally had not been in Congress on July 4th to vote for the Declaration (e.g., Benjamin Rush and James Smith); conversely, many who had voted for the Declaration on July 4th were not there to sign it on August 2nd (e.g., Robert Livingston and George Clinton). This was because several States had changed their delegates to the Congress between the

The object of this Declaration was twofold.

First, to proclaim the people of the thirteen united colonies One People; and in their name and by their authority, *to dissolve the political bands which had connected them with another* people – that is, the people of Great Britain. [†]

Secondly, *to assume* – in the name of this One People of the thirteen united Colonies – *among the powers of the earth, the separate and equal station to which the Laws of Nature, and of Nature's God entitled them.*

With regard to the first of these purposes, the Declaration alleges *a decent respect to the opinions of mankind* as requiring that the one People separating themselves from another *should declare the causes which impel them to the separation.* The specification of these causes and the conclusion resulting from them constitute the whole paper. The Declaration was a manifesto issued from *a decent respect of the opinions of mankind* to justify the people of the North American Union for their voluntary separation from the people of Great Britain by alleging the causes which rendered this separation necessary. . . .

For the second object of the Declaration (the *assumption among the powers of the earth of the separate and equal station to which the Laws of Nature and of Nature's God entitled them*), no reason was assigned – no justification was deemed necessary. . . .

---

vote on July 4th and the signing on August 2nd (e.g., George Clinton was called home to lead military forces in New York, while Benjamin Rush had been sent by Pennsylvania to replace a delegate who had voted against the Declaration on July 4th). On January 18th, 1777, Congress authorized the printing and public distribution of the signed Declaration. In the time between August 2nd when the fifty delegates had first signed and January 18th when the Declaration was authorized for printing, five more had signed: Matthew Thornton (NH), George Wythe (VA), Oliver Wolcott (CT), Richard Henry Lee (VA), and Elbridge Gerry (MA). Therefore, at the time of the congressional order to print the Declaration, fifty-five delegates had signed. Thomas McKean became the fifty-sixth to sign the Declaration – doing so nearly a year after the January 18th order to print and distribute the Declaration. (Although McKean had voted for the Declaration on July 4th, 1776, he did not sign until after January, 1778.) Therefore, at the time that Congress first printed and distributed the Declaration, it had only fifty-five signatures on the document; but within a year it had risen to fifty-six – the number at which it stands today.

† The italicized lines in this part of the oration indicate direct quotes from the Declaration of Independence (unless otherwise identified).

Six years of war – cruel, unrelenting, merciless war – war at once civil and foreign – were waged, testing the firmness and fortitude of the One People in the inflexible adherence to that separation from the other which their representatives in Congress had proclaimed. By the signature of the preliminary Articles of Peace on the 30th of November 1782, their warfare was accomplished and the Spirit of the Lord – with a voice reaching to the latest of future ages – might have exclaimed (like the sublime prophet of Israel), *Comfort ye, comfort ye My people, saith your God* (ISAIAH 40:1). . . .

George the Third believed that the Parliament of Great Britain had the right to enact laws for the government of the people of the British Colonies in all cases. An immense majority of the people of the British Islands believed the same. . . . Here was a conflict between two first principles of government resulting from a defect in the British Constitution: the principle that sovereign power in human government is in its nature unlimited; and the principle that property can lawfully be taxed only with the consent of its owner. Now these two principles carried out into practice are utterly irreconcilable with each other. . . . [T]he King and Parliament [and t]he people of Great Britain appealed for the right to tax the Colonies to the unlimited and illimitable sovereignty of the Parliament, (and) [t]he Colonists appealed to the natural right of property and the articles of the Great Charter. [†] The collision in the application of these two principles was the primitive [root] cause of the severance of the North American Colonies from the British Empire.

The grievances alleged in the Declaration of Independence [††] were . . . causes amply sufficient to justify before God and man the

---

[†] The Great Charter is the Magna Charta, enacted in 1215 AD by Englishmen demanding protection from the arbitrary actions of King John against their persons and property. The Magna Charta was the first step in limiting governmental authority and granting rights to citizens – it was, in essence, the world's first Bill of Rights.

[††] The Declaration listed 27 grievances against Great Britain, including the abuse of representative powers (11 clauses), the abuse of military powers (seven clauses), the abuse of judicial powers (four clauses), and one clause each about Britain fostering domestic instability, opposing immigration, increasing government size and intrusiveness, interfering with foreign trade, and imposing taxation without representation.

separation itself; and that resolution – to the support of which the fifty-five representatives of the one people of the United Colonies *pledged their lives, their fortunes, and their sacred honor* † – after passing through the fiery ordeal of a six years war, was sanctioned by the God of Battles and by the unqualified acknowledgment of the defeated adversary [Great Britain]. . . .

The members of the Congress who signed their names to the Declaration style [call] themselves *the representatives* not of the separate colonies but *of the United States of America in Congress assembled.* No one colony is named in the Declaration – nor is there anything on its face indicating from which of the colonies any one of the signers was delegated.

They proclaim the separation of One People from another. They affirm *the right of the people to institute, alter, and abolish their government*; and their final language is, *we do, in the name and by the authority of the good people of these colonies, solemnly publish and declare that these United Colonies are, and of right ought to be, free and independent States.* . . . And by this paper, this One People did notify the world of mankind that they thereby did *assume among the powers of the earth the separate and equal station to which the Laws of Nature and of Nature's God entitled them.*

This was indeed a great and solemn event. The sublimest of the prophets of antiquity – with the voice of inspiration – had exclaimed, *Who hath heard such a thing? Who hath seen such things? Shall the earth be made to bring forth in one day? Or shall a nation be born at once?* [ISAIAH 66:8]. In the two thousand-five-hundred years that had elapsed since the days of that prophecy, no such event had occurred. . . . [But with America] the earth was made to bring forth in one day! A nation was born at once!

Well indeed may such a day be commemorated by such a nation from year to year! But whether as a day of festivity and joy, or of humiliation and mourning – that, fellow-citizens – that, in the various turns of chance below – depends not upon the event itself but

---

† See previous note three pages earlier on why JQA cites 55 rather than 56 signers.

upon its consequences. . . . [A]s early as the age of Solomon, that wisest of men told the people of Jerusalem that *as a good name was better than precious ointment, so the day of death was better than the day of one's birth* (ECCLESIASTES 7:1).

Are you then assembled here, my brethren – children of those who declared your national independence – in sorrow, or in joy? In gratitude for blessings enjoyed, or in affliction for blessings lost? In exultation at the energies of your fathers, or in shame and confusion of face at your own degeneracy [slippage] from their virtues? Forgive the apparent rudeness of these inquiries – they are not addressed to you under the influence of a doubt what your answer to them will be. You are not here to unite in echoes of mutual [con]gratulation for the separation of your forefathers from their kindred freemen of the British Islands [the American Revolution]. You are [here]. . . . to turn your final reflections inward upon yourselves and to say, "These are the glories of a generation passed away; what are the duties which they devolve upon us?"

The Declaration of Independence . . . explicitly unfolded the principles. . . . [and] the exposition of these principles will furnish the solution to the question of the purpose for which you are here assembled.

In recurring to those principles, let us remark:

First, that the people of the thirteen Colonies announced themselves to the world – and solemnly bound themselves with an appeal to God – to be One People. And this One People, by their Representatives, declared the United Colonies free and independent States.

Secondly, they declared the People – and not the States – to be the only legitimate source of power; and that to the People alone belonged the right to institute, to alter, to abolish, and to reinstitute government. And hence it follows that as the people of the separate Colonies or States formed only parts of the One People assuming their station among the powers of the earth, so the people of no one State could separate from the rest but by a revolution similar to that by which the whole people had separated themselves from the people of the British Islands – nor without the violation of that solemn covenant by which they bound themselves to support and maintain the United Colonies as free and independent States.

An error of the most dangerous character – more than once threatening the dissolution by violence of the Union itself – has occasionally found countenance and encouragement in several of the States by an inference not only unwarranted by the language and import of the Declaration but subversive of its fundamental principles. [†] This inference is that because by this paper the United Colonies were declared free and independent States, therefore each of the States separately was free, independent, and sovereign. . . .

The origin of this error was of a very early date after the Declaration of Independence; and the infusion of its spirit into the Articles of Confederation – first formed for the government of the Union – was the seed of dissolution sown in the soil of that compact which palsied [enfeebled] all its energies from the day of its birth and exhibited it to the world only as a monument of impotence and imbecility. [††]

[†] There had occasionally been times when States or movements wrongly invoked the principles of the Declaration as a justification for weakening or dissolving the Union, such as in the Whiskey Rebellion (1794), the Kentucky and Virginia Resolutions (1798, 1799), the Hartford Convention (1814), and the South Carolina Nullification Convention (1832). In each case, the group - or State - threatened to declare its own independence from the United States, or unilaterally – as a single State – to declare national acts unlawful. It was this perversion of the principles of the Declaration that eventually was invoked by the South to justify its secession from the Union in order to form its own separate nation, thus precipitating the War Between the States.

[††] It became clear during the American Revolution that some type of national government was needed; the war could not be effectively conducted through thirteen separate State governments. Consequently, in June, 1776, Congress appointed a Committee of thirteen delegates – one from each State – to work out some agreement under which they could operate jointly while still maintaining their individual State sovereignty. Those on the Committee were a distinguished group, most of whom would eventually sign the Declaration of Independence and some of whom would later sign the US Constitution. This Committee constructed what became known as the Articles of Confederation, approved by Congress on November 15, 1777, but not ratified by the States until three-and-a-half years later on March 1, 1781.

The reason for this delay primarily lay in resolving questions surrounding the future ownership principally of the Ohio territory then claimed by Virginia. Each State had long-standing and universally acknowledged claims on territories that were within its State jurisdiction. For example, New York held the lands that in 1792 became Vermont; North Carolina held the

The Declaration did not proclaim the separate States free and independent, much less did it announce them as sovereign States or affirm that they separately possessed the war-making or the peace-making power. The fact was directly the reverse.

The Declaration was that the United Colonies, forming One People, were *free and independent States* – *that they were absolved from all allegiance to the British Crown* – *that all political connection between them and the State of Great Britain was and ought to be totally dissolved* – *and that as free and independent States, they had full power to levy war, conclude peace, contract alliances, establish commerce, and do all other acts and*

---

lands that in 1796 became Tennessee; Delaware was part of Pennsylvania until 1776; Kentucky was part of Virginia until 1785; Maine was part of Massachusetts until 1820; etc. The Ohio territory (claimed by Virginia) was a massive area stretching from the Great Lakes in the north, along the length of the Mississippi River, and all the way to the "South Sea" (the Gulf of Mexico). Many of the other States wanted parts of this territory; however, Virginia ceded her rights to the Ohio Territory with the stipulation that the land would be used for the common good of the new nation rather than for any particular State. In short, several States had been reticent to approve a national government until the disposition of that (and other) territory had been settled.

Under the Articles of Confederation, a national Congress was established, but each State had equal power with all others without regard to representation. Additionally, agreement was not by the majority but rather by two-thirds of the States, thereby giving power to a block of any five States to thwart the will of the other eight. Furthermore, under the national government there was no judiciary and no "head" or executive and therefore no way to enforce the laws.

The weakness of this system – weaknesses incorporated because of the ardent State jealousies that caused the scope of powers of the national government to be over-restricted – soon became apparent to all. Congress had conducted its business throughout most of the Revolution (until the Articles of Confederation were officially ratified late in the war) on the majority vote principle. Had Congress been required to operate under the Articles of Confederation during the Revolution, it would have been completely powerless and ineffective – a fact that was made clear in the few years in which the nation did flounder under the Articles.

Further fueling discontent with the Articles was the fact that they actually protected and encouraged inequality rather than justice among the States . For example, States that had contributed the most during the Revolution (e.g., Connecticut and Massachusetts) were unable to receive their proper reimbursement because their repayment was opposed by States that had provided much less than their proportionate share (e.g., Georgia and South Carolina). The Articles indeed were "exhibited to the world only as a monument of impotence and imbecility."

For additional information on the problems with the Articles of Confederation, see the note on pp. 109-110.

things which independent States may of right do. But all this was affirmed and declared not of the separate, but of the United, States. . . .

In constituting themselves One People, it could not possibly be their intention to leave the power of concluding peace to each of the States of which the Union was composed. The war was waged against all. The war itself had united the inhabitants of the thirteen Colonies into One People. The lyre of Orpheus was the standard of the Union. †
By the representatives of that One People and by them alone could the peace be concluded. Had the people of any one of the States pretended to the right of concluding a separate peace, the very fact would have operated as a dismemberment of the Union and could have been carried into effect only by the return of that portion of the people to the condition of British subjects.

Thirdly, the Declaration of Independence announced the One People *assuming their station among the powers of the earth* as a civilized, religious, and Christian people – acknowledging themselves bound by the obligations and claiming the rights to which they were entitled by *the laws of nature and of nature's God.* ††

---

† The "lyre of Orpheus" refers to a constellation of stars named "Lyre" (also spelled "Lyra") that form a circle – like the bottom part of a stringed lyre. In Greek mythology, Orpheus had played the lyre skillfully and beautifully; when he was treacherously killed, Zeus retrieved the instrument and set it among the stars as a permanent memorial to Orpheus – thus the "lyre of Orpheus." The thirteen stars that formed a circle in the first American flag were likened to the "lyre of Orpheus" – a permanent memorial (just like the stellar constellation) – a memorial that became "the standard [the symbol] of the Union." Interestingly, the "lyre of Orpheus" was also a part of the Adams' family seal, and it may well have been John Adams in 1777 (at that time serving on the American Board of War) who suggested the circle of stars as part of the flag. In short, Adams is saying that the non-ending circle of stars, reminiscent of "the lyre of Orpheus" and signifying the non-ending Union of the States then appearing on the American flag, had become the symbol for the Union.

†† The phrase "the laws of nature and of nature's God" was taken from one of the most famous and widely-used legal works of that generation: *Blackstone's Commentaries on the Laws* by Sir William Blackstone (1723-1780). So influential was Blackstone on the thinking of the Founders that he is documented as the second most-invoked political authority during the Founding Era (1760-1805).

Blackstone's *Commentaries* eventually became the official law book adopted by the US Senate, and Supreme Court Justice James Iredell (appointed by President George Washington) declared that Blackstone's views were heavily relied upon during the framing of the

They had [originally] formed a subordinate portion of an European Christian nation in the condition of Colonies. The European Colonies in America had all been settled by Christian nations; and the first of them (settled before the reformation of Luther) had sought their justification for taking possession of lands inhabited by men of another race in a grant of authority from the successor of Saint Peter at Rome for converting the natives of the country to the Christian code of religion and morals.[†] After the Reformation, the kings of

---

Bill of Rights. So important was Blackstone to America that Thomas Jefferson even commented that American lawyers used Blackstone's with the same dedication and reverence that Muslims used the Koran.

With the Founders' heavy reliance on Blackstone, it is not surprising that many of them (including James Madison, James Wilson, John Adams, Henry Laurens, Thomas Jefferson, John Marshall, James Madison, James Otis, James Kent, Joseph Story, Fisher Ames, and many others) either endorsed or relied on Blackstone in their own legal writings.

So how did Blackstone define "the laws of nature" and the laws "of nature's God" (also called by Blackstone "the law of revelation") – the phrase incorporated into the Declaration of Independence by the Founders? According to Blackstone:

> Man, considered as a creature, must necessarily be subject to the laws of his Creator, for he is entirely a dependent being. . . . And consequently, as man depends absolutely upon his Maker for everything, it is necessary that he should in all points conform to his Maker's will. This will of his Maker is called *the law of nature*. . . . This law of nature, being coeval [coexistent] with mankind and dictated by God Himself is, of course, superior in obligation to any other. It is binding over all the globe, in all countries, and at all times; no human laws are of any validity if contrary to this; and such of them as are valid derive all their force and all their authority, mediately or immediately, from this original. . . . The doctrines thus delivered we call the revealed or divine law and they are to be found only in the holy Scriptures [i.e., the "*law of nature's God*"]. These precepts, when revealed, are found upon comparison to be really a part of the original law of nature. . . . Upon these *two* foundations, the law of nature and the law of revelation, depend all human laws; that is to say, no human laws should be suffered [permitted] to contradict these.

While today "the laws of nature and of nature's God" is not understood to be a significant legal phrase or even to carry any religious implications, the fact is clear that under the philosophy articulated by Blackstone and embraced and set forth in the Declaration by the Founders, civil laws could not contradict the laws of God revealed either through nature or the Bible – i.e., "the laws of nature and of nature's God."

† The "grant of authority from the successor of Saint Peter at Rome" (the Pope) for "converting the natives of the country to the Christian code of religion and morals" was actually more of an indirect grant of authority. That is, the Pope would sanction a Catholic

England (substituting themselves in the place of the Roman Pontiff as heads of the Church) granted charters for the same benevolent purposes; † and as these colonial establishments successively arose, worldly purposes, the spirit of adventure, and religious persecution took their place (together with the conversion of the heathen) among

---

monarch to develop the New World (or a particular region of it) and the Catholic monarch, when sending an expedition to that part of the New World, would dispatch Catholic missionaries to the Indians as part of the expedition. For example, after Pope Alexander VI (Pope from 1492-1503), a Spaniard, recognized Spain's right to take possession of the entire New World following its "discovery" by Columbus, Spain dispatched numerous expeditions into Mexico, Central, and South America; on every expedition were missionary priests (usually Dominican, Franciscan, or Jesuit) to convert the Indians. Therefore, while "the grant of authority" for the New World came from the Pope, it was the Catholic monarchs — both French and Spanish — who implemented the missionary aspects of "converting the natives."

The soldiers and leaders on these Catholic expeditions often resorted to violence "for taking possession of lands inhabited by men of another race," although the forcible conversion of natives more frequently characterized Spanish than French missions. Pope Paul III (Pope from 1534-1550) later tried to change the "forcible conversion" policy, but his words were largely ignored by the monarchs. Spain and France both had been particularly unaffected by the Reformation and — providentially for American liberty — those two nations did not have much lasting influence in the settling of the eastern shore of America. (France's influence primarily was to the far north, in and along Canada, while Spain's influence primarily was in the far southern, southwestern, and western regions of the continent.) The colonists who arrived to settle America's eastern seaboard were largely English and were steeped in the ideas of the Reformation rather than the Spanish and French models; and it was a notable distinction that they purchased rather than took lands from the Indians (e.g., the Pilgrims of Plymouth Plantation Colony, the Puritans of the Massachusetts Bay Colony, the settlers of the New Haven Colony, etc.) — a practice in direct contrast to the methods of settlement used in Mexico, Central and South America. That early favorable practice of the English religious settlers in the east regrettably was largely abandoned in America's later westward expansion.

† Examples of charters granted by English kings "for the same benevolent purposes" included the Charter of Virginia, issued by King James in 1606 for the purpose — among others — of "propagating of Christian religion to such people as yet live in darkness and miserable ignorance of the true knowledge and worship of God, and may in time bring the infidels and savages living in those parts to human civility and to a settled and quiet government." Other charters with similar declarations included the Charter of New England (issued by King James in November 1620), the Charter of Maryland (issued by King Charles in 1632), the Charter of Rhode Island (issued by King Charles II in July 1663), and the Charter of Pennsylvania (issued by King Charles II in March 1681) with its declared purpose "to reduce the savage natives *by gentle and just manners* to the love of civil society and Christian religion."

the motives for the European establishments in this Western Hemisphere. † Hence had arisen among the colonizing nations a customary law under which the commerce of all colonial settlements was confined exclusively to the metropolis or Mother Country. The Declaration of Independence cast off all the shackles of this dependency. The United States of America were no longer Colonies. They were an independent Nation of Christians. . . .

In setting forth the justifying causes of their separation from Great Britain, your fathers opened the fountains of the great deep. For the first time since the creation of the world, the act which constituted a great people laid the foundation of their government upon the unalterable and eternal principles of human rights. They were comprised in a few short sentences and were delivered with the unqualified confidence of self-evident truths.

We hold, says the Declaration, *these truths to be self-evident: that all men are created equal; that they are endowed by their Creator with certain unalienable rights; that among these are life, liberty, and the pursuit of happiness; that to secure these rights, governments are instituted among men, deriving their just powers from the consent of the governed; that whenever any form of government becomes destructive of these ends, it is the right of the people to alter or to abolish it and to institute a new government, laying its foundations on such principles, and organizing its powers in such form, as to them shall seem most likely to effect their safety and happiness. . . .*

[T]he history of mankind had never before furnished an example of a government directly and expressly instituted upon this principle. . . . [until t]he Declaration of Independence. . . . And never from that to the present day has there been one moment of regret on

---

† The "spirit of adventure" that replaced the "benevolent purposes" of evangelization was seen in charters such as that of Georgia (1732) that declared one of its purposes was to "not only gain a comfortable subsistence . . . but also strengthen our colonies and increase the trade, navigation and wealth of these realms." The 1ˢᵗ Virginia Charter (1606) issued by King James I authorized the colonists "to dig, mine, and search for all manner of mines of gold, silver, and copper . . . and have and enjoy the gold, silver, and copper to be gotten." The New York Charter (1663) issued by King Charles II similarly authorized the colonists to collect "revenues and profits" from the lands. In each case, the Mother Country (whether France, Spain, Holland, or England) wanted all the profits and commerce coming out of her colonies.

the part of the people whom they thus declared independent at this mighty change of their condition, nor one moment of distrust of the justice of that declaration. . . .

Every individual whose name was affixed to that paper has finished his career upon earth, and who at this day would not deem it a blessing to have had his name recorded on that list? The act of abolishing the government under which they had lived – of renouncing and abjuring [disavowing] the allegiance by which they had been bound . . . – stands recorded in the annals of the human race as one among the brightest achievements of human virtue, applauded on earth, ratified and confirmed by the fiat [decree] of Heaven. . . .

The position thus assumed by this One People consisting of thirteen free and independent States was new in the history of the world. It was complicated and compounded of [formed from] elements never before believed susceptible of being blended together. . . . By the affirmation that the principal natural rights of mankind are unalienable, it placed them beyond the reach of organized human power; and by affirming that governments are instituted to secure them – and may and ought to be abolished if they become destructive of those ends – they made all government subordinate to the moral supremacy of the people. . . . This was a novelty in the moral philosophy of nations and it is the essential point of difference between the system of government announced in the Declaration of Independence and those systems which had until then prevailed among men. A moral Ruler of the Universe – the Governor and Controller of all human power – is the only unlimited sovereign acknowledged by the Declaration of Independence, and it claims for the United States of America (when assuming their equal station among the nations of the earth) only the power to do all that may be done of right.

Threescore and one years have passed away since this Declaration was issued and we may now *judge of the tree by its fruit* [MATTHEW 12:33; LUKE 6:44]. It was a bold and hazardous step when considered merely as the act of separation of the Colonies from Great Britain. Had the cause in which it was issued failed, it would have subjected every individual who signed it to the pains and penalties of treason –

to a cruel and ignominious [shameful] death. † But inflexible as were the spirits and intrepid [courageous] as were the hearts of the patriots (who by this act set at defiance the colossal power of the British Empire), bolder and more intrepid still were the souls which at that crisis in human affairs dared to proclaim the new and fundamental principles upon which their incipient [newborn] Republic was to be founded. It was an experiment upon the heart of man. . . .

The Declaration had laid the foundation of all civil government in the unalienable natural rights of individual man of which it had specifically named three: *life, liberty, and the pursuit of happiness,* declaring them to be among others not enumerated [specifically mentioned]. The Revolution had been exclusively popular and democratic, and the Declaration had announced that the only object of the institution of governments among men was to secure their unalienable rights, and that they *derived their just powers from the consent of the governed.* . . .

They reported on the twelfth of July (eight days after the Declaration of Independence) a draft of Articles of Confederation and perpetual union between the Colonies, naming them all from New Hampshire to Georgia. . . . [I]n the original draft reported by the select committee †† on the twelfth of July, the first words of the second ar-

---

† A "cruel and ignominious death" was definitely a certainty if the Revolution failed since the very act of separation was viewed by the king as an act of treason and therefore would have subjected the signers to the most painful forms of death. However, even though victory and independence were ultimately achieved for America, many of the signers still suffered a cruel death at the hands of the British. For example, of the 56 signers of the Declaration, nine died during the American Revolution, including three directly at the hands of the British; two others were so abused by the British as prisoners of war that they died shortly after the Revolution; two lost wives at the hands of the British (and four lost children in the same way); 17 had their homes, estates, or property pillaged or destroyed by the British; and many others paid similarly high prices. Therefore, even though death was a certainty if the signers lost the Revolution, it was no less a reality for many of them in fulfillment of their personal pledge of their "lives, fortunes, and sacred honor" to achieve American independence.

†† The select committee assigned to draft the Articles of Confederation consisted of one delegate from each State: Josiah Bartlett (NH), Samuel Adams (MA), Stephen Hopkins (RI), Roger Sherman (CT), Robert Livingston (NY), John Dickinson (PA), Thomas Mc-

ticle were, "The said Colonies unite themselves so as never to be divided by any act whatever." Precious words! Words pronounced by the infant nation at the instant of her rising from the baptismal font! Words bursting from their hearts and uttered by lips yet glowing with the touch from the coal of the Declaration! [c.f., ISAIAH 6: 5-7] . . .

From the twentieth of August, 1776, to the eighth of April, 1777 – (although the Congress was in permanent session without recess but from day to day) no further action upon the revised draft reported by the committee of the whole was had. The interval was the most gloomy and disastrous period of the war. † The debates on the draft

---

Kean (DE), Thomas Stone (MD), Thomas Nelson (VA), Joseph Hewes (NC), Edward Rutledge (SC), and Button Gwinnett (GA). There was no delegate from New Jersey because at the time the committee was formed, New Jersey was sending new delegates to the Continental Congress and none had as yet arrived; the former New Jersey delegates had resigned to attend to new posts and responsibilities, with an effective resignation date prior to the committee appointment by Congress (e.g., John DeHart resigned and went home to help draft the State constitution; William Livingston resigned to take a military commission; Jonathan Dickinson Sargeant resigned to take a seat at the State level; etc.).

† From mid-August 1776 to mid-August 1777, nothing seemed to go right for the American army. On August 27-29, 1776, Washington's forces were crushed by British General Howe at the Battle of Long Island, forcing the Americans to beat a hasty retreat; on September 11, a peace conference between the British and the Americans failed; on September 16, a massive fire broke out in upper Manhattan, destroying over 300 buildings; on September 22, Nathan Hale was caught by the British and summarily executed; on October 11, the American navy was almost destroyed at the Battle of Lake Champlain; two weeks later on October 22, Washington was defeated in the Battle of White Plains; in November, Washington suffered two additional defeats with almost 3,000 American casualties and the loss of 100 cannons, thousands of muskets, and an important American fort; on December 6, the British took an American naval base in Rhode Island; and on December 11, Congress evacuated Philadelphia, fearing an imminent British attack. On December 25-26, 1776, following Washington's famous crossing of the Delaware River, he did win two minor military victories at Trenton and Princeton; nevertheless, overall this was indeed "the most gloomy and disastrous" period in the Revolution. In fact, even in the weeks following that period, more difficulty was forthcoming for General Washington. American General Horatio Gates won a major American victory at Saratoga but Washington lost the battles of Brandywine and Germantown. This resulted in a move among some military officers to oust Washington from command and replace him with General Gates (a failed insurrection called the "Conway Cabal"). Indeed, mid-1776 through 1777 was unquestionably "the most gloomy and disastrous period of the war" both for the nation collectively and for Washington personally.

of articles reported by the first committee had evolved and disclosed all the sources of disunion existing between the several sections of the country. . . . State prejudice, State jealousy, were soon embodied under the banners of State sovereignty. And while the cause of freedom and independence itself was drooping under the calamities of war and pestilence, with a penniless treasury and an all but disbanded army, the Congress of the people had no heart to proceed in the discussion of a confederacy overrun by a victorious enemy and on the point – to all external appearance – of being crushed by the wheels of a conqueror's triumphal car. . . .

[T]he fifteenth of November, 1777, the Articles of Confederation as finally matured and elaborated were concluded and sent forth to the State legislatures for their adoption. They were to take effect only when approved by them all, and ratified with their authority by their delegates in Congress. . . . The first article in them all gave the name (or as it was at last called, the "style") of the confederacy: "The United States of America" – the name by which the nation has ever since been known, and now illustrious among the nations of the earth. The second article of the plans reported to the Congress by the original committee and by the committee of the whole constituted and declared the Union in the first project commencing with those most affecting and ever-memorable words: "The said Colonies united themselves so as never to be divided by any act whatever." In the project reported by the committee of the whole, these words were struck out. . . . [and the] reservation of the rights of the separate States was made to precede the institution of the Union itself. . . . How different from the spirit of the article which began – "The said Colonies unite themselves so as never to be divided by any act whatever!"

The institution of the Union was now postponed to follow and not to precede the reservations, and cooled into a mere league of friendship and of mutual defense between the States. . . . It [the Articles of Confederation] was the statue of Pygmalion before its animation – beautiful and lifeless. And where was the vital spark which was to quicken this marble into life? It was in the Declaration of Independence. †

Analyze – at this distance of time – the two documents with cool and philosophical impartiality and you will exclaim, "Never – never since the creation of the world – did two state papers emanating from the same body of men exhibit more dissimilarity of character or more conflict of principle!" The Declaration: glowing with the spirit of union – speaking with one voice the vindication of One People for the act of separating themselves from another, and ascending to the First Cause, the Dispenser of Eternal Justice, for the foundation of its reasoning. The Articles of Confederation: stamped with the features of contention, beginning with niggardly [stingy] reservations of corporate rights, and in the grant of powers seeming to have fallen into the frame of mind described by the sentimental traveler bargaining for a post chaise [a carriage for rent] and viewing his conventionist [the owner of the carriage] with an eye as if he were going with him to fight a duel!

Yet let us not hastily charge our fathers with inconsistency for these repugnances [contradictions] between their different works. Let us never forget that the jealousy of power is the watchful handmaid to the spirit of freedom. . . . Let the obstacles which they encountered and surmounted teach us how much easier it is in morals and politics (as well as in natural philosophy and physics) to pull down than to build up, to demolish than to construct. . . . Providence watched over, protected, and guided our political infancy and led our ancestors finally to retrace their steps, to correct their errors, and resort to the whole People of the Union for a constitution of government emanating from themselves which might realize that union so feelingly expressed by the first draft of their confederation so as "never to be divided by any act whatever."

---

† Pygmalion – a talented sculptor in ancient Greek mythology – once carved (according to the legends) the figure of a woman that was so beautiful that he fell in love with the lifeless statue, treating it as if it were alive – he clothed it, jeweled it, and even brought it gifts. Pygmalion went to the temple of Aphrodite (the goddess of love) to pray for a wife. Aphrodite heard his prayers and went to his home to see the statue. She was so impressed that she brought the statue to life and it became Pygmalion's wife. JQA is saying that like Aphrodite in the story, the Declaration of Independence was the source of life, while the statue (the Articles of Confederation) was in and of itself lifeless.

The origin and history of this Constitution is doubtless familiar to most of my hearers and should be held in perpetual remembrance by us all. It was the consummation of the Declaration of Independence. It has given the sanction of half a century's experience to the principles of that Declaration. The attempt to sanction them by a confederation of sovereign States was made and signally [miserably] failed. It was five years in coming to an immature birth, and expired after five years of languishing and impotent existence.

On the seventeenth of next September [1837], fifty years will have passed away since the Constitution of the United States was presented to the people for their acceptance. . . . And what a happy – what a glorious – career have the people passed through in the half-century of their (and your) existence associated under it! . . .

Are the blessings of good government manifested by the enjoyment of liberty, by the security of property, by the freedom of thought, of speech, of action, pervading every portion of the community? Appeal to your own experience, my fellow citizens; and after answering without hesitation or doubt, affirmatively, all these inquiries (save the last) – if, when you come to them, you pause before you answer – if, within the last five or seven years of your history, ungracious recollections of untoward [disturbing] events crowd upon your memory and grate upon the feelings appropriate to this consecrated day [†] – let them not dis-

---

† The events that occurred "within the last five or seven years" that would include "ungracious recollections of untoward events" involve primarily the nullification and secession crisis of 1832. The controversy – according to the "offended" parties – had stemmed from tariff acts passed by Congress (1816, 1824, 1828). The South Carolina legislature objected to those tariffs, claiming they harmed her economy. She therefore unilaterally declared the federal tariff laws to be null and void (i.e., nullification) and threatened armed resistance as well as secession if the tariff laws were enforced. President Andrew Jackson was not to be bullied, threatened, or intimidated. He sent Gen. Winfield Scott and US troops to Charleston to enforce the act and warned of a full invasion of South Carolina by military force. Significantly, it had been Jackson's own Vice-President, John C. Calhoun of South Carolina, who had fueled the nullification convention and the secession movement precipitating the crisis. In Congress, Henry Clay of Kentucky worked out the passage of a federal law that gradually reduced tariffs over the next decade, thus averting the immediate crisis. Nevertheless, a civil war and the destruction of the Union had been seriously threatened "in the last five or seven years" before this oration – an incident still fresh on the minds of the citizens and therefore an "ungracious recollection of an untoward [disturbing] event."

turb the serenity of your enjoyments or interrupt the harmony of that mutual gratulation in which you may yet all cordially join. But fix well in your minds what were the principles first proclaimed by your fore-fathers as the only foundations of lawful government upon earth. . . .

And this, my fellow citizens – or I have mistaken the motives by which you have been actuated [motivated] – is the purpose for which you are here assembled. It is to enjoy the bounties of Heaven for the past and to prepare for the duties of the future. It is to review the principles proclaimed by the founders of your empire – [and] to exam-ine . . . what portion of them it is your first of duties to retain, to preserve, to redeem, to transmit to your offspring to be cherished, main-tained, and transmitted to their posterity of unnumbered ages to come.

We have consulted the records of the past and I have appealed to your consciousness of the present, and what is the sound which they send forth to all the echoes of futurity but "Union" – Union as one People – Union so as to be divided by no act whatever. We have a sound of modern days; could it have come from an American voice that the value of the Union is to be calculated? Calculated by what system of arithmetic? By what rule of proportion? [If you c]alculate the value of maternal tenderness and of filial affection – calculate the value of nuptial [marriage] vows, of compassion to human suffering, of sympathy with affliction, of piety to God, and of charity to man – calculate the value of all that is precious to the heart and all that is binding upon the soul – and then you will have the elements with which to calculate the value of the Union. But if cotton or tobacco, rocks or ice, metallic money or mimic paper are to furnish the mea-sure, the stamp act was the invention of a calculating statesman. "Great financier! Stupendous calculator!" † . . .

---

† John Quincy Adams is here referring to points of contention between the North and the South. For example, "cotton or tobacco" referred to the slave crops of the South, and "metallic money or mimic paper" referred to the national bank controversy (the North was for a national bank, the South opposed it). The South was threatening secession over these issues, and John Quincy Adams is stating that the Union should be measured by values more important than "cotton or tobacco, rocks or ice, metallic money or mimic paper." He then sarcastically notes that *if* such inferior standards are to be used to measure the value of the nation, then the odious 1765 Stamp Act of Lord Grenville (1759-1834; British Prime Minis-

The calculators of the value of the Union who would palm upon you in the place of this sublime invention a mere cluster of sovereign confederated States do but *sow the wind to reap the whirlwind* [HOSEA 8:7]. One lamentable evidence of deep degeneracy from the spirit of the Declaration of Independence. . . . has, indeed, presented itself in its most malignant form in that portion of the Union, the civil institutions of which are most infected with the gangrene of slavery [the South]. The inconsistency of the institution of domestic slavery with the principles of the Declaration of Independence was seen and lamented by all the southern patriots of the Revolution – by no one with deeper and more unalterable conviction than by the author of the Declaration himself [Thomas Jefferson]. No charge of insincerity or hypocrisy can be fairly laid to their [the Southern Founders'] charge. Never from their lips was heard one syllable of attempt to justify the institution of slavery. † They universally considered it as a reproach fastened

ter) that became a principal focal point in America's separation from Great Britain "was the invention of a calculating statesman" – that is, those attempting to calculate the worth of the Union by their own right of nullification will fail just as badly as did Lord Grenville in calculating that the Stamp Act would bring new revenues into British coffers.

† Interestingly, the fact that the Founding Fathers neither justified slavery nor desired it to remain in America was even confirmed in a speech by congressional Democrat Alexander Stephens (1812-1883) of Georgia, the slave-holding Vice-President of the Confederate States of America. In an 1862 speech entitled *African Slavery: the Corner-Stone of the Southern Confederacy*, Stephens explained that the Founding Fathers – even those from the South – did not intend for slavery to remain a part of the nation. According to Stephens:

> The prevailing ideas entertained by him [Thomas Jefferson] and most of the leading statesmen at the time of the formation of the old Constitution were that the enslavement of the African was in violation of the laws of nature – that it was wrong in principle, socially, morally, and politically. It was an evil they knew not well how to deal with; but the general opinion of the men of that day was that, somehow or other, in the order of Providence, the institution would be evanescent [temporary] and pass away. . . . Those ideas, however, were fundamentally wrong. They rested upon the assumption of the equality of races. This was an error, and the idea of a government built upon it; when the "storm came and the wind blew, it fell." Our new government [the Confederate States of America] is founded upon exactly the opposite idea; its foundations are laid – its cornerstone rests – upon the great truth that the Negro is not equal to the white man. That slavery – subordination to the superior race – is his natural and moral condition. This – our new government – is the first in the history of the world based upon

upon them by the unnatural stepMother Country, and they saw that
before the principles of the Declaration of Independence, slavery – in
common with every other mode of oppression – was destined sooner
or later to be banished from the earth. † Such was the undoubting

this great physical, philosophical, and moral truth.

Hence, the justification of slavery was a doctrine neither introduced nor promulgated by
the Founders – a fact acknowledged by subsequent pro-slavery leaders such as Stephens,
thus confirming Adams' statement regarding the Founders that "never from their lips was
heard one syllable of attempt to justify the institution of slavery."

† Even though the issue of slavery is often raised as a discrediting charge against the
Founding Fathers, as noted above by Confederate Vice-President Alexander Stephens, the
Founding Fathers had no intention of allowing slavery to remain a permanent fixture in the
United States. Slavery was not the product of, nor was it an evil introduced by, the Founding
Fathers; it had been introduced into America nearly two centuries before the Founders. As
President of Congress Henry Laurens explained:

> I abhor slavery [but] I was born in a country where slavery had been established
> by British Kings and Parliaments, as well as by the laws of the country, ages before
> my existence. . . . [T]he day, I hope, is approaching when – from principles of
> gratitude as well as justice – every man will strive to be foremost in showing his
> readiness to comply with the Golden Rule ["Do unto others as you would have
> them do unto you" MATTHEW 7:12].

Many of the Founders openly complained about the fact that Great Britain had forcefully
imposed the evil of slavery upon the Colonies. For example, Thomas Jefferson complained:

> He [King George III] has waged cruel war against human nature itself, violating
> its most sacred rights of life and liberty in the persons of a distant people who
> never offended him, captivating and carrying them into slavery in another hemi-
> sphere or to incur miserable death in their transportation thither. . . . Determined
> to keep open a market where men should be bought and sold, he has prostituted
> his negative for suppressing every legislative attempt to prohibit or to restrain this
> execrable commerce [that is, he has opposed efforts to prohibit the slave trade].

And Benjamin Franklin, in a 1773 letter to Dean Woodward, confirmed that whenever
the Americans had attempted to end slavery, the British government had thwarted those
attempts. Franklin explained that

> . . . a disposition to abolish slavery prevails in North America, that many of Penn-
> sylvanians have set their slaves at liberty, and that even the Virginia Assembly
> have petitioned the King for permission to make a law for preventing the impor-
> tation of more into that colony. This request, however, will probably not be granted
> as their former laws of that kind have always been repealed.

The Revolution – the opportunity for America to create a new nation with new policies
– was a turning point in the national attitude against slavery. Although a few Founding
Founders supported slavery, the clear majority of them opposed it, and many of them who

had owned slaves as British citizens released them in the years following America's separation from Great Britain (e.g., George Washington, John Dickinson, Caesar Rodney, William Livingston, George Wythe, John Randolph, and others). Furthermore, many of the Founders had *never* owned a slave. As John Adams thundered, "[M]y opinion against it [slavery] has always been known . . . [N]ever in my life did I own a slave."

Notice a few additional examples of the strong anti-slavery sentiments held by great numbers of the Founders:

> Christianity, by introducing into Europe the truest principles of humanity, universal benevolence, and brotherly love, had happily abolished civil slavery. Let us who profess the same religion practice its precepts . . . by agreeing to this duty. RICHARD HENRY LEE, PRESIDENT OF CONGRESS, SIGNER OF THE DECLARATION

> I hope we shall at last – and if it so please God, I hope it may be during my lifetime – see this cursed thing [slavery] taken out. . . . For my part, whether in a public station or a private capacity, I shall always be prompt to contribute my assistance towards effecting so desirable an event. WILLIAM LIVINGTON, SIGNER OF THE CONSTITUTION, GOVERNOR OF NEW JERSEY

> Slavery, or an absolute and unlimited power in the master over the life and fortune of the slave, is unauthorized by the common law. . . . The reasons which we sometimes see assigned for the origin and the continuance of slavery appear – when examined to the bottom – to be built upon a false foundation. In the enjoyment of their persons and of their property, the common law protects all. JAMES WILSON, SIGNER OF THE CONSTITUTION, US SUPREME COURT JUSTICE

> As much as I value a union of all the States, I would not admit the Southern States into the Union unless they agree to the discontinuance of this disgraceful [slave] trade. GEORGE MASON, "FATHER OF THE BILL OF RIGHTS"

> [W]hy keep alive the question of slavery? It is admitted by all to be a great evil. CHARLES CARROLL, SIGNER OF THE DECLARATION, A FRAMER OF THE BILL OF RIGHTS

> Domestic slavery is repugnant to the principles of Christianity. . . . It is rebellion against the authority of a common Father. It is a practical denial of the extent and efficacy of the death of a common Savior. It is an usurpation of the prerogative of the great Sovereign of the universe who has solemnly claimed an exclusive property in the souls of men. BENJAMIN RUSH, SIGNER OF THE DECLARATION

For many of the Founders, their feelings against slavery went beyond words. For example, in 1774, Benjamin Franklin and Benjamin Rush founded America's first anti-slavery society, and John Jay was president of a similar society in New York. In fact, many prominent Founding Fathers were members of societies for ending slavery, including William Livingston, Richard Bassett, James Madison, James Monroe, Bushrod Washington, Charles Carroll, William Few, John Marshall, Richard Stockton, Zephaniah Swift, and many more. Based in part on the efforts of these Founders, Pennsylvania and Massachusetts began abolishing slavery in 1780; Connecticut and Rhode Island did so in 1784; Vermont in 1786; New Hampshire in 1792; New York in 1799; and New Jersey in 1804.

As John Quincy Adams noted, the Founders saw that "slavery . . . was destined to be

conviction of Jefferson to his dying day. In the *Memoir of his Life* (written at the age of seventy- seven), he gave to his countrymen the solemn and emphatic warning that the day was not distant when they must hear and adopt the general emancipation of their slaves. "Nothing is more certainly written," said he, "in the book of fate, then that these people are to be free." [JEFFERSON'S *WRITINGS* (1830), VOL. 1, p. 40.] My countrymen! It is written in a better volume than the book of fate – it is written in *the laws of nature and of nature's God!* †

We are now told (indeed, by the learned doctors of the nullification school) that color operates as a forfeiture of the rights of human nature – that a dark skin turns a man into a chattel [personal property] – that crispy [curly] hair transforms a human being into a four-footed beast.

The master-priest [i.e., slave-owning Southern clergymen] informs you that slavery is consecrated and sanctified by the Holy Scriptures of the Old and New Testament – that Ham was the father of Canaan and that all his posterity were doomed by his own father to be hewers of wood and drawers of water to the descendants of Shem and Japheth [c.f., GENESIS 9:25-27] – that the native Americans of African descent are the children of Ham, with the curse of Noah still fastened upon them; and the native Americans of European descent are children of Japheth – pure Anglo-Saxon blood, born to command and to live by the sweat of another's brow.

The master-philosopher [i.e., slave-owning Southern philosopher] teaches you that slavery is no curse but a blessing! – that Providence – Providence! – has so ordered it that this country should be inhabited by two races of men: one born to wield the scourge [the whip] and the other to bear the record of its stripes upon his back – one to earn through a toilsome life the other's bread and to feed him on a bed of

---

banished from the earth." Although the end of slavery did not occur in the Founders' lifetime (or for nearly a century afterwards), it was not because they lacked the desire; they simply were ahead of the rest of the nation – and this was especially true with the Founding Fathers from the South (e.g., George Mason, George Washington, James Madison, etc.) who were far ahead of most citizens in their own States on this issue. (For additional information on the Founders' views toward slavery, see *Original Intent* by David Barton, pp. 289-295.)

† See previous note about this phrase on pp. 197-198.

roses; that slavery is the guardian and promoter of wisdom and virtue; that the slave, by laboring for another's enjoyment, learns disinterestedness [a lack of desire for personal improvement] and humility, and to melt with tenderness and affection for his master; that the master – nurtured, clothed, and sheltered by another's toils – learns to be generous and grateful to the slave and sometimes to feel for him as a father for his child; that released from the necessity of supplying his own wants, he acquires opportunity of leisure to improve his mind, to purify his heart, to cultivate his taste; that he has time on his hands to plunge into the depths of philosophy and to soar to the clear empyrean of seraphic morality [highest heaven of pure angelic morality].

The master-statesman [i.e., the slave-owning Southern political leader] – ay, the statesman in the land of the Declaration of Independence, in the halls of national legislation with the muse of history recording his words as they drop from his lips, [†] with the colossal figure of American liberty leaning on a column entwined with the emblem of eternity over his head, [††] with the forms of Washington

---

[†] The US Constitution requires in ARTICLE 1, SECTION 5, PARA. 3 that everything said on the floor of the House and Senate be recorded in official records; thus is "the muse of history recording his words as they drop from his lips" in the "halls of national legislation."

[††] John Quincy Adams – who was at this time a Member of the US House and often engaged in contentious debates with Southern pro-slavery House Members – is describing several pieces of art and sculpture found in the House Chambers that all Members, whether from the North or the South, saw each day – sculptures and art that carried an unequivocal message of freedom, not slavery. Specifically, in a compartment above the Speaker's desk in the House was a sculpture named "Liberty and the Eagle," placed there between 1817-1819 when the Capitol was rebuilt after the fire of 1814. This "colossal figure of American liberty" was looking down on the pro-slavery Members; they ignored its clear message.

STATUE OF "LIBERTY AND THE EAGLE"
IN THE OLD HOUSE CHAMBER

and Lafayette speaking to him from the canvas [†]– turns to the image of the Father of his Country and (forgetting that the last act of his life was to emancipate his slaves) to bolster the cause of slavery says, "That man was a slaveholder!" [††]

[†] By noting the "forms of Washington and La Fayette speaking … from the canvas," Adams is referring to the only two paintings that hang within the chamber of the US House: one of George Washington (painted in 1834) and one of Lafayette (given to the Capitol in 1824).

PICTURE OF WASHINGTON (LEFT) AND
LAFAYETTE (RIGHT) IN THE HOUSE CHAMBER

Significantly, both Washington and Lafayette were leaders in efforts to end slavery. Adams notes that the Southern statesmen were in a chamber surrounded by emblems of liberty and paintings of anti-slavery leaders but still refused to recognize what their eyes daily saw.

[††] Adams here is referring to statements made by John C. Calhoun (1782-1850), a slaveholder from South Carolina and prominent political leader. Ironically, when John Quincy Adams – an ardent abolitionist – was elected President by the US House, John C. Calhoun – an ardent pro-slavery leader and active opponent of Adams – was elected Adams' Vice-President by the US Senate. As can be imagined, the relationship between the two was at best rocky. Furthermore, Calhoun was the father of the South Carolina nullification/secession movement (vehemently opposed by Adams) that later became the impetus for the Civil War.

Calhoun invoked George Washington as an authority to justify slavery – as he did in a Senate speech on March 4, 1850, declaring of Washington: "He was one of us – a slaveholder and a planter." Adams, of course, points to the side of Washington ignored by Calhoun:

My countrymen! These are the tenets of the modern nullification
school. Can you wonder that they shrink from the light of free discussion? That they skulk from the grasp of freedom and truth? . . .
No! No! Freedom of speech is the only safety valve which – under
the high pressure of slavery – can preserve your political boiler from
a fearful and fatal explosion. [†] . . . Quench not the spirit of freedom.

Washington's anti-slavery side – a side little discussed today but nonetheless very significant.

Washington had been born into a world in which slavery was accepted; he himself had
became a slave owner at the tender age of 11 when his father died, leaving him slaves as an
inheritance. As other family members died, Washington inherited even more slaves. Although he had grown up from his earliest youth as a slave owner, he worked to overthrow
the very system in which he had been raised.

For example, as a member of the Virginia Assembly, he announced:

> I can only say that there is not a man living who wishes more sincerely than I do
> to see a plan adopted for the abolition of it [slavery]; but there is only one proper
> and effectual mode by which it can be accomplished, and that is by legislative
> authority; and this – as far as my suffrage [vote and support] will go – shall never
> be wanting [lacking].

Washington even chaired legislative committees that called for an end to slavery, but his
own State never agreed to his proposals. He therefore lamented:

> I wish from my soul that the legislature of this State could see the policy of a
> gradual abolition of slavery.

Washington had committed himself to seeking a legal remedy by which slaves might be
freed in his State and he also did so on the national level. In fact, the first federal law
limiting slavery in America (passed on August 7, 1789) carried the approving signature of
President George Washington. It was because of this law that Ohio, Indiana, Illinois, Michi-
gan, Minnesota, and Wisconsin, etc., prohibited slavery. (This policy unfortunately was
changed by Congress in 1820 to allow the expansion of slavery.)

Although Washington had been unable to end slavery in his own State of Virginia, he
circumvented State law by emancipating his slaves upon his death. Regrettably, State laws
were then stiffened to close this loophole so that it became virtually impossible for anyone
to emancipate his slaves – even at death.

The anti-slavery character of George Washington – especially the fact that he freed his
own slaves – caused JQA to be mystified when Southerners such as Calhoun pointed to
Washington as a justification for owning slaves.

[†] It was common that ardent supporters of slavery would employ brutal tactics to suppress anti-slavery speech. In fact, shortly after this oration, JQA personally authored the
introduction to a book about a man martyred simply because he published his opinions
against slavery (*Memoir of the Rev. Elijah P. Lovejoy; Who Was Murdered in Defence of the
Liberty of the Press at Alton, Illinois, Nov. 7, 1837; with an Introduction by John Quincy Adams*

(New York: John S. Taylor, 1838).

Elijah Lovejoy (1802-1837) – a Presbyterian minister and publisher of a St. Louis, Missouri, newspaper – printed several articles against slavery. Following numerous threats against his life, he moved his paper to Alton, Illinois, a city in an anti-slavery State. Because he continued the inclusion of anti-slavery articles, pro-slavery mobs three times within a single year attacked and destroyed his press. On the fourth attack, Lovejoy was killed – shot five times by his attackers. In describing this incident, JQA explained:

> [Lovejoy] there fell a victim to the fury of a band of ruffians, stung to madness and driven to despair for the fate of their darling slavery by the terrors of a printing press. That an American citizen, in a State whose constitution repudiates all slavery, should die a martyr in defence of the freedom of the press, is a phenomenon in the history of this Union. . . . [He is] the first American Martyr to THE FREEDOM OF THE PRESS, AND THE FREEDOM OF THE SLAVE.

The constitutional guarantees for freedom of speech and freedom of press were regularly ignored by pro-slavery advocates.

In fact, in 1835, the American Anti-Slavery Society mailed 75,000 anti-slavery tracts throughout the South, inciting slave owners to enact State laws that – according to famous historian J.T. Headley – resulted in "pains and penalties inflicted on 'abolitionists' (as all were termed who dared to express sentiments condemnatory of slavery by the southern states); and men – and even women – were subjected to treatment that would disgrace barbarians."

As an example of this intolerance of anti-slavery speech, in 1860 the Rev. Stephen Hodgman of Kentucky visited Texas and privately mentioned that if the South should secede, he thought the Union would eventually win and that slavery would be abolished; he therefore advised against the South seceding. For uttering these remarks in a _private_ conversation, a town meeting was called and he was placed on "trial" against five leading citizens and political leaders of Hempstead, Texas. It was eventually proved that he was not an "abolitionist" and therefore – according to Hodgman – "I was released and, of course, I was free once more – but not to express my opinions." Others did not fare as well, however; according to Hodgman, "hundreds of men had, during the past few months, fallen victims and been hung" for speech offenses.

The pro-slavery intolerance of anti-slavery speech was not limited solely to Southern States, for in May 1856, when anti-slavery Republican US Senator Charles Sumner (1811-1874) of Massachusetts spoke out against the evil and against slavery-promoters on the floor of the US Senate, pro-slavery Democrat US Representative Preston Brooks of South Carolina came from the House over to the Senate floor and brutally and repeatedly clubbed Sumner over the head, causing such serious injuries that it was four years before Sumner could resume his duties in the Senate. Similarly, at an 1860 Boston lecture on "How Shall Slavery be Abolished?," a pro-slavery mob attacked and broke up the meeting – and that in a State which not only outlawed slavery but also provided education, property, voting, and other rights for blacks.

These examples are simply a few from among scores; and while some occurred after JQA delivered this speech, the same flagrant disregard for the Constitution that so often characterized pro-slavery advocates had caused JQA to proclaim that "freedom of speech is the only safety valve which – under the high pressure of slavery – can preserve your political boiler from a fearful and fatal explosion."

Let it go forth, not in the panoply [armor] of fleshly wisdom but with the promise of peace and the voice of persuasion, clad in the whole armor of truth, *conquering and to conquer* [REVELATION 6:2]!

Friends and fellow citizens! I speak to you with the voice as of one risen from the dead. Were I now (as I shortly must be) cold in my grave, and could the sepulchre unbar its gates and open to me a passage to this desk devoted to the worship of Almighty God, † I would repeat the question with which this discourse was introduced: "Why are you assembled in this place"? And one of you would answer me for all: Because the Declaration of Independence, with the voice of an angel from Heaven, *put to his mouth the sounding alchemy* [brass trumpet] †† and proclaimed universal emancipation upon earth! . . .

[T]he first words uttered by the genius of our country in announcing his existence to the world of mankind was, "Freedom to the slave! Liberty to the captives! Redemption! Redemption forever to the race of man from the yoke of oppression!" It is *not* the work of a day; it is *not* the labor of an age; it is *not* the consummation of a century that we are assembled to commemorate. It *is* the emancipation of our race – it *is* the emancipation of man from the thralldom [bondage] of man!

And is this the language of enthusiasm [an active imagination]? The dream of a distempered fancy [hallucinating mind]? Is it not rather the Voice of Inspiration? The language of Holy Writ? Why is it that the Scriptures – both of the Old and New Covenants – teach

---

† John Quincy Adams delivered this oration in a church; hence he notes that he is speaking from "a desk [pulpit] devoted to the worship of Almighty God."

†† This quote comes from John Milton's (1608-1674) *Paradise Lost* (1667), Book II. Milton is considered one of the most famous of English poets, and *Paradise Lost* is considered the greatest epic poem in the English language. That work is the story of Satan's rebellion against God, and of Adam and Eve in the Garden of Eden. The full passage from which the above quote is taken states:

> Toward the four winds four speedy cherubim,
> *Put to their mouths the sounding alchemy* [brass trumpet],
> By herald's voice explained: the hollow abyss,
> Heard far and wide, and all the host of hell,
> With deafening shout returned them loud acclaim.

you upon every page to look forward to the time when *the wolf shall dwell with the lamb and the leopard shall lie down with the kid?* [ISAIAH 11:6]. Why is it that six hundred years before the birth of the Redeemer, the sublimest of prophets – with lips touched by the hallowed fire from the hand of God [c.f., ISAIAH 6:5-7] – spake and said, *The Spirit of the Lord God is upon me because the Lord hath anointed me to preach good tidings unto the meek; He hath sent me to bind up the broken hearted, to proclaim liberty to the captives, and the opening of the prison to them that are bound?* (ISAIAH 61:1) And why is it that at the first dawn of the fulfillment of this prophecy – at the birthday of the Savior in the lowest condition of human existence – the angel of the Lord came in a flood of supernatural light upon the shepherds (witnesses of the scene) and said, *Fear not, for behold I bring you good tidings of great joy which shall be to all people.* Why is it that there was suddenly with that angel a multitude of the heavenly host, praising God and saying, *Glory to God in the highest, and on earth peace, good will toward men?* (LUKE 2:9-10, 13-14).

What are the *good tidings of great joy which shall be to all people?* The prophet had told you six hundred years before: . . . *good tidings to the meek, mercy to the afflicted, liberty to the captives, and the opening of the prison to them that are bound* (ISAIAH 61:1).

It is generally admitted by Christians of all denominations that the fulfillment of this prophecy commenced at the birth of the Redeemer six hundred years after it was promulgated. That it did so commence was expressly affirmed by Jesus Himself Who, on His appearance in his missionary character at Nazareth (we are told by the gospel of Luke), went into the synagogue on the Sabbath-day and stood up to read. And there was delivered to Him the book of the prophet Isaiah. And when He had opened the book, He found this very passage which I have cited: *The Spirit of the Lord God is upon me because the Lord hath anointed me to preach good tidings unto the meek; he hath sent me to bind up the broken hearted; to proclaim liberty to the captives, and the opening of the prison to them that are bound! And he closed the book and gave it again to the minister and sat down* (LUKE 4:17-18, 20-21).

This was the deliberate declaration of the earthly object of His mission. He merely read the passage from the book of Isaiah [ISAIAH 61:1-2]. He returned the book to the minister and without application of what He had read, sat down. But that passage had been written six hundred years before. It was universally understood to refer to the expected Messiah. With what astonishment then must the worshippers in the synagogue of Nazareth have seen Him – an unknown stranger in the prime of manhood – stand up to read; on receiving the book, deliberately select and read that particular passage of the prophet and without another word, close the volume, return it to the minister, and sit down! The historian adds, *and the eyes of all them that were in the synagogue, were fastened on him. And he began to say unto them, This day is this scripture fulfilled in your ears* [LUKE 4:20-21]. . . .

The prophecy will therefore be fulfilled not only in the ears but in the will and in the practice of mankind. But how many generations of men – how many ages of time – will pass away before its entire and final fulfillment? Alas! More than eighteen hundred years have passed away since the fulfillment of that Scripture which announced the advent of the Savior and the blessed object of His mission. How long – O how long! – will it be before that object itself shall be accomplished? Not yet are we permitted to *go out with joy and to be led forth with peace.* Not yet shall *the mountains and the hills break forth* before us *into singing and all the trees of the field clap their hands.* Not yet shall *the fir tree come up instead of the thorn nor the myrtle-tree instead of the brier.* But let no one despair of the final accomplishment of the whole prophecy. Still *shall it be to the Lord for a name – for an everlasting sign that shall not be cut off* (ISAIAH 55:12-13).

The prediction of the prophet – the self-declaration of the Messiah and His annunciation of the objects of His mission – have been and are fulfilled so far as depended upon His own agency [actions]. He declared Himself anointed to preach good tidings to the meek, and faithfully that mission was performed. He declared Himself sent to bind up the broken hearted, and this, too, how faithfully has it been performed! Yes, through all ages since His appearance upon earth, He has preached – and yet preaches – good tidings to the meek.

He has bound up – He yet binds up – the broken hearted. He said He was sent to proclaim liberty to the captives and the opening of the prison doors to them that are bound. But the execution of that promise was entrusted to the will of man.

Twenty centuries have nearly passed away and it is yet to be performed. But let no one surrender his Christian faith that the Lord of Creation will – in His own good time – realize a declaration made in His name – made in words such as were never uttered by the uninspired lips of man – in words worthy of omnipotence. The progress of the accomplishment of the prophecy is slow. It has baffled the hopes and disappointed the wishes of generation after generation of men. Yet, observe well the history of the human family since the birth of the Savior and you will see great, remarkable, and progressive approximations [gradual steps] towards it. . . .

It is because this day is consecrated to the cause of human liberty that you are here assembled; and if the connection of that cause with the fulfillment of those clear, specific predictions of the greatest of the Hebrew prophets – re-announced and repeated by the unnumbered voices of the heavenly host at the birth of the Savior – has not heretofore been traced and exhibited in the celebrations of this day, may I not hope for your indulgence in presenting to you a new ray of glory in the halo that surrounds the memory of the day of your national independence?

Yes, from that day forth shall the nations of the earth hereafter say with the prophet, *How beautiful upon the mountains are the feet of him that bringeth good tidings, that publisheth peace!* (ISAIAH 52:7). From that day forth shall they exclaim, *Sing, O heavens, and be joyful, O earth; and break forth into singing, O mountains! for the Lord hath comforted His people and will have mercy upon His afflicted* (ISAIAH 49:13, 24-25). From that day forth, to the question: *Shall the prey be taken from the mighty or the lawful captive be delivered [freed]?*, shall be returned the answer of the prophet: *But thus saith the Lord, "Even the captives of the mighty shall be taken away, and the prey of the terrible shall be delivered; for I will contend with him that contends with thee, and I will save thy children"* [ISAIAH 49:24-25]. From that day forth (shall they say) commenced the opening of the last seal of prophetic felicity [heavenly joy] to the race of man upon earth when *the Lord God shall judge among the nations and shall rebuke many people; and they shall beat their swords into plowshares and their spears into pruninghooks; nation shall not lift up sword against nation neither shall they learn war any more.* (ISAIAH 2:4)....

Turn, then, your faces and raise your hands to God and pray that in the merciful dispensations of His providence, He would hasten that happy time! Turn to yourselves and in the Declaration of Independence of your fathers, read the command to you − by the unremitting [never-ending] exercise of your highest energies − to hasten yourselves its consummation! ■

An Oration by

Samuel Davies

1755

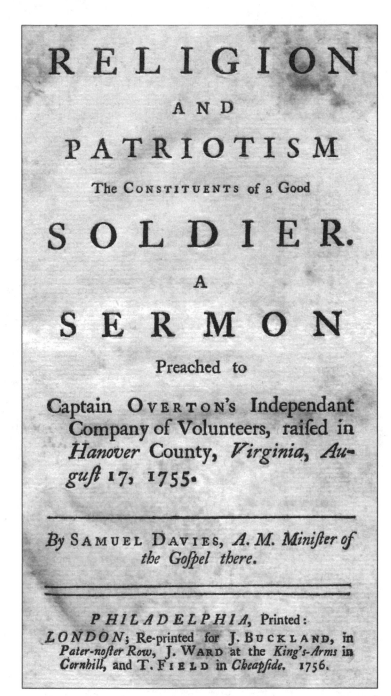

RELIGION

AND

PATRIOTISM

The Constituents of a Good

SOLDIER.

A

SERMON

Preached to

Captain Overton's Independant Company of Volunteers, raised in *Hanover* County, *Virginia, August* 17, 1755.

By Samuel Davies, *A. M. Minister of the Gospel there.*

PHILADELPHIA, Printed: *LONDON*; Re-printed for J. Buckland, in *Pater-noster Row*, J. Ward at the *King's-Arms* in *Cornhill*, and T. Field in *Cheapside*. 1756.

The Rev. Samuel Davies

The Rev. Samuel Davies
(1723-1761)

Samuel Davies was one of the two most noted clergyman in America in his day, the other being the Rev. George Whitefield. Both men were leaders in the First Great Awakening – a national religious revival that lasted from 1730 to 1770, with some of its most active years occurring from 1734 to 1745. Whitefield was considered the most noted traveling evangelist of that movement, and Davies its most noted (and perhaps its most widely published) pulpit minister. The first Great Awakening directly impacted and personally touched nearly one-half of America's two million inhabitants. The Rev. Davies was not only a clergyman but also an educator, serving as the President of Princeton.

The First Great Awakening actually laid much of the foundation for the changes in thinking that eventually led to the success of the American Revolution. For example, it caused the people to discover that they were actually a nation rather than just thirteen separate colonies – that they had much more in common than different – that they had one common Christian faith, even though distinguished by different creeds and denominations.

As an example of this unifying effect, both John Adams and Benjamin Franklin cited the Rev. George Whitefield's "Father Abraham" sermon in which Whitefield argued that in Heaven there were no Baptists, Catholics, Presbyterians, Lutherans, Quakers, etc., but only Christians. (This was indeed a revolutionary idea since most of the Colonies at that time had a single State-established denomination, often promoted to the exclusion of all others.) The Great Awakening also lowered many of the distinctions based on race or class. In short, it was a direct precursor to and influence on American independence. As John Adams later confirmed: "The Revolution was effected *before* the War commenced. The Revolution was in the mind and hearts of the people and change in their _religious_ sentiments and obligations." The Rev. Samuel Davies played a prominent role in that national transformation.

Davies had been licensed to preach as a Presbyterian in 1746; the following year he was ordained as an evangelist and dispatched to Virginia for missionary work in that Anglican-controlled State. In Virginia, dissenters and non-conformists (the non-Anglicans) were frowned upon, persecuted, imprisoned, or put to death for offenses such as preaching without a license or holding prohibited gatherings (non-Anglican services).

Davies became an advocate for the non-conformists (Presbyterians, Baptists, Quakers, etc.), working to defend their civil and religious liberties in both Virginia and North Carolina. He is credited with almost single-handedly building the Presbyterian denomination in that region.

Davies also spent extended time in the British Isles raising money from Presbyterians in Scotland for the work of their brethren in America. While in the Isles, Davies delivered some sixty sermons, many of which were published and received broad distribution on both sides of the ocean.

Returning from Great Britain, Davies lived and preached another eight years in America before dying of pneumonia. In the half-century following his passing, it is reported that his sermons were more widely read than those of any other minister from his era.

This 1755 sermon was preached by the Rev. Davies in Virginia during the early part of the French and Indian War – a war in which the French and Indians were united against the British and Americans, fighting for control of the inland of North America (e.g., the Ohio territory, western Pennsylvania, lands along the Mississippi River, etc.). The British and Americans had formed four expeditions to drive the French out of the country, and Virginians had been part of the expedition of Gen. Edward Braddock that had suffered a resounding defeat. In fact, a young Col. George Washington had led 100 Virginians to join Braddock's 1,200 British soldiers in that battle, and of the 100 Virginians, 68 were shot down (as well as nearly half the British soldiers). This devastating defeat left the middle Colonies (Virginia, Maryland, Pennsylvania, etc.) unprotected from enemy attacks.

Captain Samuel Overton of Hanover, Virginia – only a month after Braddock's defeat – organized an independent company of Virginia volunteers to go to the "western" frontier (e.g., the area near Ohio, Kentucky, etc.) to help protect the Colonies. It was at a gathering of this unit immediately preceding its deployment that the Rev. Davies was asked to deliver his sermon.

At the time of this oration, a new paradigm of thinking was being planted in America that would grow to maturity by the time of the American Revolution. For example, the Rev. Jonathan Mayhew had just preached a sermon in Massachusetts attacking the divine right of kings and condemning British ecclesiastical absolutism – a direct affront to two fundamental British philosophies. Additionally, America was learning that she could defend herself from danger (as evidenced by this sermon to a local group that had formed itself into a militia for defense) rather than rely solely on the British – an important first step toward what two decades later would become crucial for victory in the American Revolution. Furthermore, Benjamin Franklin had just proposed a plan to unite all the Colonies to operate under one government – the first such attempt at any national union. And, two important symbols that would eventually be associated with American independence had made their first appearance: the Liberty Bell had just arrived in America, and the tune "Yankee Doodle" had recently been composed.

Davies' oration is not only a powerful exhortation from the Scriptures on the duties and characteristics of patriotism (as well as the veneration rightly accorded to soldiers) but it is also a wonderful glimpse into a war about which most Americans today know little. Pay special attention to notice the insightful (and even prophetic) comments about a very young George Washington – at that time almost universally unknown in the nation, and still largely unknown even in Virginia.

®ration.

Be of good courage and let us play the men for our people and for the
cities of our God; and the Lord do that which seemeth Him good.
[II SAMUEL 10:12; I CHRONICLES 19:13]

An hundred years of peace and liberty in such a world as this is a
very unusual thing, and yet our country has been the happy spot that
has been distinguished with such a long series of blessings with little
or no interruption. . . . [W]hile other nations have been involved in
war we have not been *alarmed with the sound of the trumpet* [JEREMIAH
4:19] nor seen *garments rolled in blood* [ISAIAH 9:5].

But now the scene is changed; now we begin to experience in our
turn the fate of the nations of the earth. Our territories are invaded
by the power and perfidy [treachery] of France, our frontiers ravaged
by merciless savages, and our fellow subjects there murdered with all
the horrid arts of Indian and Popish torture. † Our General, unfortu-

---

† An almost continual state of war between Britain and France had existed during the
1700s, often involving America. Prior to the French & Indian War (1754-1763), there had
been King William's War (1689-1697), Queen Anne's War (1702-1713), and King George's
War (1744-1748). The frequency of war between the two powers resulted in that period
being called the "Second Hundred Years' War."

Throughout the lengthy time that France had been fighting England, France had been
Catholic and England Protestant, resulting in the belief – especially from the British and
American viewpoint – that it was Catholics warring against Protestants rather than just the
French against the English. Of specific concern to American settlers, the French Catholics
had inflicted numerous atrocities and barbaric tortures upon Americans that were indistin-
guishable from the identical depredations of the Indians upon the Americans. This behavior caused the French – and their religion – to be hated and despised by Americans.

The French Catholic behavior during this time was so atrocious that even French Catholic
historian and university professor Ferdinand Brunetire (1849-1906) described the 1700s as
"the *least Christian* and *least French* century in the history of France." In fact, many of the
French immigrants to America in the 1680s were French Protestants (e.g., the Huguenots)
who had been forced to flee their beloved homeland because of deadly persecution by French
Catholics against Protestants, even though they were native citizens. And England's negative experience with coercive behavior by Catholics went well beyond her experiences with
the French. King Phillip II of Spain (a Catholic) had sent the Spanish Armada against England to effect the forcible conversion of the Britons to Catholicism. He had also been responsible for the brutal Spanish Inquisition against Protestants.

As a result of her experiences, England became so anti-Catholic that in the 1600s she
began to retaliate in kind against Catholic leaders in Britain. By 1700, so fearful and suspicious

did England become against Catholics that she even passed laws specifically prohibiting Catholics from holding land or having legal rights in England (laws largely repealed by 1778). Therefore, early American (i.e., British) rhetoric regarding Catholics was often vitriolic and harsh (as in this oration).

This unfriendliness of American Protestants toward Catholics continued into the early stages of the American Revolution. In the minds of many American independence leaders, not only had Catholics often been the most ardent defender of monarchies but they also supported the vesting of total, absolute, and irrevocable power in a single body (i.e., the Papal authority) with no recourse by the people – two beliefs that Americans opposed. In short, while the patriot leaders opposed autocracy in any form, Catholics appeared to support it vigorously.

Further fueling negative generalizations about Catholics in the early stages of the Revolution were specific instances of Catholics attempting to impede American independence. For example, Dr. David Ramsay (a member of the Continental Congress and noted historian) observed that during America's struggle for independence:

> [T]he Roman Catholic clergy [in Canada]. . . . used their influence in the next world as an engine to operate on the movements of the present. They refused absolution [forgiveness of sins] to such of their flocks as abetted [helped] the Americans.

John Adams similarly criticized the Roman Catholic "power of deposing princes and absolving [releasing] subjects from allegiance" to civil authorities.

Understandably, the Founders did not want individuals influencing American government who maintained a sworn oath of allegiance to a "foreign power" (the Pope). As Supreme Court Justice Joseph Story later explained:

> [T]he civil magistrate. . . . is bound, indeed, to protect. . . . papists [Roman Catholics]. . . . But while they [Catholics] acknowledge a foreign power superior to the sovereignty of the kingdom, they cannot complain if the laws of that kingdom will not treat them upon the footing of good subjects.

Consequently, the 1776 Massachusetts constitution provided "for the exclusion of these from offices who will not disclaim these principles of spiritual jurisdiction which Roman Catholics in some centuries have held and which are subversive of a free government established by the people."

This deep-rooted suspicion against Catholics began to change dramatically during the Revolution when many Catholics sided with the Americans to help them win their independence (e.g., military leaders such as General Marquis de Lafayette, General Casimir Pulaski, General Stephen Moylan, and Commodore John Barry; signers of the Declaration such as Charles Carroll; and signers of the Constitution such as Thomas Fitzsimmons and Daniel Carroll). This willingness of Catholics to fight side by side with Protestants against tyranny forced a rethinking of the American stereotype of Catholics and began a new era in the political landscape in America in which all – including Catholics – were welcomed, so long as they held beliefs not "subversive of a free government established by the people."

However, at the time of this oration this progress had not yet occurred; and it was an indisputable fact that Catholics were then joining with the Indians to ravage, murder, and scalp settlers, and therefore were enemies in the minds of Americans.

nately brave, is fallen; an army of 1300 choice men routed; our fine train of artillery taken; and all this (oh mortifying thought!) – all this by 4 or 500 dastardly, insidious barbarians. †

These calamities have not come upon us without warnings. We were long ago apprized of the ambitious schemes of our enemies and their motions to carry them into execution. And had we taken timely measures they might have been crushed before they could have arrived at such a formidable height. But how have we generally behaved in such a critical time? Alas, our country has been sunk in a deep sleep; a cupid [an intense desire for] security has unmanned [blinded] the inhabitants; they could not realize a danger. . . . And now – when the cloud thickens over our heads and alarms every thoughtful mind with its near approach – multitudes, I am afraid, are still dissolved in careless security or enervated [weakened] with an effeminate [unmanly], cowardly spirit. . . .

We have also suffered our poor fellow subjects in the frontier counties to fall a helpless prey to bloodthirsty savages without affording them proper assistance which – as members of the same body politic – they had a right to expect. They might as well have continued in a state

of nature as be united in society if in such an article of extreme danger they are left to shift for themselves. The bloody barbarians have exercised on some of them the most unnatural and leisurely tortures, and others they have butchered in their beds or in some unguarded hour. Can human nature bear the horror of the sight! See yonder? The hairy scalps clotted with gore! The mangled limbs! Women ripped up! The heart and bow-

---

† This refers to General Edward Braddock (1695-1755), shot down from ambush by the French and Indians as he was nearing what is now the city of Pittsburg, Pennsylvania. For a complete account of this battle – not only of General Braddock's death but also of God's Divine intervention that sovereignly saved the life of a young George Washington – see the book *The Bulletproof George Washington* by David Barton.

els still palpitating with life and smoking on the ground! See the savages swilling [drinking down] their blood and imbibing a more outrageous fury with the inhuman draught [drink]! Sure these are not men; they are not beasts of prey; they are something worse; they must be infernal furies [hellish spirits] in human shape. And have we tamely looked on and suffered them to exercise these hellish barbarities upon our fellow men, our fellow subjects, our brethren? Alas! With what horror must we look upon ourselves as being little better than accessories to their blood?

And shall these ravages go on unchecked? . . . No, I am agreeably checked by the happy encouraging prospect now before me. Is it a pleasing dream? Or do I really see a number of brave men without the compulsion of authority – without the prospect of gain – voluntarily associated in a company to march over trackless mountains . . . to succor [help] their helpless fellow-subjects and guard their country? Yes, gentlemen, I see you here upon this design. . . .

I am gratefully sensible of the unmerited honor you have done me in making choice of me to address you upon so singular and important an occasion. [†] . . . I cannot begin my address to you with more proper words than those of a great general which I have read to you [Joab, leading Israel's troops against the Syrians and Ammonites]: *Be of good courage and play the men for your people and for the cities of your God; and the Lord do what seemeth Him good* [II SAMUEL 10:12; I CHRONICLES 19:13]. . . .

---

† This sermon was delivered at a special religious service called by the soldiers just before they left for military action against the French and Indians.

The words were spoken just before a very threatening engage-
ment by Joab, who had long served under that pious hero King
David as the general of his forces and had shown himself an officer
of true courage, conducted with prudence. The Ammonites, a neigh-
boring nation at frequent hostilities with the Jews, had ungrate-
fully offered indignities to some of David's courtiers [official en-
voys] whom he had sent to condole [grieve with] their king upon
the death of his father, and congratulate his accession to the crown
[I CHRONICLES 19:1-4]. Our holy religion teaches us to bear personal
injuries without private revenge, but national insults and indignities ought to excite the public resentment.

Accordingly, King David, when he heard that the Ammonites with
their allies were preparing to invade his territories and carry their
injuries still farther, sent Joab his General with his army to repel
them and avenge the affronts they had offered his subjects.

It seems the army of the enemy were much more numerous than
David's: their mercenaries from other nations were no less than
31,000 men – and no doubt the Ammonites themselves were a still
greater number. These numerous forces were disposed in the most
advantageous manner and surrounded Joab's men that they might
attack them both in flank and front at once and cut them all off,
leaving no way for them to escape. Prudence is of the utmost importance in the conduct of an army, and Joab, in this critical situation, gives a proof of how much he was master of it and discovers
the steady composure of his mind while thus surrounded with danger. He divides his army and gives one party to his brother, Abishai,
who commanded next to him, and the other he kept the command
of himself, and resolves to attack the Syrian mercenaries who seemed
the most formidable; he gives orders to his brother in the mean-
time to fall upon the Ammonites, and he animates [strengthens]
him with this noble advice: *"Be of good courage and let us play the men
for our people and the cities of our God, which are now at stake; and the
Lord do what seemeth Him good."*

"Be of good courage and let us play the men": courage is an essential
character of a good soldier – not a savage ferocious [cruel] violence,

not a foolhardy insensibility of danger or headstrong rashness to rush into it, not the fury of inflamed passions broken loose from the government [restraint] of reason, but calm, deliberate, rational courage; a steady, judicious, thoughtful fortitude; the courage of a man and not of a tiger – such a temper [disposition of mind] as Addison ascribes with so much justice to the famous Marlborough [†] and Eugene: [††]

> Whose courage dwelt not in a troubled flood
> Of mounting spirits and fermenting blood;
> But lodged in the soul, with virtue overruled,
> Inflam'd by reason, and by reason cooled. [†††]

This is true courage and such as we ought all to cherish in the present dangerous conjuncture [situation]. This will render men vigilant and cautious against surprises, prudent and deliberate in concerting [coordinating] their measures, and steady and resolute in executing them. But without this they will fall into unsuspected dangers which will strike them with wild consternation [panic]; they will meanly [foolishly] shun dangers that are surmountable or precipitantly [hastily] rush into those that are causeless or evidently fatal and throw away their lives in vain.

There are some men who naturally have this heroic turn of mind. The wise Creator has adapted the natural genius of mankind with a surprising and beautiful variety to the state in which they are placed in this world. To some He has given a turn for intellectual improvement and the liberal arts and sciences; to others a genius for trade; to

---

† Marlborough refers to John Churchill (1650-1722), the 1st Duke of Marlborough. He served as Supreme Commander of British forces and successfully defended the country from aggression in a number of important battles.

†† Prince Eugene (1663-1736) was a military leader who laid the foundation of the Hapsburg empire in central Europe (the Germany area). He won major battles against numerous nations, including the French, Turks, and Hungarians. He also fought alongside British leader Marlborough as an ally in several important battles against the Spanish. Eugene is considered one of the greatest military commanders in modern history.

††† This is part of a very lengthy 1705 Addison (1672-1719) poem titled "The Campaign. A Poem to His Grace the Duke of Marlborough." Addison was a noted English poet as well as a member of Parliament.

others a dexterity in mechanics and the ruder arts necessary for the support of human life [the making of basic utensils, implements, and tools]. The generality of mankind may be capable of tolerable improvements in any of these, but it is only they whom the God of nature has formed for them that will shine in them – every man in his own province [profession].

And as God well knew what a world of degenerate, ambitious, and revengeful creatures this is – as He knew that innocence could not be protected, property and liberty secured, nor the lives of mankind preserved from the lawless hands of ambition, avarice and tyranny without the use of the sword – as He knew this would be the only method to preserve mankind from universal slavery – He has formed some men for this dreadful work and sired them with a martial [military] spirit and a glorious love of danger. Such a spirit (though most pernicious [destructive] when ungoverned by the rules of justice and benevolence to mankind) is a public blessing when rightly directed. . . .

He that winged the imagination of an Homer or a Milton, He that gave penetration to the mind of Newton, He that made Tubal-Cain an instructor of artificers [craftsmen] in brass and iron, and gave skill to Bezaleel and Aholiab in curious works; † nay, He that sent out Paul and his brethren to conquer the nations with the gentler weapons of plain truth, miracles, and the love of a crucified Savior; He – even that same Gracious Power – has formed and

---

† Davies is here listing some of the greatest names in their professions. *Homer* and *Milton* were two of the greatest poets in history. Homer (circa 850 BC), a Greek, is considered the greatest poet of classical antiquity (his two most famous works are the *Iliad* and the *Odyssey*), while John Milton (1608-1674) is considered the greatest poet of the English language, especially famous for his work *Paradise Lost*. *Newton* refers to Isaac Newton (1642-1727). Considered the greatest scientist who ever lived, Newton was the center of the scientific revolution of the 17th century, establishing the laws of gravity, theories on optics and light, inventing calculus and contributing greatly to the fields of physics and math. *Tubal-Cain* is the figure in the Bible specifically singled out and described as "an instructor of *every* artificer [craftsman] in brass and iron" (Genesis 4:22). *Bezaleel* and *Aholiab* were two master craftsman described in the Bible (Exodus 31:2; 35:30; 36:1-2; 38:22) who supervised the work of the other artisans on the temple built in the wilderness and oversaw the metal working, masonry, carpentry, engraving, embroidery, and weaving. Davies is noting that all of these individuals – each in a different craft from the others – received his skill from God.

raised up an Alexander, [†] a Julius Caesar, [††] a William, [†††] and a Marlborough [§] and inspired them with this enterprising, intrepid [courageous] spirit – the two first to scourge a guilty world, and the two last to save nations on the brink of ruin. There is something glorious and inviting in danger to such noble minds, and their breasts beat with a generous ardor [excitement] when it appears.

Our continent is likely to become the seat of war; and we, for the future (till the sundry European nations that have planted colonies in it have fixed their boundaries by the sword), have no other way left to defend our rights and privileges. And has God been pleased to diffuse some sparks of this martial [military] fire through our country? I hope He has; and though it has been almost extinguished by so long a peace and a deluge of luxury and pleasure, now I hope it begins to kindle – and may I not produce you, my brethren who are engaged in this expedition, as instances of it? [§§] Well cherish it as a sacred Heaven-born fire, and let the injuries done to your country administer fuel to it and kindle it in those breasts where it has been hitherto smothered or inactive. . . .

---

† Alexander the Great (356-323 BC) was a conqueror who subdued nation after nation to build himself a great personal empire.

†† Julius Caesar (100-44 BC) was a military leader of the Roman Empire, winning battles and repulsing foes across several continents from Asia to Spain, France to Britain, and Egypt to Syria. He eventually became a dictator and ushered in absolutism and imperial rule.

††† William refers to William the Conqueror (1027-1087). William was from France. He conquered all of Britain and became king, enjoying a lengthy reign in Britain even though he spoke no English. (Every monarch of England since has been a descendent of William the Conqueror.) William not only conquered the country and installed Normans in place of the Anglo-Saxons but he also implemented an effective system of governmental administration that resulted in making England the most powerful government in Europe. He had a direct impact on the English language through the inclusion of many French and Latin words into the language – words that still appear in English dictionaries today.

§ See previous note on Marlborough on page 236.

§§ At this point in the sermon, Davies inserted the following note in the original text:

"As a remarkable instance of this, I may point out to the public that heroic youth Col. Washington, whom I cannot but hope Providence has hitherto preserved in so signal [remarkable] a manner, for some important service to his country."

I need not tell you that it is of great importance for this end that you should be at peace with God and your own conscience and prepared for your future state. . . . The most important periods of our existence, my brethren, lie beyond the grave; and it is a matter of much more concern to us what will be our doom in the world to come than what becomes of us in this. . . .

O my countrymen – and particularly you brave men that are the occasion of this meeting – repent! Fall down upon your knees before the provoked Sovereign of Heaven and Earth against whom you have rebelled. Dissolve and melt in penitential sorrows at His feet and He will tell you *"arise; be of good cheer; your sins are forgiven you"* [MATTHEW 9:2]. . . . *I bring you glad tidings of great joy: to you is born a Savior* [LUKE 2:10] – a Savior of no mean [common] character: He is Christ the Lord. And have you never heard that He has made reconciliation for iniquity and brought in everlasting righteousness [c.f., II CORINTHIANS 5:19-21]? That He suffered, the just for the unjust [c.f., I PETER 3:18]? That God is well pleased for His righteousness sake and declares Himself willing to be reconciled to all that believe in Him and cheerfully accept Him as their Savior and Lord [ROMANS 10: 9-13]? Have you never heard these joyful tidings, O guilty, self-condemned sinners? Sure you have! Then away to Jesus – . . . . fly to Jesus on the wings of faith – all of you, of every age and character, for you all stand in the most absolute need of Him and without Him you must perish, every soul of you. . . .

This I earnestly recommend to all my hearers – and especially to you gentlemen and others that are now about generously to risk your lives for your country. Account this the best preparative to encounter danger and death – the best incentive to true, rational courage. What can do you a lasting injury while you have a reconciled God smiling upon you from on high, a peaceful conscience animating you within, and a happy immortality just before you? Sure you may bid defiance to dangers and death in their most shocking forms. You have answered the end of this life already by preparing for another; and how can you depart off this mortal stage more honorably than in the cause of liberty, of religion, and your country? . . .

It is also of great importance to excite and keep up our courage in such an expedition that we should be fully satisfied we engage in a righteous cause and in a cause of great moment [importance], for we cannot prosecute a suspected or a wicked scheme which our own minds condemn but with hesitation and timorous [fearful] apprehensions; and we cannot engage with spirit and resolution in a trifling [insignificant] scheme from which we can expect no consequences worth our vigorous pursuit. This Joab might have in view in his heroic advice to his brother, *"Be of good courage,"* says he, and *"let us play the men, for our people, and for the cities of our God." q. d.* †

We are engaged in a righteous cause – we are not urged on by an unbounded lust of power or riches to encroach upon the rights and properties of others and disturb our quiet neighbors. We act entirely upon the defensive, repel unjust violence, and avenge national injuries; we are fighting for our people and for the cities of our God. . . . He has condescended to be a God to our nation and to honor our cities with His gracious presence and the institutions of His worship – the means to make us wise, good, and happy. But now these most invaluable blessings lie at stake – these are the prize for which we contend; and must it not excite all our active powers to the highest pitch of exertion? Shall we tamely submit to idolatry and religious tyranny? No! God forbid! Let us play the men since we take up arms for our people and the cities of our God.

I need not tell you how applicable this advice (thus paraphrased) is to the design of the present associated Company. The equity of our cause is most evident. The Indian savages have certainly no right to murder our fellow-subjects, living quiet and inoffensive in their habitations; nor have the French any power to hound them [the Indians] out upon us nor to invade the territories belonging to the British

---

† *"q. d."* is Latin for *"quaque die"* and is translated "every day." This is the phrase that a pharmacist uses on the instructions for the administration of certain dosages – *"q. d."* or "every day." Davies is "issuing" this thought as if it were a medical "prescription" for their spiritual well-being – that is, think about this every day. The same is true with the other *"q. d."*'s throughout this piece. This would be similar to the use of the word "selah" in the Psalms of David - i.e., "stop and think about this" – *q. d.* (every day).

Crown and secured to it by the faith of treaties. This is a clear case. And it is equally clear that you are engaged in a cause of the utmost importance. To protect your brethren from the most bloody barbarities – to defend the territories of the best of kings against the oppression and tyranny of arbitrary power – to secure the inestimable blessings of liberty, British liberty, from the chains of French slavery – to preserve your estates (for which you have sweat and toiled) from falling a prey to greedy vultures . . . and hungry Gallic [French] slaves, or not-more-devouring flames – to guard your religion, the pure religion of Jesus streaming uncorrupted from the sacred fountain of the Scriptures, the most excellent, rational and Divine religion that ever was made known to the sons of men – to guard so dear, so precious a religion (my heart grows warm while I mention it) against ignorance, superstition, idolatry, tyranny over conscience, massacre, fire, and sword, . . . to secure the liberties conveyed to you by your brave forefathers and bought with their blood that you may transmit them uncurtailed [fully intact] to your posterity – these are the blessings you contend for. . . . Yes, this view of the matter must fire you into men; methinks the cowardly soul must tremble lest the imprecation of the prophet fall upon him, *cursed be the man that keepeth back his sword from blood* [JEREMIAH 48:10].

To this shocking but necessary work the Lord now calls you, and cursed is he that doeth the work of the Lord deceitfully – that will not put his hand to it when it is in his power or that will not perform it with all his might. The people of Meroz lay at home in ease while their brethren were in the field delivering their country from slavery. [†] And what was their doom? *"Curse ye Meroz," said the angel of the Lord, "Curse ye bitterly the inhabitants thereof, because they came not to the help of the Lord, to the help of the Lord against the mighty"* [JUDGES 5:23].

I count myself happy that I see so many of you generously engaged in such a cause; but when I view it in this light, I cannot but be

---

† This is a reference to the Old Testament story of Deborah and Barak from Judges 5 in which Israel was called out to fight against Sisera, king of the Canaanites; however, the people of Meroz remained behind, ignoring the call and refusing to confront the danger or fight the enemy.

concerned that there are so few to join you. Are there but 50 or 60 persons in this large and populous county that can be spared from home for a few weeks upon so necessary a design or that are able to bear the fatigues of it? Where are the friends of human nature – where are the lovers of liberty and religion? Now is the time for you to come forth and show yourselves. Nay, where is the miser? Let him arise and defend his mammon or he may soon have reason to cry out with Micah, *They have taken away my gods, and what have I more?* [JUDGES 18:24]. Where is the tender soul on whom the passions of a husband, a father, or a son have a peculiar energy? Arise and march away – you had better be absent from those you love for a little while than see them butchered before your eyes or doomed to eternal poverty and slavery.... I do invite and entreat all of you who have not some very sufficient reason against it, voluntarily to enlist and go out with those brave souls who have set you so noble an example....

The event, however, is in His hands; and it is much better there than if it were in yours. This thought is suggested with beautiful simplicity in the remaining part of my text, *"the Lord do that which seemeth Him good."* This may be looked upon in various views, as:

1. It may be understood as the language of uncertainty and modesty. *q. d.* † Let us do all we can, but, after all, the issue is uncertain; we know not (as yet) to what side God will incline the victory. Such language as this, my brethren, becomes us in all our undertakings; it sounds creature-like, and God approves of such self-diffident [modest] humility. But to indulge sanguine [optimistic] and confident expectations of victory – to *boast when we put on our armor as though we were putting it off* [I KINGS 20:11] and to derive our high hopes from our own power and good management without any regard to the Providence of God – this is too lordly and assuming for such feeble mortals; such insolence is generally mortified and such *a haughty spirit is the forerunner of a fall* [PROVERBS 16:18]. Therefore, though I do not apprehend your lives will be in any great danger in your present expedition to range the frontiers and clear them of the

---

† See previous note on *q. d.* on page 240.

skulking Indians, yet I would not flatter you, my brethren, with too high hopes either of victory or safety. I cannot but entertain the pleasing prospect of congratulating you with many of your friends upon your successful expedition and safe return; and yet it is very possible our next interview may be in that strange untried world beyond the grave. You are, however, in the hands of God and He will deal with you as it seemeth Him good; and I am persuaded you would not wish it were otherwise – you would not now practically retract the petition you have so often offered up, *"Thy will be done on earth, as it is in Heaven"* [MATTHEW 6:10; LUKE 11:2].

2. This language, *"the Lord do as seemeth Him good,"* may be looked upon as expressive of a firm persuasion that the event of war entirely depends upon the Providence of God. *q. d.* Let us do our best; but after all, let us be sensible that the success does not depend on us – that [it] is entirely in the hands of an all-ruling God. That God governs the world is a fundamental article of natural as well as revealed religion. It is no great exploit of faith to believe this – it is but a small advance beyond atheism and downright infidelity. I know no country upon earth where I should be put to the expense of argument to prove this. The heathens gave striking proofs of their belief of it by their prayers, their sacrifices, their consulting oracles before they engaged in war and by their costly offerings and solemn thanksgivings after victory. And shall such a plain principle as this be disputed in a Christian land? No; we all speculatively believe it, but that is not enough; let our spirits be deeply impressed with it and our lives influenced by it; let us live in the world as in a territory of Jehovah's empire. Carry this impression upon your hearts into the wilderness whither you are going. Often let such thoughts as these recur to your minds: "I am the feeble creature of God and – blessed be His name – I am not cast off His Hand as a disregarded orphan to shift for myself. My life is under His care; the success of this expedition is at His disposal. Therefore, O Thou all-ruling God, I implore Thy protection – I confide in Thy care – I cheerfully resign myself and the event of this undertaking to Thee." Which leads me to observe:

3. That these words, *"the Lord do what seemeth Him good,"* may express a humble submission to the disposal of Providence, let the event turn out as it would. *q. d.* We have not the disposal of the event nor do we know what will be, but Jehovah knows – and that is enough. . . . Thus, my friends, do you resign and submit yourselves to the Ruler of the World in the present enterprise. He will order matters as He pleases; O let Him do so by your cheerful consent! Let success or disappointment – let life or death – be the issue, still say, "Good is the will of the Lord"; *"let Him do what seemeth Him good"* [II SAMUEL 10:12; I CHRONICLES 19:13]. Or if nature biases your wishes and desires to the favorable side (as no doubt it will), still keep them within bounds and restrain them in time, saying after the example of Christ, *"Not my will, but Thine be done"* [MATTHEW 26:39,42; LUKE 22:42; MARK 14:36]. You may wish, you may pray, you may strive, you may hope for a happy issue – but you must submit; *be still and know that He is God* [PSALM 46:10] and will not be prescribed to or suffer a rival in the government of the world He has made. Such a temper [disposition of mind] will be of unspeakable service to you; and you may hope God will honor it with a remarkable blessing, for submission to His will is the readiest way to the accomplishment of our own.

4. These words, in their connection, may intimate that let the event be what it will, it will afford us satisfaction to think that we have done the best we could. *q. d.* We cannot command success; but let us do all in our power to obtain it; and we have reason to hope that in this way we shall not be disappointed. But if it should please God to render all our endeavors vain, still we shall have the generous pleasure to reflect that we have not been accessory to the ruin of our country but have done all we could for its deliverance. . . .

Having thus made some cursory remarks upon the sundry parts of the text, I shall now conclude with an address first to you all in general, and then to you gentlemen and others who have been pleased to invite me to this service [i.e., the soldiers and officers]. I hope you will forgive my prolixity [wordiness]: my heart is full, the text is copious, and the occasion singular and important. I cannot therefore dismiss you with a short hurrying discourse.

It concerns you all seriously to reflect upon your own sins and the sins of your land which have brought all these calamities upon us. If you believe that God governs the world . . . you must acknowledge that all the calamities of war and the threatening appearances of famine are ordered by His Providence; there is no *evil in a city or country but the Lord hath done it* [AMOS 3:6]. And if you believe that He is a just and righteous ruler, you must also believe that He would not thus punish a righteous or a penitent people. We and our countrymen are sinners – aggravated sinners: God proclaims that we are such. . . . Our consciences must also bear witness to the same melancholy truth. And if my heart were properly affected, I would concur with these undoubted witnesses – I would *cry aloud and not spare, I would lift up my voice like a trumpet, to show you your transgressions and your sins* [ISAIAH 58:1]. . . .

Pass over the land, take a survey of the inhabitants, inspect into their conduct, and what do you see? What do you hear? You see gigantic forms of vice braving the skies and bidding defiance to Heaven and earth while religion and virtue is obliged to retire to avoid public contempt and insult. You see herds of drunkards swilling down their cups and drowning all the man within them. You hear the swearer venting his fury against God and man, trifling with that name which prostrate angels adore and imprecating [calling down] that damnation under which the hardiest devil in Hell trembles and groans. You see avarice [greed] hoarding up her useless treasures, dishonest craft planning her schemes of unlawful gain, and oppression unmercifully grinding the face of the poor. . . . You see cards more in use than the Bible, the backgammon table more frequented than the table of the Lord, plays and romances more read than the history of the blessed Jesus. . . . You see swarms of prayerless families all over our land – ignorant, vicious [unruly and poorly mannered] children, unrestrained and untaught by those to whom God and nature hath entrusted their souls. You see thousands of poor slaves in a Christian country, the property of "Christian masters" as they will be called. . . .

You see the best religion in all the world abused, neglected, disobeyed, and dishonored by its professors; and you hear infidelity scattering her ambiguous hints and suspicions or openly attacking the Christian cause with pretended argument, with insult and ridicule. You see crowds of professed believers that are practical atheists, nominal Christians that are real heathens, many abandoned [totally committed] slaves of sin that yet pretend to be the servants of the Holy Jesus. . . .

You may indeed see some degree of civility and benevolence towards men . . . but O how little sincere homage – how little affectionate veneration for the great Lord of Heaven and Earth! You may see something of duty to parents, of gratitude to benefactors, and obedience to superiors, but if God be a Father, where is His honor? If He be a master, where is His fear? If He be our benefactor, where is our gratitude to Him? You may see here and there some instances of proud, self-righteous virtue, some appearances of morality; but O how rare is vital, evangelical religion and true Christian morality, animated with the love of God, proceeding from a new heart and a regard to the Divine authority, full of Jesus, full of a regard to Him as a mediator on Whose account alone our duties can find acceptance? O blessed Redeemer!. . . how few earnest prayers, how few penitential groans do You hear! Pass over the land and bring me intelligence: is not this the general character of our country? I know there are some happy exceptions – and I hope sundry such might be produced from among you – but is not this the prevailing character of a great majority? . . .

And is there no relief for a sinking country? Or is it too late to administer it? Is our *wound incurable, that refuseth to be healed?* [JEREMIAH 15:18]. No – blessed be God! – if you now turn every one of you from your evil ways, if you mourn over your sins and turn to the Lord with your whole hearts, then your country will yet recover. God will appear for us and give a prosperous turn to our affairs. He has assured us of this in His own word; *"At what instant,"* says He, *"I shall speak concerning a nation, and concerning a kingdom, to pluck up and to pull down and to destroy it, if that nation against whom I have pro-*

nounced turn from their evil, I will repent of the evil that I thought to do unto them" (JER. XVIII. 7, 8). . . .

And now, my brethren, in the last place I have a few parting words to offer to you who are more particularly concerned in this occasion; and I am sure I shall address you with as much affectionate benevolence as you could wish.

My first and leading advice to you is: labor to conduct this expedition in a religious manner. Methinks this should not seem strange counsel to creatures entirely dependent upon God and at His disposal. As you are an independent company of volunteers under officers of your own choosing, † you may manage your affairs more according to your own inclinations than if you had enlisted upon the ordinary footing – and I hope you will improve this advantage for the purposes of religion. Let prayer to the God of your life be your daily exercise.

When retirement [privacy] is safe, pour out your hearts to Him in secret; and when it is practicable, join in prayer together morning and evening in your camp; how acceptable to Heaven must such an unusual offering be from that desert wilderness! Maintain a sense of Divine Providence upon your hearts and resign yourselves and all your affairs into the hands of God. You are engaged in a good cause – the cause of your people and the cities of your God – and therefore you may the more boldly commit it to Him and pray and hope for His blessing. I would feign hope there is no necessity to take precautions against vice among such a select Company; but lest there should, I would humbly recommend it to you to make this one of the articles of your Association before you set out that every form

---

† Many militia groups at that time were local volunteer associations, each of which would annually elect its own officers. It was a regular practice in the New England area to preach sermons (called "Artillery Sermons") before the group, usually at the election of officers. (This early practice of ministers delivering Biblical injunctions and sermons to the military was later replaced with military chaplains who performed the same functions but who were also able to minister to the spiritual needs of the soldiers during the heat of battle.) The first militia group formed in America – the Ancient and Honorable Artillery Company of Massachusetts – was formed in 1638 by Puritan leader John Winthrop. It is now the world's third oldest chartered military organization.

of vice shall be severely discountenanced and – if you think proper
– expose the offender to some pecuniary [monetary] or corporal
[physical] punishment. † It would be shocking indeed – and I cannot bear the thought – that a Company formed upon such generous
principles should commit or tolerate open wickedness among them;
and I hope this caution is needless to you all, as I am sure it is to
sundry [many] of you.

---

† This request to set high moral standards for the group (to "severely discountenance"
"every form of vice") and to impose a fine or punishment for a violation of those standards
was a practice adhered to throughout early American military history. For example, during
the French & Indian War, Col. George Washington issued an order to his troops declaring:

> Colonel Washington has observed that the men of his regiment are very profane
> and reprobate. He takes this opportunity to inform them of his great displeasure
> at such practices and assures them that if they do not leave them off, they shall be
> severely punished. The officers are desired if they hear any man swear or make use
> of an oath or execration, to order the offender twenty-five lashes immediately
> without court-martial. For the second offense, he will be more severely punished.

Washington's firm opposition to "every form of vice" (as the Rev. Davies called it) in the
military never wavered – as evidenced by military orders he issued as Commander-in-Chief
on several occasions throughout the American Revolution. For example:

> The General is sorry to be informed that the foolish and wicked practice of pro-
> fane cursing and swearing (a vice heretofore little known in an American Army)
> is growing into fashion; he hopes the officers will, by example as well as influence,
> endeavor to check it and that both they and the men will reflect that we can have
> little hopes of the blessing of heaven on our arms if we insult it by our impiety and
> folly; added to this, it is a vice so mean and low, without any temptation, that
> every man of sense and character detests and despises it. GENERAL ORDERS, NEW
> YORK, AUGUST 3, 1776

> It is much to be lamented that the foolish and scandalous practice of profane
> swearing is exceedingly prevalent in the American Army. Officers of every rank
> are bound to discourage it, first by their example, and then by punishing offend-
> ers. As a mean to abolish this and every other species of immorality, Brigadiers are
> enjoined to take effectual care to have Divine Service duly performed in their
> respective brigades. GENERAL ORDERS, MIDDLEBROOK, MAY 31, 1777

> Purity of morals being the only sure foundation of public happiness in any coun-
> try, and highly conducive to order, subordination, and success in an army, it will be
> well worthy the emulation of officers of every rank and class to encourage it both
> by the influence of example and the penalties of authority. It is painful to see
> many shameful instances of riot and licentiousness among us; the wanton practice
> of swearing has risen to a most disgusting height. A regard to decency should

And now, my dear friends – and the friends of your neglected country – in the name of the Lord, lift up your banners! *Be of good courage and play the men for the people and the cities of your God, and the Lord do what seemeth Him good.* . . . May the Lord of Hosts – the God of the armies of Israel – go forth along with you! May *He teach your hands to war* [II SAMUEL 22:35; PSALM 144:1] and *gird you with strength to battle* [II SAMUEL 22:40]! May He bless you with a safe return and long life, or a glorious death in the bed of honor and a happy immortality! May He guard and support your anxious families and friends at home and return you victorious to their longing arms! May all the blessings your hearts can wish attend you wherever you go! These are wishes and prayers of my heart – and thousands concur in them; and we cannot but cheerfully hope they will be granted through Jesus Christ! Amen! ■

---

conspire with a sense of morality to banish a vice productive of neither advantage or pleasure. GENERAL ORDERS, FREDERICKSBURG, OCTOBER 21, 1778

Washington so firmly opposed "every form of vice" that General Henry Lee once observed of Washington:

[V]ice shuddered in his presence, and virtue always felt his fostering hand.

In fact, records of the Continental Army show that dozens of soldiers were court-martialed and received dishonorable discharges solely for their unrelenting use of profanity.

Therefore, while Rev. Davies' request to "severely discountenance" "every form of vice" might seem unusual today, it was a request to which virtually every patriotic officer and solider in that day – as well as in succeeding generations – acceded.

WallBuilder's Sampler

A few of our resources . . .

To learn about _ALL_ our great resources,
call 800-873-2845 for a free catalog,
or visit www.wallbuilders.com

Books such as . . .

Original Intent: The Courts, The Constitution, and Religion
Reveals how the Court has reinterpreted the Constitution, diluting the principles upon which it was based. This book is filled with hundreds of the Founders' quotes. (B16) $12.95
Available on CD-Rom (CDR02) $9.95

America: To Pray or Not To Pray?
A statistical look at what has happened since religious principles were separated from public affairs by the Supreme Court in 1962. (B01A) $7.95

Benjamin Rush: Signer of the Declaration of Independence
Features the life and writings of this dedicated Christian statesman, including numerous historical illustrations. (B20) $9.95
Available on CD-Rom (CDR03) $7.95

Celebrate Liberty! Famous Patriotic Speeches & Sermons
A collection of orations by John Quincy Adams, Daniel Webster, George Bancroft and many others – also includes historical annotations and brief biographies of each orator. (B30) $10.95

Reprints such as . . .

Lives of the Signers of the Declaration of Independence
This reprint of an 1848 original features biographic sketches on the lives of each of the 56 men who signed the Declaration of Independence. (B14A) $10.95

Noah Webster's "Advice to the Young"
A reprint from 1792 and 1832, that "will be useful in enlightening the mind of youth in religious and moral prinicples." (B10A) $6.95

Videos such as . . .

The Spiritual Heritage of the U.S. Capitol (120 min.) A personal tour of the US Capitol with WallBuilders' founder David Barton, complete with dramatic reenactments. Also available in DVD, CD, audio, and transcript. (V06) $29.00* Donation

The Role of Pastors & Christians in Civil Government (60 min.) A look at the role played by faith in early America – inspiring today's Christians to also become involved. Also available in DVD, CD, audio and transcript. (V02) $19.95

DVDs such as . . .

America's Godly Heritage (60 min.) Explains the Founding Fathers' beliefs concerning the role of Christian principles in the public affairs of the nation. Also available in video, CD, audio, and transcript. (DVD01) $19.95

Foundations of American Government (25 min.) Surveys the historical statements and records surrounding the drafting of the First Amendment, showing the Founders' intent. Also available in video, audio, and transcript. (DVD04) $9.95

Audio CDs such as . . .

Keys to Good Gov't & Faith , Char. & the Con. (2 CDs) *Keys. . .* Presents beliefs of the Founders concerning the proper role of Biblical thinking in education, government, and public affairs. *Faith. . .* Does character matter? Does religious faith have a part in today's society? Learn what the Founders believed on both issues. (CD02) $11.95

Spirit of the Am. Rev. & America's Birthday (2 CDs) *Spirit. . .* A look at the motivation that caused the Founders to pledge their "lives, fortunes, and sacred honor" to establish our nation. *America's. . .* A fascinating look at our nation's birth and the great men and events involved in bringing us to the occasion. (CD04) $11.95

Audio Cassettes such as ...

Developing a Biblical Worldview
Provides insight on how to apply Biblical principles in every area of your life. (A28) $4.95

The Influence of the Bible on America
America's founding documents were heavily influenced by the Bible, and many of America's political and social customs were derived from its teachings. (A29) $4.95

American Heritage Poster Series such as ...

George Washington
(P06) $4.95

Black Legislators
(P11) $4.95

Thomas Jefferson
(P03) $4.95

The Signing of the Declaration
(P10) $4.95

American Heritage Resources in Spanish such as ...
La Herencia De Cristiana De Estados Unidos
Claves Para Un Buen Gobierno
El Papel Desempeñado por los Pastores y Cristianos en el Gobierno Civil

And many **Additional Resources** including CD-Roms, historical prints, documents, pamphlets, etc.

Shipping and Handling are additional.
Prices subject to change without notice.
Quantity & case-lot discounts available.

WallBuilders, P.O. Box 397, Aledo, TX 76008 (817) 441-6044

For Visa or MasterCard orders call
(800) 873-2845 or order online at
www.wallbuilders.com